WHO WAS ROBERTO?

WHO WAS ROBERTO?
A Biography of Roberto Clemente

PHIL MUSICK

1974
AN ASSOCIATED FEATURES BOOK
PUBLISHED BY
DOUBLEDAY & COMPANY, INC.
GARDEN CITY, NEW YORK

PHOTOGRAPH CREDITS

1–9 United Press International Photo
10 Pittsburgh *Press*
11 United Press International Photo
12 Wide World Photos
13–15 United Press International Photo
16 Pittsburgh *Press*
17–21 United Press International Photo
22 Pittsburgh *Press*
23–25 United Press International Photo
26 Pittsburgh *Press*
27 United Press International Photo
28 Pittsburgh *Press*
29 United Press International Photo
30 Pittsburgh *Press*
31 United Press International Photo
32 Pittsburgh *Press*
33 Malcolm W. Emmons

Library of Congress Cataloging in Publication Data

Musick, Phil.
  Who was Roberto?

"An Associated Features book."
  1. Clemente, Roberto, 1934–1972. I. Title.

GV865.C45M87   796.357'092'4 [B]

ISBN: 0-385-08421-8

Library of Congress Catalog Card Number 73-15358

Copyright © 1974 by Associated Features Inc.
Printed in the United States of America
All Rights Reserved
First Edition

For Sandy, Kristi, and Keri, the sunshine in one guy's life, and for Pop, a catcher who has never failed to give more than receive

Now you will not swell the rout
of lads that wore their honors out,
Runners whom renown outran
and the name died before the man.

>—A. E. Housman

To an Athlete Dying Young.

ACKNOWLEDGMENTS

No book is ever the product of one man's labor; this one is certainly no exception. Now comes the difficult part. Where to begin bestowing thanks?

No better point could be found than the family hearth and Sandy Musick, gentle but honest critic, who kept the roast warm and ever buoyed the sagging spirit, and two small, indefatigable blondes who sacrificed many a piggyback ride and backyard romp so that Daddy might become an "arthur."

Conceived by wise, old pro Zander Hollander of Associated Features, this project produced its share of labor pains, and it would be unappreciative of me not to note that he suffered them graciously, and offered patience and encouragement beyond the call of duty or profit.

I would also be remiss in failing to acknowledge the aid

of Lou Prato, longtime Clemente watcher and good friend, who shipped me his voluminous files and copious notes, both gathered over the years and of inestimable value in trying to solve the riddle that was Roberto Clemente.

Pittsburgh Pirate public relations director Bill Guilfoile and his secretary, Sally O'Leary, gave me access to their files and their unfailing cooperation, no matter the number of times they were imposed upon. The same might be said for those unsung keepers of the morgue at various newspapers, including the Pittsburgh *Press* and the Pittsburgh *Post-Gazette*.

And, though it will surely embarrass him, I would like to thank Roy McHugh of the Pittsburgh *Press*, merely for being the definitive professional reporter and writer. He never lectured me; no one ever taught me more about our mutual craft. Without his teaching, you would not be reading this.

Another fine newspaperman, Dave Ailes of the Greensburg (Pa.) *Tribune-Review*, offered suggestions, and over a hundred drinks in my kitchen, he never once failed to venture the opinion that this would be a readable book. For these and other considerations, he gets a free copy and my undying gratitude.

Where to end the thank yous? Surely not without overlooking those whose names will immediately come to mind the day this book is published. But I would not want to forget the people of Puerto Rico, in particular Luis Mayoral and R. Elfren Bernier, who lavished warmth and help on a stranger who came away from their lovely land with an affection for it that will never die.

And, last but . . . Judy Anderson, who typed the manuscript with never a flagging smile, gently pointed out grammatical errors, kept the faith, and proved to be to secretaries what Roberto Clemente was to right fielders.

Phil Musick
August 8, 1973
Pittsburgh, Pennsylvania

PREFACE

If the truth were known, most of us figure we're hard-boiled and cynical and tough enough not to be scared too often, and smart enough not to be hustled too often. That's the reporters' image that survived Front Page. Secretly, we all covet that image. It's what they give us in lieu of money. If I died tomorrow, I'd want chiseled on my tombstone a conversation I once had with a pro basketball hustler named Mark Binstein. One day he sneered at me, "You don't believe in anything, do you?" And, shades of all those good lines you should've laid on people and didn't think of until you got home, I sneered back, "Not unless it's negotiable or trying to kiss me."

But the truth is that few of us are all that tough. And once in a while, a jock comes along and he gets closer to our hearts and our heads than most. Such a jock was Roberto Clemente.

I covered the Pittsburgh Pirates during parts of Clemente's final four years. We weren't close. Once we got in a loud argument; once he was mad at some other reporter and twisted up one of my shirts. Most of the time we treated each other civilly enough, and in time I came to needle him about being an old man without him finding it necessary to hit me with a blunt object. A few times we talked seriously about things other than baseball.

Like most people with bodily orifices, he was anything but perfect. He was vain, occasionally arrogant, often intolerant, unforgiving, and there were moments when I thought for sure he'd cornered the market on self-pity. Mostly, he acted as if the world had just declared all-out war on Roberto Clemente, when in fact it lavished him with an affection few men ever know.

He used to say "newspaper reporters are scared of me," but it's the truth that I was never afraid of him, I guess primarily because I figured if he started beating hell out of me, somebody would realize that I was wearing glasses and weighed maybe 165 and would pull him off quick. One of the great ironies I've ever seen in this business was that Clemente thought reporters disliked him when, in fact, very few felt anything about him save admiration and respect. Pity.

This is a hell of a thing to admit, but after countless hours of research and writing about the man, there have been times when I've gone out and swallowed a lot of whiskey because the feeling suddenly came over me that I wasn't sure I really knew him.

But I know some things about him. I know that through all of his battles—Roberto Clemente did not engage in skirmishes—with managers, teammates, and reporters, there was about him an undeniable charisma. Perhaps that was his true essence—he won so much of your attention and affection that you demanded of him what no man can give, perfection.

"What do they want me to do, kill myself?" he would cry. "They" was anyone or any group with whom he presently was unhappy. Mostly, though, "they" were the demons who drove him headlong in the pursuit of excellence.

When the *machismo* was upon him, and it usually was, he could invoke from teammate Manny Sanguillen the enraptured expression, "He is the inspiration." Or he could turn an antagonist to stone with one withering glance, the derision fairly pouring from his eyes. Sometimes he would bitterly berate an honest reporter, or turn away from a kid pleading for an autograph, and the urge was almost overpowering to grab him and shake him and say, "Wise up, schmuck, you're Roberto Clemente; act like it."

But he could also speak warmly and personally on any subject when the mood struck him, and when the precise meaning of an English word escaped him, he would cock his head like a confused puppy looking around for the newspapers. And there were times when the tension of being Roberto Clemente would drain from him and he would smile and converse with you—most jocks don't engage in conversation, they talk over your head trying to write the story for you in their mind's eye. In those moments, and others, he owned nothing less than real charm.

If he confused his managers and teammates, and

angered reporters, what he was as a human being found its way through to the fans of Pittsburgh, and they adored him, and he held them in abiding affection.

He feuded endlessly and needlessly and pettily with the press. Reporters were shaken by the fury he could summon in an instant; baffled when he would turn from angelic to apoplectic in even less time. They were publicly suspicious of his injuries—with reason—and for that he never forgave them. He would rail at them—and at anything he considered an injustice—with words as heartfelt as a nun's. "I played mad all the time," he once confessed. "It helped me. If I would be happy, I would not be a good ballplayer." Yet he gave his most prized trophy —a silver bat he received for winning the batting championship a year after he felt he had been overlooked as the National League's most valuable player—to Pirate broadcaster Bob Prince.

To see him angry was to conjure up a vision of some African prince standing in the surf and brandishing his spear at a slave ship retreating into the horizon. Yet I heard him say often and defiantly, "I am not afraid to cry."

He was prouder than a lion—"for me, I am the best"— and he paid a price, because his pride was interpreted as arrogance. He had the dignity of an English butler; many took it for aloofness. And many confused his passion for all the things of his life for something so shallow as a hunger for attention.

He was all fire and instinct and sensitivity and grace and drive. A zealot. "No one drives himself more than Clemente," a psychologist once said. "I've never seen such an intense person. If Clemente were a football player, he'd make Ray Nitschke look like a pussycat."

And so he would have. Already he's a memory, which the years will strip bare or falsely inflate. A friend of his said, "He wasn't a devil and he wasn't an angel . . . but I'd like it to be remembered that he was a lot closer to the one than the other."

I think he was, too. I never got around to telling him I thought on those occasions when he wasn't being a horse's ass, I thought he was a hell of a guy. I'm sorry I didn't.

CONTENTS

PREFACE		13
1.	MISSION . . . IMPOSSIBLE	23
2.	ADIOS, AMIGO	35
3.	TOO SLOW FOR SHORT	49
4.	"THE GREATEST NATURAL ATHLETE I EVER SAW"	67
5.	HIDDEN IN MONTREAL	77
6.	A ROOKIE'S RAGE	95
7.	DAMN PRESS!	119
8.	THE PROMISED LAND	135
9.	FAT CITY . . . MOSTLY	155
10.	DR. CLEMENTE	177
11.	MOST VALUABLE AT LAST	193
12.	THE LEADER	213
13.	WHO RETIRES AT .350?	233
14.	THE GREAT ONE	255
15.	NO 3,001	281
EPILOGUE		301

WHO WAS ROBERTO?

Chapter 1

MISSION . . . IMPOSSIBLE

He had seen enough of 1972, Gregorio Rivera decided with three hours of the year remaining. It hadn't been much anyway, so when long shadows crawled over his salmon-colored, cinderblock house and the relentless tune of the waves had quieted the children and the dogs, he went to bed.

Some five miles away at the San Juan International Airport, Art Rivera slumped in the copilot's seat of his hoary old DC-7, his fertile, twenty-seven-year-old mind spinning. He worried because the teen-agers handled the cargo with abandon instead of loading it with the required care; he worried because his new pilot, Jerry Hill, was late, and the flight had already been delayed sixteen hours; he worried because the DC-7 was old and wounded and still owned the mortgage on his business future; he worried because that morning, as he frantically sought a crew, his wife, Mary Eileen, informed him she was pregnant; he worried because the plane had not been test flown since new props had been installed on the inboard engines and was overloaded by two tons; and he worried because it was his nature to do so.

As much of the world abandoned itself to a final fling, either decrying the end of 1972 or wishing it good riddance, another worrier did his thing. Roberto Clemente worried about the airplane that would take five men and sixteen thousand pounds of relief supplies to survivors of the December 23 earthquake in Managua, Nicaragua; he worried about being away from his family on the day that meant more to him than any other; he worried about reports that the black market was feeding on the supplies he had so painstakingly gathered; he worried because after flying hundreds of thousands of miles, he still feared he would die in an airplane; he worried about a small, legless Nicaraguan boy; and he worried because it was his nature to do so. "If there is one more delay, we will leave this for tomorrow," Clemente the worrier told an equally worried Art Rivera.

Some fifteen miles out Highway No. 3, in houses at opposite ends of sprawling Carolina, Robertito Clemente and his grandfather Melchor Clemente, also worried. "Daddy's going to Nicaragua, but he's not coming back," Robertito Clemente cried to his maternal grandmother. "Call the airport. Don't let him go. Please." The boy was only seven years old and susceptible to nightmares. His grandmother quieted him. Across Carolina, Melchor Clemente awoke from an evening nap. "I had a dream the airplane crashed into the sea," he told his wife, Luisa.

Melchor Clemente was ninety-two and just weeks from his death. His wife urged him to return to sleep.

The boy and the old man were joined in anxiety by others on a night usually devoted to its absence. In Washington, Richard Nixon worried about his Washington Redskins and extended an invitation to their coach, George Allen, to come to the White House and discuss the strategy that would be used against Miami a fortnight later in the Super Bowl. In Phoenix, Mary Jo Creed, a pretty nineteen-year-old model, worried about her vocal cords. In a few days she was to be sworn in as the United States Air Force's very first female vocalist, striking a tardy blow for women's liberation. In New York, British film star Michael Caine worried about the necessity of his impending marriage to the most recent Miss Guyana; in Hollywood, American film star Edward G. Robinson worried about the results of tests being conducted on him at Mount Sinai Hospital; in Madrid, Generalissimo Francisco Franco fretted over rumors that age was slackening his tenacious grip on Spain.

At Roberto Clemente's majestic "House on the Hill" in the exclusive San Agustin section of Rio Piedras, Vera Clemente, sure her husband was safely in Managua by now, entertained friends from Allentown, Pennsylvania. She had taken her husband to the airport at four-thirty that afternoon and tried to dissuade him from making the trip after watching the young volunteers load the DC-7. "When your time comes, it comes; if you are going to die, you will die," said her husband, who was at once both a fatalist and a man certain his destiny was in its adolescence. "And babies are dying there. They need these supplies."

Actually Roberto Clemente didn't want to make the trip to Managua. "I can do more staying here," he had argued. Events conspired to argue otherwise. The day after Managua had been leveled by an earthquake for the third time in its history, Clemente threw himself into work as honorary chairman of the Nicaraguan Relief Committee, formed by a San Juan television personality, Luis Vigoreaux. For sixteen hours a day, Clemente arranged for the collection of food and clothing to be stored in San Juan's Hiram Bithorn Stadium; went door-to-door in his fashionable neighborhood soliciting money; hired trucks and chartered airplanes and helped load both; and sought money for the NRC on radio and television. "He never did anything 99 percent," sighed his attorney and close friend, Elfren Bernier.

At 2:00 A.M., some fourteen hours before he was to leave for the airport, Clemente had returned to the House on the Hill, where a party he had given for some friends had been concluded without him. Only Roberto Marin, a stocky, coppery rice salesman and part-time Pittsburgh Pirate scout, who had discovered him whacking tin cans on a barrio sandlot, remained. They sat in the living room having a snack. Clemente relaxed at the organ, which he had taught himself to play. "He was getting pretty good," says Marin. "I kept calling him the Liberace Negro. I said, 'I'm getting you a . . . what do you call it . . . candelabra.' He was very tired. It wasn't in his mind to go to Nicaragua."

At 5:00 A.M. the telephone rang, and Clemente changed

his mind. Anastasio Somoza, a West Point graduate and one of the world's richest chiefs of state until he loosened the reins on Nicaragua ten months before, was calling. They discussed the earthquake that had killed three thousand and injured countless thousands more. Managua had no water, no electricity; the city, which had just entered the modern era, was littered with uncollected corpses, "like the end of the world," a Managuan said. More than a hundred thousand refugees streamed from the city toward the port of Masayas, a town thirty miles distant with a normal population of thirty thousand. Somoza's advisers had warned him that the existing food supply would sustain Managua only seventy-two hours, and the tall aristocrat would take no chances of offending neighbors who held a piece of the city's lifeline in their hands. Spain had sent a team of doctors; Britain, planeloads of medical supplies and plasma. Japan assured financial assistance, and help was coming from thirty-nine other countries, including the United States, which had mounted a massive effort. But Clemente's NRC had responded immediately, sending two planeloads of supplies, and at that very moment the Puerto Rican freighter *San Expedito* was steaming south with 210 tons of clothing and 36 tons of food. Still, Somoza informed Clemente, the Nicaraguan government would accept "only money and food."

"That made Roberto think reports were true that the military was getting supplies shipped from Puerto Rico," said Bernier. "He was enraged. He said, 'I'll go down there and distribute the supplies myself.'" No one who knew him was at all surprised.

Reasons other than suspicion also dictated Clemente's decision to go to Nicaragua. In Managua the year before, where he managed the Puerto Rican team in the world amateur baseball championships, he had been graciously treated. If he was a man who rarely forgave, he was also a man who rarely forgot. And while there he had visited a hospital and formed a bond with a young boy who had lost both legs. "He made arrangements for the boy to be fitted for artificial legs, and he was worried because he knew the earthquake had damaged many hospitals," said Bernier.

The fate of the boy evidently wore on Clemente. "He would say to his wife, 'Vera, I wonder how the kid is . . . I wonder how the kid is,'" remembered Luis Mayoral, a friend and Clemente's assistant in planning Ciudad Deportiva, a sports city for the youth of Puerto Rico, which had long been the ballplayer's dream.

Finally, Clemente was concerned about his countrymen who had gone to Managua on two earlier flights. Narciso Rabell Mendes, executive director of the Engineers, Architects, and Surveyors Association of San Juan, and the association president, Rafael Lopez Vega, had stayed in Nicaragua to coordinate distribution of the supplies with the National Guard. They and twelve others had rushed to the stricken city without passports. Clemente worried that they might have difficulty in trying to return on a commercial flight. "And he felt he couldn't ask others to give up their holiday if he wouldn't," said Pittsburgh Pirate general manager Joe L. Brown.

For most people, New Year's Eve was party time.

Elfren Bernier was surprised when Clemente agreed to

go to Nicaragua on New Year's Eve. Bernier is a thoughtful, immensely likable man, and president of the San Juan Bar Association. Wisdom seems to flow from his luminous brown eyes, which are accentuated by lustrous, curly gray hair. "Why this particular day?" he asked. "It must be something very special . . . very urgent."

Bernier speaks English softly and precisely, slowing as unfamiliar phrases come to mind. "You must understand . . . New Year's Eve is the most important holiday of the year in Puerto Rico. A day entire families gather together."

As the plane was loaded and mechanical difficulties were corrected, on the twenty-seventh floor of a condominium overlooking the Atlantic, guests at a party thrown by Pittsburgh Pirate pitcher Bob Johnson paused in conversation while jets howled their escape from the nearby airport.

Not long after Gregorio Rivera had gone to bed, Jerry Hill eased Art Rivera's anxiety by appearing at the airport. Faulty lights aborted one takeoff, and new spark plugs were installed on the No. 3 engine. And after Robertito Clemente's premonition had been dismissed and Melchor Clemente's dream had been lost to sleep; after Roberto Clemente's visions of hungry children had triumphed over the warnings of his wife and friends; after a pilot named David Joyner grew comfortable in his new suit and had forgotten his buddy Art Rivera's desperation; after all of these things, the mercy flight to Managua was finally ready to depart.

While Air Indies pilot Tom Klocinski chatted with a

mechanic and ran through his preflight checklist at Gate 28, a DC-7, retired from service a year before by a Florida airline but sporting two new propellers, a new set of spark plugs, and a noble purpose, waddled down a taxiway toward runway No. 7.

In the salmon-colored house in which he had lived all of his fifty-three years, Gregorio Rivera tossed and turned. He, too, knew concern. He had not worked in 1972. The welfare check came each week, but six dogs and nine children and four grandchildren and chattering women were not fit company for a Jibaro, a man of pride. Perhaps 1973 would be better. Perhaps the sand company out on Point Maldonado would again be hiring men to load the bags.

The wind increased, swirling through the mango trees in the deep ravine behind his house and up the slope to whip the saw grass clinging to the edges of the bluff that overlooked the Atlantic. As it coaxed the swells higher against the bluff, the holiday meal lay heavily against Rivera's ribs, and he slept. No more than a thousand feet above the house, a DC-10 banked left and headed for New York, the thrust of its engines shaking the rusty 7-Up sign that served as Gregorio Rivera's front door. No one stirred, not even the dogs that sprawled in the dust outside. The only members of the household still awake were Juan Angel Rivera, who was fourteen and would not go to bed so early on La Vispera de Nueve Ano as a matter of principle, and his sister-in-law, Flor Maria Ortiz, who was pregnant and would have gladly gone to bed had her back not ached. They chatted quietly. Finally the girl dozed, and only the boy was awake.

Aboard the DC-7 that sat awaiting takeoff just in front of Air Indies Flight 407, the three-man crew busied itself. The pilot, Jerry Hill, had accepted the charter after four other fliers had turned it down. Frank Matias, a mechanic for Caribair, was serving as flight engineer, a critical role on a DC-7 but one for which he was not qualified. Art Rivera, who had no formal instruction on DC-7s and whose pilot's license had been revoked two years before, nevertheless was the copilot. All three were there out of necessity. Hill had six children and had recently been furloughed by Airlift International in Miami. Matias, whose neighbor was ex-Boston Red Sox pitcher José Santiago, needed the money. In two weeks his wife Margarita would give birth to their fifth child. Rivera had even less choice than the other two; he couldn't find a qualified copilot.

Dave Joyner was a friend of Art's. He is a veteran pilot with Shamrock Air Freight. Mention his name around the San Juan airport and other fliers grin. A while back Joyner became a man of intrigue and infamy in San Juan. He was flying some antique guns back to his collection in San Juan. In the process of being divorced, Joyner had incurred the antipathy of his mother-in-law. She phoned the cops. Joyner was arrested and his bail set at forty-five thousand dollars. "The papers splashed it all over page one," chortles an acquaintance. "They called him a gun runner."

In fact, Joyner is a gregarious Texan of mellifluous drawl. He served as Art Rivera's friend and adviser for two years. "You couldn't have met a nicer fellow than Art," says Joyner, but in his voice there is the implication he feared that one day the old DC-7 would kill someone. "He just wanted his airplane up there to be making some money. He was an enterprising young man."

Three weeks earlier, the brakes had failed on Rivera's plane as it was being taxied to another hangar. It slammed into an abutment and nosed over into a shallow canal. "The tips of two of the propellors were bent," Joyner said. "I flew Art to Miami to buy new ones. His regular pilot, Bill Shearer, had gone home for the holidays, but he was adamant the plane be test flown. But the charter came up suddenly."

When Clemente had contacted Art Rivera about the trip to Nicaragua, the young businessman hadn't hesitated. Shearer was on holiday, but Art Rivera was by necessity and by instinct a gambler. Hadn't he two years before found a loophole in FAA regulations that allowed him, at twenty-five, to enter the competitive air freight business in Puerto Rico by leasing his plane instead of operating it? Hadn't he promoted a DC-3 and used it so skillfully that in no time his clients were demanding he acquire a plane with a larger payload? Hadn't he done so, increasing both his business and his responsibilities? And how do you run an airline with your airplane on the ground?

"Art worked hard," Joyner said, "but I've known Bill Shearer a long time. If he'd been here, Art would've unloaded that plane and Bill would've tested it."

But Bill Shearer was in Charleston, South Carolina, and Art Rivera was in a hurry and Jerry Hill was available. And then there was Dave Joyner's new suit. When Rivera had shown up at Joyner's Yagrumo Heights home at ten-thirty on the morning of December 31, he was an hour too late to persuade the Texan to take the charter to Nicaragua, on which Hill would've provided an experienced copilot. "Art was desperate for a crew," Joyner said. "I had just spent two hundred dollars on a new suit. And we'd been planning to go to this party. I thought about that suit. I turned him down."

So, at 9:22 P.M. Atlantic Standard Time, on a clear, crisp evening while millions were busy having fun or pretending to be, each of the four engines were revved to the 4,000 horsepower they could maintain for only the two minutes required to get the DC-7 airborne. Hill released the brakes, shoved the throttles to the control panel, and the plane rolled up the macadam runway and lurched into the sky. One engine exploded almost immediately.

"I'm turning back," Hill radioed the San Juan control tower, tugging the DC-7 into a left turn. He never made it. There were two more explosions, and then a third as the DC-7 nosed into the Atlantic, whipped into hard, heavy swells by the wind. For the second time in fifteen years an airplane had fallen from the sky within view of Gregorio Rivera's salmon-colored house.

This time there would be no survivors.

Roberto Clemente—who once said, "I want to be remembered as one who gave all he had to give"—had done so.

In Bob Johnson's twenty-seventh-floor apartment, the party was interrupted as the guests watched flares falling off Isla Verde, a five-mile ribbon of land that runs from the airport to the fashionable tourist area of Condado.

"We heard about a plane crash," said Pirate Richie

Zisk. "We saw search crews looking for debris and bodies, and we started to talk about how terrible it was for the people on the plane . . . what a terrible New Year's Eve for the people who knew the victims. We watched the searchlights as one year went out and a new one came in."

Chapter 2

ADIOS, AMIGO

Perhaps a single break in a chain of events would have prevented Roberto Clemente's death. If he had not met a legless boy in Nicaragua; if Art Rivera's DC-7 had been test flown; if Clemente could have done one thing 99 percent; if General Somoza had not called; if Dave Joyner had not bought a new suit. Such conjecture is, of course, worthless.

A baseball player who had said when your number's up, you go, had gone. A few paused to note his absence. Richard Nixon officially marked Clemente's death, and two weeks later grieved again. His Washington Redskins were humbled in the Super Bowl. That week, Mary Jo Creed, the Air Force's first female vocalist, brought feminism to the wild blue yonder and began a new career she hoped would "lead to travel, education, and promotional opportunities." In New York and Hollywood, respectively, two actors learned the worst. Michael Caine's bride-to-be, Miss Guyana, was three months pregnant. A date for their wedding was not immediately set, but a spokesman for the English film star said it would take place "definitely before July." Tests indicated Edward G. Robinson had a terminal illness. In Madrid, the eighty-year-old Francisco Franco retrenched and warned his countrymen he could in future months be expected to rule Spain "with the same firmness as in past years."

Meanwhile, Tom Klocinski cursed certain unknown control tower officials at San Juan International Airport. Perhaps one or more passengers survived the crash of Art Rivera's DC-7, he told friends. But even he doubted it. Presumably killed upon impact were the crew; San Juan trucking executive Rafael Lozano, a friend of Clemente's who had assisted him in the relief operation; and Roberto Clemente y Walker, a man who invested himself passionately in all endeavors, large and small.

Tom Klocinski is a thirty-two-year-old captain for Air Indies. On the night of December 31, he piloted a Beechcraft out of the San Juan airport directly behind the ill-fated DC-7. As Klocinski's Beechcraft headed east on its nightly forty-five-minute run to Mayaguez, Juan Angel Rivera, who had watched the exploding DC-7 hit the water, was shaking his father. "We ran to the top of the bluff and the plane was in the water, maybe a mile out," Gregorio Rivera said, rubbing a scrawny hand over his gray wool scalp and down the lined, ebony neck. "I sent Juan for the police and ran to tell the others. When I went back to the bluff five minutes later, I could see nothing. I wondered if anyone had lived."

It is a moot point, but one that angers Klocinski, who spent four years with a civilian airline in Southeast Asia and has flown dozens of search-and-rescue missions. "When I came back from Mayaguez two hours later, the Coast Guard was searching in the wrong place. Hell, they were five miles away. I had circled the plane in the water and asked if they wanted me to stay, but they said the Coast Guard knew where the plane was and was on its way. Three times in the four hours after I got back from Mayaguez, I asked if I could be of assistance. They told me to forget it. It's my opinion there wasn't anyone alive after impact, but if anyone had been unconscious in the tail section, well . . . that would have been another story."

Klocinski is still bitter. "The next day, I was called and asked if I would help them locate where the plane went down. I showed them."

Later a Federal Aviation Agency report would dispassionately state that the two inboard engines on the DC-7 "suffered massive internal failures." But the report would be incomplete to Dave Joyner's way of thinking.

"That plane would've flown with two engines out, but the crew would've had to be on their toes," theorized Joyner, who had flown the plane in the past. "Art was inexperienced. And Matias was just a mechanic, not a flight engineer. The engines on a DC-7 are extremely critical—they can literally burn themselves up—and it takes a good engineer to handle them. Obviously the engines were damaged in the previous accident.

"I think I know what happened. When Hill tried to

come back to the airport, the landing gear was exerting a tremendous drag. The control for the gear is in the center of the pedestal; the control for the flaps is to its right. On a standard takeoff in a DC-7, you need 25 percent flaps, and the gear produces a strong drag. I'm sure as they were coming back, Hill said, 'Gear up.' Art had very little training in the plane. I'm sure he pulled the flaps up. When he did, with the gear drag slowing the plane, all the lift they had was killed, and they stalled and went in at a sharp angle."

An underwater picture taken later seemed to confirm Joyner's hypotheses: The landing gear on the DC-7 was down and locked.

Pilot error could've resulted in major league baseball losing its third player in recent years to an airplane crash. Within the past twenty years, the Chicago Cubs' brilliant young second baseman, Ken Hubbs, and a rookie catcher for the Baltimore Orioles, Tommy Gastall, died in similiar accidents. But the entire sports world has not been immune to air tragedy. Notre Dame's Knute Rockne, who transformed an obscure little Indiana college into a national college football power beloved by fans all across the country, was killed in 1931 when a small plane crashed into a Kansas cornfield. Rocky Marciano, the only heavyweight boxing champion to retire undefeated, died in a similar accident thirty-eight years later. Whole athletic teams have perished in airplane accidents: Eighteen U. S. Olympic figure skaters in Belgium in 1961, and eighteen Italian soccer players twelve years earlier; the California Polytechnic Institute and the Marshall University football teams almost a decade apart to the day.

Other sports figures to have died in air tragedies included golfer Tony Lema, former middleweight boxing champion Marcel Cerdan, and seven members of the world soccer champions, Manchester United of England.

The plane that carried Clemente to his death crashed in 120 feet of lovely aqua water off Point Maldonado, a half-mile slice of rock that juts into the Atlantic from a gently curving half-mile stretch of brown sand called Pinonas Beach. The Navy and Coast Guard established a search in the area, a place favored in quieter times by surfers and San Juan's drug addicts, who use it as a shooting gallery. On the first day a rainbow hovered over the site, and hundreds of Puerto Ricans waited on the beach, many of them standing knee-deep in the surf.

It would not be melodramatic to say that some part of the Puerto Rican spirit was lost in the accident. Luis Mayoral is a bright, educated young man of the type that is briskly attacking problems that have plagued the island for centuries. But he says, almost mystically, "I am not mad at God, but sometimes I cannot even imagine that Roberto is dead. He had everything in life, but with his death God showed us material things are not important. I think Roberto would've liked to die that way. His death had meaning. It will influence the youth of Puerto Rico because the Ciudad Deportiva will be built and they will benefit."

For each of the following eleven days, even though police cordoned the area for the last week, Pinonas Beach was overrun. While cows with crescent-shaped horns grazed in the groves beyond the palm trees and coppery kids raced among them, the spectators stood quietly and studied the sea, breaking into an excited chatter only when something was spotted floating in the water.

Steve Blass, a Pirate pitcher who had gone to San Juan after Clemente's death, carried the scene in his mind for weeks. "Those people didn't know what to do, so they went to the beach," he said. "Roberto was out there somewhere, so they just went to the beach and waited."

In a roped-off area away from the crowds, Vera Clemente waited, too. Each afternoon she would come to the beach and stand in the sand, allowing grief to flood her face but never quite claim it completely. One day she quit coming. "The youngest boy does not understand he is dead," she said. "I do not go to the beach. Once I went and there were fifty boats with people throwing flowers into the water. For two months, every day I would receive a big package of mail, letters from all over the world. I knew from traveling that everyone loved him. When I received all that mail, I knew how far it went."

Vera Clemente is a striking woman. Strands of midnight black hair, piled high on her head, peek out to frame a wide, oval face the color of the mahogany furniture exported from the island. Her nose is patrician, her eyebrows gracefully arched, her mouth lovely and generous. If she is not the classical Spanish beauty, she is very close, and the general effect is one of rich, warm loveliness. And strength.

In Puerto Rico, when a man dies, it is customary to open his house to those who grieve him. Vera Clemente followed that custom, and day after day, while divers searched for her husband's body, those who mourned him crowded into his house. There was not room to sit in eleven of the twelve rooms of the rambling house, and the moat that stood in front of the main entrance seemed entirely appropriate. The house sits majestically on a hill. From the front porch the view is breathtaking, especially to the east, where the rain forest rises abruptly from the lush, green countryside. In the days following Clemente's death, it was possible to stand on the porch and watch endless lines of people climbing the hill, encircling the house, and retreating down the hill toward the Rio Piedras business district. A blue 1962 sedan stood watch outside the house, a black handkerchief fluttering from its radio antenna. A uniformed patrolman, part of a twenty-four-hour guard provided by the governor, lolled under a tree. In a small room beyond the spacious living room, dominated by a lavish, thousand-dollar blue-and-gold sofa and two huge paintings of her husband, Vera Clemente and her family spoke softly to friends. Reports that visitors stole Clemente's trophies proved false, though some took ashtrays as mementos. Mostly they walked around the ocelot skin and llama rug, studied the pastel waterfall that spread over an entire wall, and shared a sense of loss.

"The wife, she is a saint," nodded Pedro R. Dominche, owner of The Little Curve bar, a refreshment stand sought out by the hungry and the thirsty during the days of the search. "I live here sixty-six years and I never see anything like this."

Pedro R. Dominche nodded again. "I am the godfather to the second child of Clemente's sister, Rosa. He was my good friend," he said, waving a rag idly over the cracked boards that serve as a bar. "It was a terrible thing. Business was amazing. Cars were everywhere. I am godfather to his sister Rosa's second child."

While Dominche and his chubby, teen-age son feverishly dispersed Corona beer and Don Q. rum, the Navy and the Coast Guard searched diligently but with few results. The sailors grumbled that the search should be ended, that strong tides in the area made it fruitless, that if a celebrity had not been involved, they would have been back in their barracks. Hill's battered body was discovered Wednesday afternoon, and a pathologist who did the autopsy held out little hope that the remaining four bodies would be found. "The cargo went through that airplane like a shell through the barrel of a shotgun," he said. "They won't find anything else."

The doctor was right. Eight more days of scouring the area brought forth little. The cockpit was located Friday; the tail and fuselage two days later. After that only Hill's glasses and a sock belonging to Clemente were found. A week later, Clemente's briefcase drifted onto a pile of garbage near the Coast Guard station, miles from where the plane went down.

When it had been determined that the bodies were not likely to be found, a memorial service was held at the San Fernando Roman Catholic Church, across from the main plaza in bustling Carolina, where Clemente had been born and raised. Clemente had been baptized and married in the church, which recently had been repainted a dull gray, although the timbers bordering its walls had been given a coat of brilliant blue. When Clemente and Vera Christina Zabala were married, it was noted that an accurate census might've been taken by anyone standing in the plaza, so many had come to see the newlyweds. On the sunny morning of the memorial service, it would've been possible to be equally accurate in assessing the population. Hundreds of Carolinians stood quietly under the laurel trees, and the crowd flowed across the plaza and gathered under the shops that surround the main square. Inside the church, dignitaries from Pittsburgh and Clemente's teammates sat among the player's friends and relatives as seven priests officiated. A former Pirate batboy, now grown, cried through the service.

As Steve Blass and Elfren Bernier offered the eulogies in front of a pale blue altar, Manny Sanguillen, who would replace his friend and patron in the Pirate outfield, stood in a dredging boat off Pinonas Beach. As he did on each of the eleven days, Sanguillen dove with Navy divers working a great, gray coral reef fifty yards from shore. They found nothing, but continued their work as Bernier concluded his eulogy: "Roberto Clemente, image of Puerto Rico, enlighten us all through the path of serenity and the solidarity of mankind."

A man who in life had been loved, liked and disliked, admired and detested, was dead; the response was, as it always is with such men, excessive. Puerto Rico and Pittsburgh reacted officially, meaningfully and, fittingly considering the man, emotionally. Perhaps more than any Puertoriqueño, Clemente had reflected the spirit of the tiny island, its fierce pride, its sense of dignity and worth, its fervor. "When you honor Roberto Clemente, you honor all of Puerto Rico," the island's famed opera singer Ruth Fernandez once said. In Philadelphia, a countryman, Miguel Norat, agreed. "The passing of Clemente was like

... the death of God," he said. So Puerto Rico wept openly and offered its homage. The inauguration of newly elected governor, Rafael Hernandez Colon, a reserved young man in his thirties who had pulled the once-powerful Popular Party from the grave, was postponed. When it was held four days later, without the festive atmosphere that usually attends the event, Colon ended his acceptance speech with the words, "Our people have lost one of their great glories."

A resolution was introduced in the lower house of the legislature to rename the San Juan airport in honor of Clemente. A memorial fund was established to build Ciudad Deportiva. Children from a Brooklyn grade school pasted pennies to a sheet to form Clemente's uniform number, 21; the Pirates and a Pittsburgh foundation each donated a hundred thousand dollars to the Clemente fund. In a week the fund swelled to half a million dollars. After eulogizing the ballplayer, Richard Nixon called upon all Americans to donate. Throughout the island ecumenical masses were said. Dozens of wreaths were dropped into the sea off Pinonas Beach, and one day five little girls dressed in white released five white balloons that floated in the air above the flowers. A Pittsburgh congressman petitioned for a medallion to be struck in Clemente's memory, and a city park was renamed in his honor. The Washington *Post* editorialized: "In Pittsburgh, at the empty Three Rivers Stadium yesterday, the scoreboard bore the legend, 'Roberto Clemente, 1934–1972.' It might also have read, 'A man of honor played baseball here.'"

A Harlem school was one of four in New York City

seeking to change its name to the Roberto Clemente School; in Philadelphia, a Police Athletic League center was so named.

In a gritty melting pot of a town that prides itself on the fact that most of its citizens are as hard as its steel, there was a very real grief. Overlooking the downtown area from the highest of Pittsburgh's seven hills, a neon sign that usually heralds the virtues of a local beer said it for everyone in town: "*Adios, Amigo.*"

For forty years the city had patiently waited for its professional football team to play in a championship game. On the day Clemente died, the Steelers lost to Miami in a game for the American Conference title. The following day Pittsburghers took slim notice.

A nine-year-old boy spent his allowance on a bouquet of gold chrysanthemums and placed them on the altar of a suburban church. He signed the card "Robbie Yelenosky," surprising a Sunday school teacher who had no interest in baseball. "We'd been calling him Roberto Clemente since he registered in September," the teacher explained. A five-year-old informed a Pittsburgh newspaper columnist that he had named his new cloth dog "Puerto Rico" because "nice people live there . . . Clemente lived there."

Bob Wido, a salesman, said simply, "I loved that man." A tavern owner named Bill Sortino wept. "As a person he is irreplaceable," he said.

A black man, told of Clemente's death, walked directly to the Normandie Bar on Westchester Avenue in the Bronx. "Don't tell my minister," he asked a friend.

"I've got the drinking licked, but Roberto was my man. I had to have a taste."

In El Barrio, the Puerto Rican ghetto of New York City, a man joined the dozens of others who had become "Clemente cousins." "He's alive," the cousin said. "He is too smart . . . besides, he is too good of a man to leave us that way."

Norman Weiss, who teaches Puerto Rican history in El Barrio, asked his students to submit letters on the theme, "Why the world should remember Roberto Clemente."

Wrote Robert Zabala, "He cared enough." Classmate Jamie Casanova said, "He didn't care if he died; all he knew is that he tried."

Baseball, a game of people who crudely plunder the language much of the time, produced unexpected eloquence. In a moment of untypical warmth, Commissioner Bowie Kuhn said of Clemente, "He had a touch of royalty about him. Somehow he transcended superstardom. His marvelous playing skills rank him among the truly elite. And what a wonderfully good man he was."

Some of the Pirates felt the loss of the player, others the loss of the man. Willie Stargell, the gentle, thoughtful giant who had been an intimate of Clemente's, said, in a voice that sounded of velvet and thunder: "Roberto was a good man." Al Oliver, young, black, heir apparent to Clemente's role as leader, mourned the loss of a champion of equality. "Clemente was black and he spoke up," Oliver said. "People don't like that. When you are black, you are supposed to shut up."

Lumbering Charlie Sands, third-string catcher and brief escapee from a minor league team to which he shortly returned, was among the many unable to accept the death of a man who had seemed so alive. "He was such an incredible man," Sands said. "Two weeks after he was gone, I still didn't believe it. I expected him to swim ashore someplace."

Too scrupulously honest to fake emotion he didn't feel, Pirate manager Bill Virdon honestly rued the loss to the game of baseball of skills he admired since 1956, the year he and Clemente had reached the major leagues together. "He was the greatest all-around player of my era," said the thoughtful Virdon. "He gave more to baseball than he ever took from it . . . no matter how much money he made."

Among many others who ascribed saintly virtues to a man more human than most was Bing Crosby, who owns stock in the Pirates. But the singer made one pertinent observation: "Clemente felt the needs of the other fella," he said.

Few who spoke publicly of him failed to mention that Clemente had died trying to help people to whom he owed no real obligation. No one put it better than Pittsburgh television sportscaster Myron Cope, who Clemente had once refused to speak to for four years because of a magazine story Cope had written about him. Said Cope: "Honorary chairmen don't die in airplane accidents."

Chapter 3

TOO SLOW FOR SHORT

Daddy Sugar is dead now, and Carolina is a slowly fading scar on the face and heart of Puerto Rico, its thousand-year-old poverty gnawed away daily by industrialization. The sagging tin roofs of its adobe houses still throw long, quivering shadows when the wind blows down the maze of sidestreets beyond the town plaza, but scattered here and there like jewels in a dustpan, shiny brick buildings trumpet the end of a way of life.

No longer do the blazing red poinciana trees, the huge, shimmering hibiscus blooms, the ruby bougainvillea vines mask a static poverty. Now midwives are replaced by neat signs advertising the skills of *"especialadades en los niños";* old gives way to new, history to hope. A growing middle class drives a hard wedge between the legendary rich and the legion poor. If a village struggled for generations in the shadows of sugar cane, a small city has blossomed in the wake of fabricating factories and plastic plants.

Now the people of Carolina no longer hate the unseen Norteamericanos who owned most of the huge, sprawling sugar plantations. The Carolinians are part of the new Puerto Rico, a self-governing commonwealth under the protection of the United States but no longer under its thumb. The feeling of oppression wanes; each generation becomes more Americanized as the island continues to be a model for Caribbean democracy, a thriving, proud sapphire.

Yes, Daddy Sugar, the giant hand from which all blessings flowed when Roberto Clemente was a squalling brown infant born on a steamy August day in 1934, is dead. It would require perhaps three decades for Clemente to fully understand that the pride that drove him to celebrity and wealth was suckled on the toil of peasants who bore dignity like a shield in a mean battle for survival.

Melchor Clemente understood; it was his back that was bent when the heat rays of late morning would ripple across the gently swaying cane fields and worm their way through the thick walls of the processing factory to wilt Don Pepito Rubert's stiff, white collars and fill his mind with the marbled coolness of the restaurant at the El Condado Hotel. There, over a leisurely lunch and cigars and rum, the elite gathered each noon to transact much of the island's business.

Almost daily, Don Pepito would make the fourteen-mile journey from the outskirts of Carolina to San Juan, a trip that in 1940 required forty-five minutes by automobile. For the first half hour, he did not leave a road that twisted through his own fields, under constant and resolute attack by tireless men swinging dull silver machetes. From the backseat of his car, Don Pepito would wave, favoring his overseers and foremen with polite nods. In a feudal but very real sense, these were his people, twentieth-century vassals staked in his fields by bonds of tradition and necessity and ignorance. It would not have occurred to him to be unnecessarily impolite to them. Moreover, they were Jibaros, peasants descended from the island's mountain men to whom pride was as natural as tattered clothing and stomachs never quite full. Without thinking, he knew they would husband even a slight insult. So he waved and nodded, not distinguishing between the brown Indios of the hills or the plum-black Negroes of the coast. He was the patron of them all.

They came to the fields at dawn, and departed at dusk to the barrios that dotted the shallow hillsides between little Carolina and its sprawling big brother, San Juan. While they were there, they cut the cane and loaded it into carts. Each Saturday they were paid two dollars, and each Saturday night, over beer and rum, they generally agreed that Don Pepito was a good man.

Don Pepito Rubert and his younger brother, Guillermo, owned Rubert Brothers Sugar Company. They were, of course, Spanish—descendants of the sailors and noblemen who came to Puerto Rico in 1493 on Columbus' second voyage to the New World, and of the Americans and Frenchmen and Africans and Dutch who shortly followed. If the Ruberts were not pure Castilian—and obviously their bloodline had been invaded in at least one instance—they were an intrinsic part of the minuscule ruling class that commanded the destiny of the 2,300,000 Puerto Ricans who inhabited an island smaller than Connecticut but more populous than Colorado.

The poet Luis Munoz Marin might have been in the hills preaching the slogan of his new Popular Democratic Party —*"Pan, Tierra, y Libertad"*—in a quest to become the island's first elected governor. But in 1940 it was Don Pepito Rubert who controlled the bread, land, and liberty of men like Melchor Clemente.

When Don Pepito's car drew near and the patron nodded, Melchor Clemente's head bobbed forward only slightly. If one of his sons worked beside him, Clemente would stare in the direction of the car and remind, "He is no better than you."

Melchor Clemente was as straight and lean and hard as the machete. If he was poor, he felt no disgrace in his poverty, and he held firmly to certain undeniable truths. A man paid his debts, accorded and demanded respect, carried himself with dignity, provided for his own, assisted the less fortunate. A man who did these things bowed to no other. Life was meant to be hard, he felt. A test. "I want you to become a good man, a serious man," he told his youngest son. Roberto Clemente listened intently. Most people listened when Melchor Clemente spoke, for he did not use words often or idly. On the narrow, twisting streets of Barrio San Anton, which peered down at Carolina in the east and San Juan in the west, his neighbors all agreed: Melchor Clemente had about him the look of *aguioso*.

That pride remained in his face when he was ninety and in a strange land, standing before forty-five thousand people at Three Rivers Stadium on a 1970 evening when Pittsburgh honored his son. A sportswriter studied the hawkish, coppery features worn thin by the years and told a friend, "Clemente's father looks like a tired eagle."

Melchor and Luisa Clemente raised seven children in a square, white frame house set deep in a grove at the edge of San Anton, one of the smattering of barrios that are a part of Carolina, although the town proper is some five miles distant, where the hills that surround it drop into a broad, dusty plain. Two children born to Luisa by a previous marriage died before reaching middle age. Melchor fathered Roberto, Martino, Justino, Andres, and Osvaldo.

The Clementes were a patriarchy, ruled by the principles Melchor Clemente had never found reason to question, guidelines the Jibaros had carried down from the mountains generations before, when they had come to cut the cane. A man might not be educated; that was often a matter of circumstance. But only a fool did not take purchase on something in the face of a hard life. And Melchor Clemente was no fool. What he held fast to was a belief in the value of hard work and education. Because of the latter, he sent his six children to the Fernandez grammar school, located only a hundred yards from a grove of banana trees that separated the Clemente home from the red dirt road that fronted it and served as the barrio's principal artery. Because of his belief in the value of honest toil, from their eighth birthdays his sons often accompanied him to Don Pepito's fields.

Life was struggle; the sooner they accepted that fact, the better. When he was nine, Roberto Clemente wanted a bicycle the way Don Pepito's children had never wanted anything. Even though he was a foreman, Melchor Clemente received just four dollars each week, and the budget had to be severely stretched to include necessities. "Earn the bicycle," he told the boy. A neighbor was offering a penny a day for anyone willing to lug a heavy milk can from the country store a half mile away. The pennies faithfully found their way to a glass jar in Luisa Clemente's kitchen. Three years and twenty-seven dollars later there were enough to purchase a second-hand bicycle. The boy learned a lesson the man never forgot. "Six o'clock every morning, I went for the milk," Clemente said after becoming almost as wealthy as Don Pepito. "I wanted to do it. I wanted to have work, to be a good man. I grew up with that on my mind. Maybe that is why I don't smile so often."

Work is a Jibaro virtue much the way gambling is a Chinese vice. Strictly defined, the Jibaro culture belongs to the island's lush, green interior. But industrialization lured it from the mountains to the valleys, and it evolved into a code for living; an unwritten Ten Commandments for the poor; a survival kit.

"They were poor, the Clementes . . . almost dirt poor," said a friend of the family. "But they were cultured people. Not sophisticated, just good people who did right by others. The father was hard, but the children loved him. The mother they idolized."

At its core, the Jibaro code demanded that each man share his wealth, however limited it might be. No Jibaro let another one starve. Puerto Rican social security was best described as a Jíbaro, living in a one-room shack with a wife and eight children, who adopted the family of a dead neighbor. Visitors dared not admire something in a Jíbaro home, for the owner would have been insulted were it not immediately accepted as a gift. These were the principles Melchor Clemente insisted his children understand and adopt.

"Roberto thought very well of the Jíbaros," his attorney, Elfren Bernier, said. "They are a quiet people, very close to their families. They give to each other. He was like that."

If Melchor Clemente was a serious, austere man, his wife brought to the house on Calle Sabena Llanos its warmth and a sense of the practical. When her youngest son was five years old, she suspected he had already received his calling. "Roberto was," she said, "born to be a baseball player." Later, when the thought of having an engineer in the family entered her mind, it was too late. The die was cast.

A stout, dignified woman, Luisa Clemente awoke each morning at 1:00 A.M. to attend to the laundry of Don Pepito Rubert's household. In the heat of day she dealt with the dust that blew into the house from the barrio baseball field across the road, and prepared the pork and rice and pink beans that were the staples of the family diet. As she cooked, she was comforted by the omnipresent sound of a rubber ball thunking from the walls and ceilings of the house. Only when Roberto slept, it seemed to his mother, did that sound not permeate her home.

"He used to buy those rubber balls every chance he got," Luisa Clemente said. "When he was small, he would lay in bed and bounce the ball off the walls. There were times he was so much in love with baseball that he did not care for food."

If Roberto Clemente was disinterested in food it was because the excitement of adolescent thoughts dismissed anything so mundane as pink beans. "I wanted to be a ballplayer," he said. "And the more I thought about it, the more I became convinced God wanted me to. I was sure I came to this world for some reason."

God, however, did not provide the wherewithal for young dreamers, so Roberto Clemente twisted magazines into paper balls, hoarded his pennies against the purchase of balls made of rubber, and gloried in the occasional tennis ball that came his way.

Life became baseball, school, hauling the milk can, working the cane, and offering respect and affection to the quiet, good people who were raising him to escape his father's footsteps if he could, or to tread them honorably if he must. "They did so much for me," Clemente said. "I never heard my father or my mother raise their voices in our home. I never heard any hate."

By the time he was eight, and a natural need to rebel had vented itself in a refusal to comb his hair, Roberto Clemente was playing organized baseball on the palm-tree-studded field across from his home and emulating his brothers, who had graduated to the fast kid leagues of San Juan. Later, when Martino had traded his flannel uniform for one of khaki, Luisa Clemente was convinced that the family had sacrificed a chance to harbor a professional *pelotera* to the Korean War.

"Martino was never as good when he left the Army," she said, conviction set deep in the twin trenches that lined her wide, chocolate-colored face and gave it strength if robbing it of softness. But on the barrio field, Roberto seemed a candidate to succeed where the U. S. Army and/or Martino had failed. Even Melchor Clemente was impressed with his son's sincerity and skills. When Roberto Clemente hit ten home runs in a sandlot game that began at eleven o'clock in the morning and was halted at six-thirty in the evening, the father's pride issued the admission, "He played surprisingly well against boys his age or older."

World War II struck as Roberto Clemente romped the barrio sandlots. Puerto Rico sent its young men off to the highly decorated 65th Infantry Regiment and took another tuck in a belt already pulled inhumanly tight in many parts of the island. Where life before had been difficult, it now became mean. A dust-colored statue of Puerto Rico's first governor and his family guarded the entrance to Carolina. Immortalized in stone, a hometown boy who had prospered, Governor Juan Pinero smiled while the people in these mean times joked bitterly that he had lost weight, that one could now discern the ribs of his teen-age son, who stood to his left, stripped to the waist and looking not unlike a slightly older Roberto Clemente.

"My mother always fed us first, then she and my father would eat what was left," Clemente said. "She had to work hard, never went to a movie, never learned to dance.

But even the way we used to live, we were happy. We would sit down to eat and make jokes and talk and eat whatever there was. That was something wonderful . . . to grow up with people who had to struggle to eat."

As it did on the rest of the world, the war had a sobering effect on Roberto Clemente. If life was a serious business in the best of times, what must it be in the worst?

"Roberto was a very mature boy, even when he was ten or so," Martino Clemente said. A laborer for the Imperial Bottled Gas Company in Carolina, Martino Clemente lives up a sidestreet that snakes up a hill perhaps a quarter mile from the house in which he was raised. The face of the Barrio San Anton is timeless. White adobe houses, laid out with no apparent thought to geometric precision, stagger up the hillside and are separated by chain-link fences. In hardscrabble patches between them, goats graze among junked automobiles and discarded furniture. Children wander by, singly and in groups, eating flavored ice from white paper cups, red and orange and purple juices running down brown chins to mingle with a dozen other stains on torn shirts. Teenagers bunch up, hurling the taunts and teasings by which their generation seems to communicate the world over. Mock fights spring up and quickly disappear in a cloud of grins. Knots of men kneel in the street to settle political issues and inquire after the latest tactical blunder of the man who manages the local baseball team. Women string washing from handy windows to nearby trees, idly munching a mango, the tropical fruit that tastes like an apple that's been laced with turpentine. The air is sweet and heavy with the odor of jasmine. Bougainvillea is poverty's necklace.

"Basically, Roberto was a good kid," Martino Clemente said. "He did two things, played ball and stayed home. He never got into trouble. We called him 'Momen' from the time he was little. When he had grown up and become a star, no one could remember what the name meant. He was always quiet, never got whipped. We used to kid him about that."

A carbon copy of his father, the boy called Momen acquired another nickname, "Monte Irvin." By day he would squeeze the rubber ball to strengthen his wrists; by night he lay in bed and listened to radio broadcasts heralding the wizardry of Irvin, then a young outfielder with the San Juan Senators of the Puerto Rican winter league.

"I would lay in bed throwing the ball against the wall and listening to the San Juan games," Clemente said. "Irvin was my first idol because not only was he a good hitter, but he had such a good arm."

When times improved for him, Melchor Clemente would find the odd quarter and give it to his son—a dime for the bus to San Juan, fifteen cents for a bleacher seat. Afterward, Roberto Clemente, eyes averted, would wait for Irvin to leave the stadium. "I never had enough nerve to look at him straight in the face," Clemente said. "I would wait for him to pass and then look at him. I idolized him."

At fourteen, the fingers that squeezed a rubber ball could bend a ten-penny nail and were never far from a baseball. Irritated with her son's preoccupation with a game, and hopeful that as an engineer he would become part of the wave of industrialization that was washing over Puerto Rico following the war, Luisa Clemente decided on concrete action. She burned the boy's only bat.

"I got it out of the fire and saved it," Clemente said. "Many times she told me she had made a mistake; that I was right to want to play baseball."

Certainly, Roberto Clemente was well equipped for the sport. From his teens, people marveled at his hands, broad palms tapering into widely spaced, long fingers. As a boy's hands will, they outgrew the rest of him and would have looked more at home at the end of a blacksmith's arms. The hands that could hammer a baseball over distant fences could not, however, pull a comb through unruly hair.

"Why won't the boy comb his hair?" Melchor Clemente grumbled. Each morning Luisa Clemente, a powerful woman, would grab her son and clamp him between unyielding knees, drawing a hard comb through his hair. It had little effect, the kinky black strands sprouting at a hundred angles.

"Come," Melchor Clemente ordered one day, striding off to Carolina's Calle Domingo Caceres, named in grateful remembrance of an honest merchant. Hector Fidalgo's barbershop sat on the tree-lined street, and Melchor Clemente left his son there with a precise command, "Short."

"The barber broke his comb on Roberto's hair," recalled a friend. "Then he broke another. Finally he went across the street to the hardware store and got one of those steel combs they use on horses. When Roberto go, the barber stand outside and say, 'Tell your father never bring you to my shop again.'"

As Clemente prospered, so did the barber. In 1960, after the Pittsburgh Pirates defeated the New York Yankees in the World Series, Clemente walked into a barbershop in the San Juan suburb of Rio Piedras. "There was Fidalgo," the friend laughed.

Yankee pitchers who suffered Clemente's .310 average in the 1960 World Series never realized that his batting eye had first focused an empty soup cans.

Roberto Marin had grown up slashing at such cans with a broomstick on the scrub fields of the barrio and knew the first flickering of talent could be foretold by the depth of the dents in containers that had formerly held tomato soup.

Marin is one of the legion of Puerto Rican men who have informal, unofficial, unbreakable bonds with major league teams. They are, as they quickly inform a stranger, "baseball men"—which means simply that the game is vitally important to them; that somehow, some way they have remained close to it, clung to some piece of the action. Marin has been a salesman for twenty-six years, and it is probably not coincidental that his employer, Sello Rojo Rice Company, has for an equal number of years been a heavy sponsor of amateur baseball and softball.

When Roberto Clemente was fourteen, Roberto Marin was organizing a team to wear Sello Rojo's colors in a "superior" San Juan slow-pitch softball league. Each twilight, Marin would scout the barrio sandlots of San Anton,

Sabana Abajo, and Martin Gonzalez. One evening in Sabana Anton a small group of boys, using tin cans and a broomstick, were playing that ageless, international game where one player bats, the rest field. "The way they play, if you strike out, you have to pitch," Marin said. "I see this one kid . . . he never strike out Bam! Bam! Bam! Tin cans all over the field. I say, 'Who are you?' He say, 'I am Momen.' I told him to come to Carolina to try out for the softball team."

For two years, Clemente played shortstop for Marin, while also playing in a San Juan youth baseball league, where at fourteen he was selected to compete in the "future stars" competition normally dominated by sixteen-year-olds. Still, his first love was softball, and when Sello Rojo shifted to a fast-pitch league, he became the darling of San Juan's softball-crazy fans, surprising in that he could not hit.

"He was an outstanding shortstop, but we always batted him eighth," said Juan Perez, an introspective Carolina used-car dealer who oversaw the club Marin managed. "We played under the lights and he didn't hit well, but he made sensational plays in the field. His cap would always fall off and the people loved him."

Marin did not share their affection for Roberto Clemente, the capless shortstop. The baseball man in him felt that the boy was playing out of position. "I made him an outfielder," Marin said. "He was too slow for shortstop."

It was, as they say on the sports pages, a pivotal move. Clemente proved an apt pupil of the art of outfielding. "I never saw a boy who loved baseball like he did,"

Marin said. "He spent every hour he could playing. He always carried that ball to squeeze. After games we would stop to drink beer; he always drank milk and then went home to bed."

Clemente's carefree Sello Rojo teammate, Hector Alvarado, soon began to draw the attention of other San Juan baseball men. "The Dodgers (or Cards or Yanks) want Alvarado," they would assure one another.

"He could do everything; we called him 'Joe D.,'" Marin said. "But he didn't like the game like Roberto." Lacking baseball ambition, Joe D. eventually became an obstetrician; consumed by it, Roberto Clemente soon improved his batting stroke. At sixteen he was playing for Ferdinand Juncos in a Puerto Rican amateur league the equivalent of Class A professional ball on the mainland. At Julio Vizcarrando High School, he made the district all-star team three straight years, and a right arm he later considered something of a legacy threw the javelin an impressive 190 feet. "My arm is the same shape as my mother's," he said. "When she was seventy-five, she threw out the first ball to start the winter league season. And she had something on it."

When Clemente was a junior, there was considerable speculation that he would throw the javelin in the 1952 Olympic Games at Helsinki. There was also speculation that the lure of baseball was so strong that he would sign a professional contract. When Melchor Clemente envisioned his son's future, he thought in terms of slashing doubles to right-center; when Luisa Clemente undertook the same exercise, she thought of slide rules and the building of bridges.

"My mother wanted me to get an education," Clemente said. "I wanted to play baseball." Melchor Clemente was cast in the unlikely role of arbiter. "He knew I loved baseball, so he suggested I play ball and study later," Clemente said. A final decision was put off until after Clemente completed his junior year in high school.

"He was a very quiet boy," said Mrs. Mabel Caceres, a history teacher at Vizcarrando High School. "He didn't start talking until he became a professional star."

Mabel Caceres, formerly married to Roberto Marin, remembers Clemente with great affection. A chunky, gregarious woman in her sixties, she taught history for thirty years in Carolina's only high school, a gathering of light beige squares individually added to a darker main building, as though engineered by a neat but unimaginative child. At night she worked in a drugstore, uncomplainingly bearing the curse of teachers everywhere, varicose veins.

"Besides being my schoolchild, Roberto was my friend," she said. "I remembered him for three beautiful things. The first, his hands. He had such beautiful hands. Huge but gentle. I always looked at them. Then, he was such a fine son. He would do anything for his mother. And I will always remember him, because once I was sick and he was home from playing baseball and he carried me to the doctor's office in his arms. When I wanted to pay him, he got mad and said I was insulting him.

"When he first came to high school, he took a seat farthest from the front and he would not look people in the eye, he was so shy. He never got into trouble like boys will. And I teased him about the girls because he was so good-looking, even then. He was an average student . . . intelligent but not a scholar. I gave him a B in history.

Mabel Caceres would have given him an A on the athletic field. He was one of the finest schoolboy athletes on the island. In addition to throwing the javelin, Clemente triple-jumped 45 feet and high-jumped 6 feet, outstanding leaps in 1952. In a track meet against archrival Humacao in late May during Patronales (the feast of Carolina's patron saint, San Fernando), a friend, Omar Cordeiro, urged him to try the 440-yard run.

"I knew he could win," Cordeiro said. "But he didn't want to, didn't think he was good enough. We had a good 440 man named Chu-Chu Barbosa, and Humacao's runner was the best on the island. Roberto beat them both. Everybody knew he could do such things; only he didn't know."

In July, Roberto Marin told the seventeen-year-old Clemente something else he found difficult to believe.

"I told him that to me he looked better than the professional outfielders here in the winter league," Marin said. "I told him I was going to take him to a tryout that a Brooklyn Dodger scout was going to hold in Santurce."

Chapter 4

"THE GREATEST NATURAL ATHLETE I EVER SAW"

Tryout camps are the stuff of small boys' dreams and old men's memories.

You lay in bed each night of your youth, playing the scene over and over in your mind so that in time it becomes as familiar as the pattern of the bathroom wallpaper or the jiggle of the loose knob on the back door.

You cherish the dream, embellish it. But basically it is unchanging, until a girl or hard times or the years drive it from your mind.

You, the young Mantle, the adolescent Aaron, appear at a major league tryout camp in Oil City or Council Bluffs or San Juan.

Your line drives dismantle the infielders; a resigned look comes to outfielders' faces as your longer shots disappear over distant fences; base-runners drop like flies before your darting throws.

A big-league scout embraces you in his excitement. "Kid, we'll give you forty-five thou to sign a contract," he enthuses. You swallow your heart. "Make it fifty," you choke out. He hands you his pen.

That night your father buys round after round at the Elks; your mother wears a frozen smile that's half pride, half nervousness; the girl of your other, equally intense dreams becomes more malleable. Fade out to the Hall of Fame.

For some, the dream fades away. For some.

Mostly tryout camps are like rummage sales: here and there a real bargain, but for the most part, junk. Baseball teams hold them for the reasons people play the numbers: They are cheap, and once in a great while, jackpot.

Al Campanis has been a scout for more than three decades. He can count his jackpots on the gnarled fingers of one hand. A large, square man given to chain-smoking and staccato bursts of conversation punctuated by thoughtful pauses, Campanis was tutored in his formative years of scouting by the late Branch Rickey, under whom the practice became something of an art form.

Campanis is widely regarded as an excellent seer of unripened talent, having immediately recognized it in, among others, Sandy Koufax. After playing and managing in the minors in the late 1930s and early 1940s, Campanis became a public relations adviser, showing the previous year's World Series films to lunching Rotarians and any other assemblage of adults who would conceivably be inspired to purchase tickets to watch flesh-and-blood baseball after seeing the celluloid version.

Baseball also thrives by intriguing the nation's youth;

so it was that a spring morning in 1948 found Campanis showing his movies in a Long Island high school. He was interrupted by Branch Rickey's telephone call.

A Washington scout by the name of Joe Cambria had been scratching at the Caribbean baseball lode for two years when Rickey decided the Dodgers would dig deeper. Campanis was his shovel, and in three years he had become the Caribbean's best-known scout.

It was to Campanis that Roberto Marin directed his discovery. The tryout camp was held at Santurce's Sixto Escobar stadium, named for a good hit, no-field boxer of another generation. A group of seventy-two nervous teenagers appeared, one of them a lean, serious-faced boy in a T-shirt and duck-billed cap. Al Campanis studied them with skepticism. Two years earlier he had conducted a similar experiment in Aguadilla that produced not prospects but suspects. But he lined them up deep in center field with the simple but telling request to throw the ball to home plate. Ball after ball arced in lazily until one flew like an arrow.

"*Uno más*," Campanis shouted to the boy who had thrown it. Again the ball whistled in on a line, hard and true. "I couldn't believe my eyes," Campanis said. "This one kid throws a bullet, on the fly. I said, 'That's all.' Hell, you can't gild a lily."

Campanis shortly mistrusted his vision again when timing the players in the 60-yard dash. The kid in the duck-billed cap ran it in 6.4 seconds. "*Uno más*," requested Campanis. Another 6.4. "In a baseball uniform yet," Campanis said. "Hell, the world's record then was only 6.1. I couldn't believe it."

Still, Campanis remained suspicious. Diamonds are not usually discovered in garbage cans. Surely this kid who could run like the wind and throw lightning bolts could not also hit. He sent the other seventy-one players home and got down to basics. "Clemente got in the cage, and I noticed he stood far from the plate," Campanis said. "I had a minor league pitcher there and I told him to keep the ball outside." Pantalone Santiago flicked his curve ball over the distant edge of the plate for twenty minutes.

"Shots," said Campanis. "He hit line drives all over the place while I'm behind the cage telling myself we got to sign him if he can just hold the bat in his hands. How could I miss him? He was the greatest natural athlete I ever saw as a free agent."

Baseball economics being what they are, Campanis yawned and told Marin that Clemente "had great tools but needed some polish." But his mind was already reaching for a contract. However, there was a conflict. Clemente was seventeen; organized baseball teams could have no truck with him for a year.

Pedro Zorilla was not a part of organized baseball, which did not recognize the Puerto Rican winter league, something akin to the bull not recognizing the guy waving the red cape. Twelve years earlier, Zorilla had been making six hundred dollars a month as a salesman for Shell Oil. "It was not bad money then," he said.

Not bad at all. Omar Cordeiro's grandfather, who was Melchor Clemente's big boss, earned a less impressive wage and raised eleven children; supported Cordeiro, his mother, and sister; employed three maids, and drove a new car each year.

Moderately well off, Zorilla spent a thousand dollars in 1939 to organize the Santurce club of the winter league. He was also the chief Caribbean scout for the New York Giants, who had followed Brooklyn south in search of the untapped pool of talent.

Later, he dealt with all major league teams and exported such fine players as Orlando Cepeda and Reuben Gomez, while importing Willie Mays and dozens of other major leaguers for the winter season. But in 1939 Zorilla was a struggling professional entrepreneur, building his club around a skeleton of Americans and scrupulously maintaining his amateur contacts in the hopes they would lead to enough quality local players to flesh out the team.

In time, Zorilla became one of the most widely respected men in Latin American baseball, and his Santurce Crabbers became a dominant force in the Puerto Rican winter league, which thrived in the postwar years. Thus, the day after Campanis had doubted his eyes and his stopwatch, Roberto Marin appeared at Zorilla's office and left a note. It read, "Keep your eye on Roberto Clemente. He'll be playing in Manati on Sunday."

Three days later Zorilla arranged to visit his wife's parents in Manati and stopped by the ballpark. In the second inning, Roberto Clemente doubled home two runs; in the fourth, he tripled; in the seventh, he doubled again; and in the ninth, his powerful throw cut down the potential winning run.

"Bring him to my home tomorrow," Zorilla told Marin. The following morning, on the enclosed flagstone patio that serves as an entrance to Zorilla's white, Moorish-style home in a lazy San Juan residential district, the Santurce Crabbers offered Clemente a bonus of $450, and $45 a week "to learn to wear a uniform."

Clemente was uncharacteristically excited. He and Marin would immediately take the contract to Melchor Clemente, unsigned, of course. Luisa Clemente had retained an unshakable vision of an engineer in the family, but Melchor Clemente was the only lion in his house. Since he could neither read nor write, he took Pete Zorilla's contract to a neighbor who could. "Roberto got $500 to play baseball," he told the man, handing over the single-page document. The neighbor scanned it, guile clouding his eyes. "Maybe he could get $5000."

Marin was appointed negotiator and he and Melchor went to the Zorilla home. A brief impasse prevailed. Finally, for the first time, the boy took a bite out of his father. "I will do whatever you say," he told Marin. "I want to play ball."

Melchor Clemente sensed the winds of change. "Tell the man I will sign for you," he informed his son.

Pete Zorilla has qualified for Medicare, although he does not need it. Thinning, gray hair rides high on a bronzed forehead, and the years have worked two deep troughs into a long, oval face. He has always been a man with abiding faith in a judgment that has afforded him a semiretirement of dabbling in San Juan real estate and television. Zorilla's judgment told him that rookies who play regularly in a league full of major leaguers do so at the peril of deflated egos. In his first season with Santurce, Roberto Clemente batted seventy-seven times in seventy games.

"I never let the young ones play much," Zorilla said. "We had great pitchers here. Satchel Paige, pitchers like that. The ball comes to the plate looking like an aspirin tablet. A young boy like Clemente strikes out three or four times a couple of games in a row, he starts asking questions of himself: 'Can I hit? Can I really play?' It is important he does not give himself the wrong answers."

Other factors were involved. Santurce's veterans would have been ruffled playing alongside a seventeen-year-old days removed from a San Juan amateur league. And the Puerto Rican winter league fan may be baseball's most demanding. The rivalries involving Santurce, San Juan, Arecibo, and Ponce are murderous. "Our people, if they would have to kill someone for their team, they would do it . . . gladly," Zorilla said.

Thrust into a far more sophisticated brand of baseball and scared because of it, Roberto Clemente did not ask questions of himself, only of Zorilla. Clemente chafed badly in inactivity. Inserted in the ninth inning as a defensive replacement in his first game, he recorded his first putout by dropping to one knee and clutching the ball shoulder-high. But in the bottom of the inning, he doubled to beat Caguas. The following day he was back on the bench. Idled by an outfield that included Americans Bob Thurmond and Willard Brown, who would without fanfare precede Jackie Robinson across major league baseball's color line, Clemente began to hone the fine sense of outrage he would carry with him the remainder of his career.

"If I don't play tonight, I quit," he told Marin one evening. Once more the thick-set rice salesman, a quiet man unsuited for the role, was cast as mediator. "Zorilla told me, 'I pay him, he play when I say he play,'" Marin remembered. "I didn't tell Roberto that. I tell him, 'Take it easy. Your day will come.'"

Late in the year it did. Thurmond was paralyzed by left-handed pitching, and one night Clemente's pinch-hit double cleared the bases and won him steady employment in the final, brief days of the regular season.

Santurce's manager was Buster Clarkson, a husky shortstop with power who had rattled around the Negro major leagues for a dozen years, too old to really benefit from Jackie Robinson's breakthrough. Zorilla hired Clarkson in October of the year he hit .200 in fourteen games for the Boston Braves in his only major league season. If forced to obey Zorilla's dictum, Buster Clarkson offered the slim, silent rookie both affection and instruction.

Clemente was what is known to the trade as "a bailout hitter," meaning simply that he dragged his front foot toward third base as the pitch came plateward. Some bailing out may be considered part of the hitter's style; too much is frowned upon, even though a man named Al Simmons terrorized American League pitchers for years, despite a left foot that was pointing toward the third-base dugout as his home runs were disappearing over distant fences. But Clarkson never saw Al Simmons, and baseball is nothing if not a game of orthodoxy.

"Clarkson put a bat behind my left foot to make sure I didn't drag it," said Clemente. "He helped me as much as anyone. I was just a kid, but he insisted the older players let me take batting practice."

"All he ever needed from me was encouragement," Clarkson said. "He had a few rough spots the first year, but he never made the same mistake twice, and he was always willing to listen."

Clarkson led the winter league in runs-batted-in during the 1953–54 season, and Santurce, boasting major leaguers Junior Gilliam and George Crowe, won the championship and the right to meet the winners of the Cuban winter league for the Caribbean title.

Zorilla was permitted to pick up a few league stars for the Cuban series and leave some of Santurce's lesser lights at home. While his teammates played in humid Havana, recently seized by the new dictator Fulgencio Batista, Clemente steamed in San Anton. "He never forgave me for that," Zorilla said. "He never mentioned it to me, but he told some of his friends."

Although Clemente only had eighteen hits for Santurce, Campanis was not the only bird dog on his trail. Harry Craft of the Yankees, Tom Sheehan of the New York Giants, and Quincy Troupe of the Cardinals all had expressed an interest. Zorilla's sympathies were with the Giants. When the winter league season ended, he contacted the New York owner, Horace Stoneham, a man who also trusted his own judgment and was habitually surrounded by underlings who constantly assured him of its reliability.

Zorilla encouraged Stoneham to bid for Clemente, perhaps envisioning the day when Willie Mays, Roberto

Clemente, and any journeyman would have formed one of the great outfields in history.

Stoneham resisted. "The kid strikes out too much," the Giant owner said. Zorilla contacted the Dodgers. Was Campanis still interested?

On February 19, 1954, in the mahogany-paneled den leading from the patio of his home, Zorilla roughed out an informal agreement on a West Indies Cable & Wireless Ltd. telegram blank. The Dodgers would give Clemente a ten-thousand-dollar bonus, and a five-thousand-dollar salary for the 1954 season.

Once more a baseball document was taken to the barrio home. This time there was no disagreement. Melchor Clemente made his "X." When a formal contract was later drawn up, Osvaldo Clemente counterfeited his father's signature and pressed his own thumbprint to the pact, rendering it illegal. As it turned out, the contract's legality became an academic question as far as the Brooklyn Dodgers were concerned. In any case, the boy who had bounced a rubber ball from the walls of his mother's kitchen, and slashed at tin cans, and at a critical juncture fought down an instinct to be subservient, was part and parcel of the Brooklyn Dodgers. They immediately secreted him in an unlikely locale.

Chapter 5

HIDDEN IN MONTREAL

Montreal in the spring is a concrete corsage. Dogwoods bloom in pink and white profusion along its clean, sparkling streets. Dozens of parks, cacophonies of greens and golds and reds, refresh the city. Saucy Gallic girls in swirling silk; old men in dark wool huddling on park benches to grouse over separatism in reverent tones; warm breezes and soft rain and bilingual tolerance, these are the things of Montreal in the spring. The Old World charm and an easy truce between two nationalities usually at war comforts the uneasiest of strangers, assures them home is really just there, behind that nearest Laurentian peak.

Roberto Clemente was not comforted. These mountain peaks had snow on them, and the saucy girls spoke a strange language of slightly slurred consonants. And he was a nineteen-year-old Puerto Rican playing on a baseball team of Americans in a province whose heart was French. He was a stranger, thirsting with a stranger's desire to reach out and touch some piece of his homeland. Everything—habits, social customs, food, language, street signs—was different. What Roberto Clemente would accomplish here, he would accomplish in a strange and difficult land.

When he had signed with Brooklyn, dreams of Flatbush Avenue, not St. Catherine's Street, had danced in his head. After Melchor Clemente's "X" had been affixed to the telegram blank, Milwaukee had solidified its interest, and Brave scouts spoke in terms of a bonus ranging from twenty-five thousand to thirty thousand dollars. "You gave your word," Luisa Clemente reminded her son, but he needed no prodding. "Brooklyn was famous," he said. "I didn't even know where Milwaukee was."

It is a good bet he was about as familiar with Montreal. When he arrived at the Dodger spring training site at Vero Beach, Florida, in March, Clemente knew a single word of English—"Campanee"—and one less of French.

"He was a free swinger, and the only thing that concerned us in camp was him standing so far from the plate," said Dodger scout Al Campanis. "You would've had to have been a seer to predict what he would do later. There was some talk about altering his stance, but he got his hits, so we left him alone."

The Brooklyn Dodgers of 1954, the boys of author Roger Kahn's summer, came to Vero Beach fresh from two successive National League pennants and increasingly less haunted by the traumatic experience of blowing the 1951 championship to the Giants on Bobby Thomson's historic home run. It could be reasonably argued that in 1954 the Dodgers owned one of the finest collections of outfielders ever assembled on one team. This was the Golden Age of Brooklyn baseball. Carl Furillo, blocky and belligerent, led the league in 1953 with a .344 average and had the most feared arm in the game. Center field belonged to the Duke, muscular, introspective Duke Snider, the darling of Bedford Avenue, who fell eight points shy of Furillo's average but compensated with forty-two home runs. In left field much of the time was the Man, the soul of the Dodgers, Jackie Robinson, whose fierce drive fired the club and who was infinitely more valuable than his .326 average could ever hope to portray. In reserve was George Shuba, cruelly nicknamed "Shotgun" because of a woefully weak arm, but a fearsome streak hitter whose credentials included a plus .300 average in ninety-four games. No nineteen-year-old could hope to force entry to such an outfield, and following spring training, Clemente was sent to Montreal, or secreted there.

Subjected to increasing criticism that some clubs, most especially those associated with Branch Rickey, had been hoarding talent in the postwar era, baseball's lords enacted a series of "bonus rules." Each new one was as unworkable as its predecessor, and in 1953 the newest version was given some teeth: Any player signed for a bonus and salary that equaled more than four thousand dollars would be subjected to an irrevocable draft the following winter unless retained on the parent club's roster the entire season.

Faced with the prospect of losing Clemente, the Dodger front office gambled on its faculty for deceit, placing him in the care of Montreal manager Max Macon, a steely-eyed introvert with a reputation for hard work.

Whether or not the Dodgers consciously tried to hide Clemente from the prying eyes of scouts from other major league clubs is questionable—barely. The evidence insists that the Dodgers ordered him into virtual seclusion in Montreal; Macon insists otherwise. The evidence does not support his claim.

There were only four ways the Dodgers could have retained Clemente: kept him in Brooklyn; successfully hidden him in Montreal; had him jump the International League club, thus becoming ineligible for the draft; or had a major league club enter a claim for another Montreal player, which would have made the rest of the Royals untouchable. The latter was possible but risky, although it is suspected that Dodger officials saw it as a reasonable expectation.

Among the Montreal players worthy of draft consideration were outfielder Sandy Amoros, shortstop Chico Fernandez, and pitcher Joe Black, ironically Clemente's lone confidants on the club. But Amoros had been inconsistent at the plate in an earlier trial with Brooklyn, a wrist hitter awkwardly susceptible to the change-up; Fernandez' bat was even more suspect; and there were whisperings that a herculean effort in mainstaying the Brooklyn pitching staff in 1953 had been fatal to Black's arm. And, as Campanis noted, "Clemente had superior tools; you didn't have to be a scout to see that."

Macon treated such talent rather shoddily. In the first

week of the season, Clemente cleared the left-field wall at Delerimier Stadium with a shot that carried almost four hundred feet against a stiff breeze. No Montreal hitter had overpowered that wall, but the following day he was on the bench. Weeks later in Richmond, Clemente was scheduled to bat in the first inning. The bases were loaded. Macon yanked him in favor of a pinch-hitter. That month Clemente had three triples in one game and rode the bench in the next. A free swinger, Clemente suffered through stretches when he was not making contact with the ball. Fighting those slumps, he was showcased to disadvantage and stayed in the lineup days at a time.

"The idea was to make me look bad," he said. "If I struck out, I stayed in there; if I played well, I was benched. Most of the season they used me as a pinch-hitter or in second games of doubleheaders."

Max Macon's bench was no softer than Pete Zorilla's, and Clemente railed as he had before, his dreams turning to ashes. "I never thought I would reach such heights," he said. "Then I did . . . and they wouldn't let me play."

Once again he sought Roberto Marin's counsel. "He told me he was going to quit," Marin said. "I told him, 'Take it easy. You are just a kid. Take it easy.'"

In essence, Joe Black told the impatient young outfielder the same thing. A garrulous, sensitive man, Black is today a vice president with Greyhound. In 1953, he had been the pitcher the Dodgers turned to in moments of crisis, and his bursting fast ball had danced and hummed across the corners when it was most crucial. A year later it had abandoned the corners for the perilous heart of the plate, and the Dodgers abandoned Black to Montreal in hopes that his control would return. He spoke Spanish, and soon the impetuous rookie and the imperturbable veteran became an odd couple. When the Royals traveled south to segregated Richmond, Black, Clemente, and Fernandez roomed in a different part of town than the remainder of the team. Often when their conversation didn't smolder with blasts at inequality—"I thought it was childish," Clemente said—it dealt with Clemente's lack of playing time.

"Sure they were hiding him," Black said. "His inner drive wasn't being satisfied, and it was very frustrating for him. He had it and he knew he had it, and he just couldn't understand why he wasn't playing."

Clemente's life in Montreal was divided into spheres of hostility and friendship. He and Fernandez lived in a French residential neighborhood with a white family that was delighted to share its home with two young baseball players. "Montreal made blacks welcome then," Black said. "The white family they lived with had two teen-age daughters; that shows you how people treated us. Like we were human beings." Black understood the value to a young player of tolerance from others. Following the 1953 season, he gave a bottle of Scotch to the Dodger writers. Black and White scotch.

In the Montreal clubhouse, the veteran Royals were less cordial to Clemente, torn between wanting his skills in the lineup and their antipathy toward a young black "hot dog" who had the temerity to demand that he play.

"We had a lot of nuts on that team," Black said. "They

didn't appreciate a black guy who was a star. They only wanted you to go so far. But the guys on the team wondered why he wasn't playing. We had to scuffle, and when he played the second games of doubleheaders, he seemed to make the difference. But we'd lose and they still wouldn't play him."

Whether by his design or the Dodgers', Macon continued to keep Clemente under wraps, although it was not always an easy task. The flair born on the softball fields of San Juan surfaced in Montreal. One night he leaped high against a wire fence fronting the left-field bleachers at Delerimier Stadium, snatching a disappearing home run in the webbing of his glove. Like an angry god robbed of its sacrifice, the fence plucked him and held firm, Clemente's belt hopelessly snagged on the top strands. Gleeful Montreal fans extricated him at length. He played baseball with the fire their idol Maurice Richard brought to hockey; they delighted in his abandonment.

Making his way back to the Montreal dugout at the end of the inning, he passed the hitter he had victimized. "You son-of-a-bitch," the man growled. "Sank you," replied a grinning Clemente. A teammate informed him he had not been complimented; rather his ancestry had been called into serious question. Later larcenee and larcenist passed again. Clemente's vocabulary had multiplied since Vero Beach. "Son-of-a-bitch . . . son-of-a-bitch . . . son-of-a-bitch," he shouted at the transgressor.

The language he used on Max Macon was far more restrained but no less intense. As the 1954 season wore on, Macon used an outfield variously consisting of Amoros,

Gino Cimoli, Dick Whitman, and Bobby Wilson. No one ever confused it with the Dodger patrol. Amoros and Cimoli—the latter as a teammate of Clemente's—reached the majors, but Whitman was at the twilight of a mediocre career, and Wilson was a proven minor leaguer.

Nevertheless, as Montreal slowly lost ground to Toronto in a two-team sprint for the league championship, Macon played Clemente sparingly. "Bob used to say, 'That man strike out three times . . . I no strike out three times,'" Black laughed. "Some guys thought he was cocky, but he wasn't. He was just having to overcome obstacles, and he would hear things that were said, and they hurt him."

Macon's efforts at intrigue were consistent but, finally, proved ineffective. The Pittsburgh Pirates were on the scent. The 1954 Pirates were humorless forerunners of the New York Mets of the mid-1960s. They had no engaging characters, just struggling incompetents. In both 1952 and 1953, they finished a dead and well-deserved last in the National League, managing in 1952 to record the second-poorest won-loss percentage in the club's sixty-six-year history.

Branch Rickey, successful major domo in St. Louis and Brooklyn, had come to Pittsburgh four years before to rebuild the Pirates. He stayed to preside over their further demise, by 1954 having thoroughly lost the pixyish sense of humor that, along with a precise command of the language and a fearsome temper, were his personal trademarks. By July, only the mentally incompetent were unaware that the Pirates would finish last and earn the booby prize: first choice in the winter draft.

Rickey was determined not to waste that choice, and when a particularly glowing report was turned in on a prospect, he would send a favorite scout, Clyde Sukeforth, on the road. Normally a Pirate coach, Sukeforth was dispatched to Richmond in July to determine if Joe Black had regained his wandering accuracy. Rickey and Dodger vice president Buzzy Bavasi had been fencing in trade discussions. Brooklyn wanted utilityman Sid Gordon, a native son of Flatbush who had flirted with the .300 mark for nine seasons; Rickey held the hope Black could bring a semblance of respectability to the Pirate pitching staff.

"Sukey showed up one day when we were playing in Richmond," Black said. "He wanted to see if I was still any good. He was there about ten minutes, and he forgot all about old Joe Black."

Fortunate enough to have been on hand the few times Clemente batted earlier in the season, Sukeforth arrived at Richmond's Parker Field in time to watch the pregame warmup.

"I saw Clemente throwing in the outfield . . . I couldn't take my eyes off him," said Sukeforth, who was on the telephone with Rickey before the game started. Returning to his seat, he watched Clemente pinch-hit. Macon had erred, fatally.

Sukeforth was not infallible in his judgment. During the third game of the 1951 National League playoffs, Dodger manager Chuck Dressen had asked Dodger pitching coach Sukeforth which of the two pitchers warming up in the Brooklyn bullpen was the steadier. "Branca," Sukeforth told Dressen. Minutes later, Ralph Branca was touched for the Bobby Thomson home run that gave the pennant to the Giants.

On this occasion, however, Sukeforth's judgment was unerring. When the game ended, he stopped to chat with Macon. "Take care of our boy, Max," he grinned. "Make sure nothing happens to him."

Macon tried, restricting Clemente's playing time even more after Sukeforth's visit. The manager's southern drawl became increasingly less reassuring to the player's Puerto Rican ears, and the scene of Clemente hurling his uniform at Macon's feet and shouting, "I want to go home" became a familiar one in the Montreal clubhouse.

When Al Campanis came through Montreal, Clemente turned to the scout for consolation. "I know I can play better than these other guys, but they won't play me," he told Campanis. "The other night we get five runs in the first inning, they take me out. Mr. Macon does not like me."

Campanis tried to soothe his discovery. "Do you trust me?"

"I trust you."

"Then believe me. Everything will turn out all right for Roberto Clemente."

A warm reassurance, to be sure. But lacking the substance or conviction Howie Haak could bring to such a conversation. In late August, Rickey sought a further opinion on Clemente and telephoned Haak, a Pirate scout whose sphere of influence was the Caribbean.

"There's a player up in Montreal who might be our first pick," Rickey told Haak, a natural storyteller whose gray hair and easy manner fitted him for the role of father figure. "Judas Priest, Sukey says he can do everything. Go up and take a look."

Haak started shadowing Montreal in the gloaming of the season. Ironically, he and Macon had been roommates in the International League almost two decades before. If the Dodgers had been eager to seclude Clemente earlier, they were desperate when Haak appeared, and Macon used him in only one game while the Pirate scout was shadowing the Royals.

In the final game of the regular season, Clemente was scheduled to bat seventh against Rochester's Jackie Collum, a tiny junkballer. In the first inning the Royals waited patiently for Collum's assortment of off-speed pitches, scoring four runs and putting two runners on base. Clemente started plateward. He never reached the batter's box. Macon ordered Dick Whitman, who had once triggered a wild melee between the Pirates and Dodgers, to pinch-hit.

Incensed, Clemente returned to the Powers Hotel and began throwing his clothes in a suitcase, unaware that leaving the team before the playoffs would give the Dodgers the victory they were seeking. He was packing when Haak tapped on the door.

The scout's classroom Spanish and the player's ballyard English were at odds, but the message was simple: Go, and the Dodgers would retain the rights to Clemente; stay, and the Pirates would draft him. "You'll end up staying with Brooklyn if you go home," Haak cajoled. "Finish the year, and next season you'll be playing every day for the Pirates." In the battle of soft words, Haak defeated Campanis. The frustration would end for Clemente if he returned to Santurce, where Pete Zorilla was putting together a brilliant winter league entry. But Haak prevailed.

Macon, who subsequently became a territorial scout for the Pirates, is a serious man, described by colleagues as "a guy who works at his job." If he no longer owes allegiance to the Dodgers, having worked for two other clubs prior to joining Pittsburgh, Macon obviously feels a sense of loyalty to the men of the Dodger front office, proven by history to have blundered, as Horace Stoneham had when he sniffed, "The kid strikes out too much."

Macon pleads innocence for his former employer twenty years after the fact, but his pleas bring bemused grins to the faces of his contemporaries. And he is part of a baseball establishment that is superprotective of its leaders. There are no skeletons in baseball's closet: They are quickly ground to dust and scattered to the four winds, lest men of stature be embarrassed.

No one, it would seem now, was responsible for *l'affaire* Clemente. Dodger president Walter O'Malley was at the time busy badgering the New York city fathers for a new stadium to replace creaky Ebbetts Field, in reality camouflaging a far more devious plot. One dark of night three years later, the Dodgers crept from Flatbush, and the next morning when the citizens of Los Angeles awoke, right out there in the smog was their very own major league baseball team.

Campanis could see no place for Clemente among the Furillos and Sniders and Robinsons and Shubas.

O'Malley's assistant honcho, Buzzy Bavasi, had been consoled over Clemente's possible loss by some faulty arithmetic. "We thought we could get our money back if some club drafted Clemente," he said. "But we made a mistake."

A kindly word for what transpired; still Macon defends Dodger strategy. "If you had been in Montreal that year, you wouldn't have believed how ridiculous some pitchers made him look," he said. "He had a habit of always taking a strike and getting himself in a hole with men on base. I knew it was a mistake to sign him to a Triple-A contract. We couldn't protect him, and some team was bound to grab him. Hell, there was no way you could hide him even if you wanted to. Don't play him at all, everybody gets suspicious anyway."

Play him a little and suffer the anguish of being torn between orders from on high and a personal desire to win baseball games? Joe Black thinks so. "Macon knew that black guys were in baseball to stay and he wanted to win," Black said. "But he had to take orders. I think he really wanted to play the kid more."

Macon claims no lofty motives and contends his instructions were merely to win and draw as many people as possible while doing it. "Historically, the Montreal club always drew well," he said. "It was instrumental in paying a lot of the parent club's tab. Buzzy never told me to hide Clemente. The only orders I had were to win and draw big crowds.

Montreal did draw a crowd—at the winter draft—and the Dodgers would blow the biggest bonus check they'd given since Jackie Robinson had roared out of the Negro league to stomp down baseball's color barrier seven years before. Also lost was the income that would have been generated by a player who could have lured to Brooklyn the thousands of Puerto Ricans who had migrated to New York City after the war—income that conceivably might have kept the Dodgers in Brooklyn and altered baseball history. The Dodger front office had from early October to December to leisurely ponder a loss it knew was as certain as death and the Internal Revenue Service.

How painful a loss it was became evident during those weeks. If Clemente's first season with Santurce had been in its own way as painful as the Montreal misadventure, the second brought his initial fulfillment as a professional.

Pete Zorilla, trying to reignite the huge popularity the winter league had enjoyed following the war, dug deep into his bankroll and imported the New York Giants' young phenom, Willie Mays, and a nucleus of fine major leaguers, which moved veteran New York baseball writer Dick Young to observe that with three pitchers, "Santurce would've finished third in either league."

Fresh from the Army, Mays had led the National League in 1954 with a .345 average. When he made a truly incredible catch of a blast by Vic Wertz in the World Series, one of the most widely discussed defensive gems in baseball history, it was obvious to the most novice fan that here was the game's newest *enfant terrible*.

The two young Santurce outfielders had a dozen similarities. Both were young, introverted, and driven; both had physical skills so unique they excited even the blasé types who people baseball; and both played the game with a passion that inflamed spectators.

Four years older and a proven product, Mays became

the master; Clemente the watchful, willing pupil. Night after night in the hot, damp parks of San Juan and Caguas and Ponce, he watched Mays consume fly balls at his waist, palms up, and studied the batting stroke that slashed white arrows into distant corners of the park. "Don't let the pitchers up here show you up," Mays later cautioned. "Get mean when you go to bat. If they try to knock you down, act like it doesn't bother you. Get up and hit the ball. Show them."

"That was Roberto's big break, playing left field next to Mays," said the barrio scout Roberto Marin. "He watched Mays like a hawk, used to talk about how he played. Mays showed him the basket catch, how to charge the ball, told him not to worry about gambling on a catch at his ankles, because in the major leagues other outfielders would back him up."

Later, when reporters assumed Clemente had adopted Mays' waist-high catch, he balked at the notion. "Luis Olmo did that," he would snap. "I did that playing softball." But the Puerto Rican outfielder Olmo was not a consistent user of the basket catch, and no one who had seen Clemente playing softball remembered him catching the ball in any manner save the orthodox. In any case, it was an academic question. Infielder Bill Rigney had used the basket catch years before.

Mays may have been baseball's freshest *wunderkind*, but in the winter of 1954 he did not overshadow his younger teammate. Both fielded and threw superbly, the game's most awesome arms in the same outfield. Both batted over .400, Mays tuning the machinery that would soon make him unquestionably baseball's most exciting talent, Clemente readying himself to challenge for such laurels.

Branch Rickey was delighted that the difference between the Santurce outfielders was one of subtlety. Two weeks before the winter draft, he went to Puerto Rico to confirm the opinions of Sukeforth and Haak. In reality, the scouts had seen little of Clemente, who batted only 148 times in 87 games at Montreal, and Rickey, called the Mahatma, was like Zorilla and Horace Stoneham, a man with faith in his own judgment.

After watching several games, Rickey approached the young man who was to become the guts of a Pirate team that would eventually escape its role of laughingstock; a team that had lost more than a hundred games in each of the previous three seasons.

"Clemente, I like the way you play this game," Rickey said. "Can you do the same thing in the major leagues?"

Clemente's answer was falsely modest. He had few doubts. "I do not know," he offered, as canny in youth as Rickey was in age. "I have never seen, what you call it, a major league game? I do not know if the players in my country are better than the ones in the major leagues."

It was an exercise in territorial pride. Zorilla had replaced Buster Clarkson with Herman Franks and, in addition to Mays, Santurce was laced liberally with such proven National League players as Willie Kirkland, Don Zimmer, and George Crowe. Bob Thurmond, whom Clemente had unseated the previous season, had gone to the major leagues shortly before Robinson and became, in effect, the first black to play in the major leagues. Clemente knew he was, with the single exception of Mays, at least their equal. Rickey suspected as much, and returned to the mainland to back his suspicion with the four thousand dollars necessary to bring regret to Brooklyn and hope to Pittsburgh.

On Monday, November 22, 1954, Dr. Sam Sheppard told a Cleveland jury he did not kill his wife; the jury later disbelieved him. French Prime Minister Pierre Mendès-France informed friends it was merely a matter of time before his country and Great Britain would form a Western European union. Joe McCarthy, under merciless attack by the Army and his colleagues in the Senate, and in need of a brief reprieve, said he would enter the hospital to have his appendix removed. The new Kansas City Athletics, believing strongly in blood lines, announced they had drafted pitcher Cloyd Boyer, whose two younger brothers were brilliant prospects. The Chicago Cubs selected journeyman outfielder Jim King, the New York Giants' aging catcher Mickey Grasso. The woebegone Pittsburgh Pirates had already dredged the baseball draft of its single prospect. "I didn't even know where Pittsburgh was," Roberto Clemente recalled later.

Lost forever to the garrulous, growling fanatics of Ebbetts Field was perhaps the ultimate outfield: Furillo, Snider, and Clemente. Such an aggregate would not have been long united. Furillo's career was shortly strangled by a worsening knee injury; Snider was rapidly tiring of the game's pressures, its insistent question: What have you done for me lately? But Clemente would have been a cornerstone upon which to build. His power was to right-center, and the right-field wall at Ebbetts stood invitingly, 297 feet from home plate. When they became the Los Angeles Dodgers in 1958, temporarily playing in the Coliseum, a huge screen was needed to guard the left-field seats, so near the plate, it was said, that the left fielder could scratch the shortstop's back without either one of them having to move.

Considering the havoc he later wrought in the expansiveness of Forbes Field, Clemente would have been a terror in either Brooklyn or Los Angeles. "He would've knocked down the walls either place," theorized Joe Black.

But now he was a Pirate, eager to accept the legacy of Wagner and Traynor. No team at that time could have needed him more.

Chapter 6

A ROOKIE'S RAGE

Forbes Field was built generations before architects were forced to sacrifice their eye for aesthetic grace to the spectators' demand for antiseptic comfort and a roomy repository for their backsides. It was the classic baseball arena, and for more than fifty years its charm allowed the game's subtle drama to unfold in a sylvan setting. When the game palled, and it did often in Pittsburgh, Pirate fans found relief from tedium in letting their eyes wander over Forbes Field's ivy-masked brick walls and the maples that peeked over them from the park beyond. No signs extolling the virtues of beer or under-arm deodorants prostituted the view, as soft shafts of the early-evening sun streaked into the stands from behind the University of Pittsburgh's Cathedral of Learning, a forty-two-story skyscraper that peered down its nose at its ballpark neighbor.

If the baseball fans of the rough-hewn, thick-wristed city said, "Watch it, mac" rather than, "Pardon me" when they bumped into one another on the streets, they were gentler folk in the pastoral setting that was Forbes Field.

When Roberto Clemente joined the Pirates in 1955, their home was still Forbes Field, and if no one else did, the becalmed fans of Forbes Field bade him welcome.

A twenty-square-block neighborhood, Oakland, housed Pittsburgh's cultural and educational activities as well as the Pirates, and through its streets passed not only the important but the uninhibited. In the Oakland Cafe, old Irishmen wept unashamedly into their Jameson's over the strains of "Galway Bay," surrounded by the Pirates and the neighborhood's other colorful rogues. There were Mike the Drunk, who would frequently erupt from the men's room with a parakeet perched on his shoulder and rush into the street screaming, "There's an eagle attackin' me"; and newsboy Yutzie Pasquarelli, who quit Pitt the day he found out he was making more money than his professors; and the wino with no name who, for free drinks, would serve as a target for a beer salesman who aspired to become a professional knife-thrower; and Joey Diven, billed in a national magazine as "the world's greatest streetfighter," a laughing, brawling young man who built a modest political career on the strength of a Thursday evening during which he beat up, individually and collectively, a linebacker, assorted guards and tackles, and a few halfbacks on the Pitt football team.

If much of Pittsburgh in the 1950s was a steelworker trudging home with his lunchbox, Oakland was the city's high roller. Into such a place came Roberto Clemente, emerging from that twilight zone between boyhood and manhood, his cocoon thousands of miles away, still puzzled by a strange language and the people who supplemented it with hand gestures and jerks of the head and the pronoun "you-uns."

Pittsburgh was to Puerto Rico as Paris was to Peking. Where could a homesick twenty-year-old buy fried bananas? Listen to the melody of the carollo, a tiny frog that sings sweeter than any songbird? Hear a reassuring "*¿Cómo está usted, hombre?*" And why did the black people cluster in a place called The Hill? And why did strangers laugh when you abused their language without meaning disrespect? And did the sun never shine? And who was "buddy"? And what was a nigger?

"I couldn't speak English," Clemente said. "Not to speak the language . . . that is a terrible problem. Not to speak the language meant you were different." To be black meant you were different. Not to know that bananas were sliced on cereal instead of fried meant you were different. Being different was not easy. "It took guts for us just to come here," said Orlando Cepeda. The Latin players were not strangers in paradise. "Some people act as though they think I lived in a jungle," Clemente complained, astounded years later when a woman asked if he wore a loincloth in Puerto Rico.

Baseball, that was easily understood. Baseball was trying not to flinch when pitchers threw high and tight, searching the new black boy for a lack of heart. Baseball was hour after hour of fielding fungoes off the right-field fence. Baseball was a clubhouse full of strangers who quit talking when you walked in, or snickered when you were hurting.

"What stood out about Roberto was that here was a tremendous athlete, a young man of unusual talent, unusual drive," Joe L. Brown said. Brown, son of a famed prat-falling comic, also came to Pittsburgh in the spring of 1955. After sixteen years of varied sports administrative work, he was brought to the Pirates by Rickey, and before the year was out had replaced the old man. "From the very beginning, Clemente had a fantastic arm, and he hit balls so hard you wouldn't believe it. There was never a doubt he would become one of the game's great outfielders."

Brown was wrong. Roberto Clemente came to have grave doubts. He was homesick, his only friend a postal worker who befriended him on his first day in town. As Clemente's social confidence inched ahead, so did his desire to communicate, but the nuances of the English language continued to escape him.

And following the 1954 winter league season, returning from a hospital visit with a dying brother, his car had been struck broadside at a San Juan intersection by an automobile traveling sixty miles an hour. The crash—the other driver was drunk—dislodged spinal discs, and back ailments plagued Clemente the rest of his life, so much so that in time he became an expert in their treatment. In his initial season with the Pirates, Clemente moved in and out of the lineup at the behest of his back, not satisfying some of his teammates in either instance. When he played, he was accused of showboating; when he didn't, the charge was malingering.

While Clemente was pacing the Montreal dugout, the 1954 Pirates were striking, even for them, new lows. They were last in the National League in at-bats, hits, doubles, and home runs; they stole fewer bases than any team in baseball. The pitching staff had a combined earned-run average of 4.94. Their incompetence knew no boundary. In May, the Dodgers pulled off a rare triple steal against them; in August, they were victimized by a Cincinnati triple play. Fittingly, their home attendance of 475,494 was the lowest in the league. Their lone representative in the All-Star Game was Frank Thomas. He struck out.

The 1955 Pirates were fragmented, a pitiful conglomerate of had-beens and never-would-bes struggling for just another year in the pension plan. Competing players carried out a war of nerves, a purpose behind their taunting. A pitcher named Joe Trimble was constantly heckled by another pitcher and was thought to have been unnerved. In any case, he was finally sent to the minors; his antagonist remained on the roster.

Clemente found few sympathizers in the Pirate clubhouse, and could be seen signing autographs for fans, hours after home games. "I was lonely . . . I had nothing else to do," he said. If he was lonely, he was also bothered by the cool weather, and wondering on occasions if he had come too far too fast. And for the first time, he was faced with a numbing enemy: prejudice.

Fred Haney had no time to devote to a rookie's anxieties. Under Haney, the Pirates had bungled their way to 205 losses in the previous 2 seasons. Once before in his baseball career, Haney had been dumped from the manager's office to the broadcasting booth, and he had no interest in repeating the trip. A gnomelike man who had sacrificed much of his hair to the Pirate ineptitude, Haney decided early-on to be loyal to the managerial commandment that states, "Lose with experience." Loosely translated, it means, "Don't look at me, I can't play, too," and once in a while it rescues a manager's job for another season.

So it was that Haney opened the 1955 season with an outfield comprised of Frank Thomas, who had played Little League baseball in the actual shadows of Forbes Field and was developing a reputation as both a power-hitter and a grouch; Ramon Mejias, a Cuban considered a perennial prospect to the day he had played himself out of the league; and journeyman Tom Saffell, who would be best remembered for lifting a home run over the towering right-field roof at Forbes Field with a burst of power never again repeated. In reserve there was Earl Smith, one of eighty-five Smiths to have performed in the majors to that date and quite possibly the least distinguished.

The Pirates immediately capsized, losing their first eight games as Haney tried to stem the tide by replacing Saffell with Smith in a tactical move akin to trying to blot up the Johnstown flood with a hand towel. Before the second week was history, Roberto Clemente was a regular, and Smith's major league career had been concluded after five games.

Clemente opened the fourth game in right field and extracted a small measure of vengeance for Brooklyn's lack of faith. He chopped a Johnny Podres pitch into the hole at short and relished his first major league hit and the first of many bites he would take out of the Dodgers. In less than a week he ended the Pirate skid by singling and doubling to drive in a pair of runs that beat Philadelphia.

In April, Haney had said, "I want to reserve judgment on him until he plays a little up here." In May, with Clemente hitting .360, Haney said, "He likes to play . . . he learns easily . . . his fielding has been heart-warming . . . there was a report he couldn't go back on a fly ball, but he's made some fine catches." Giants' manager Leo Durocher agreed: "Whatever Haney says goes double for me; I think Clemente has a chance to be a fine player."

Clemente still fretted. His personal life pained him, and Forbes Field was poorly suited to his talents. It was mammoth, the Yellowstone of baseball: 457 feet to left-center; 365 feet down the left-field line to a 25-foot scoreboard; and only 300 feet to the right-field corner, but the foul line was guarded by a high screen, and the wall sped away on a severe angle at flank speed. He was developing real power, but the ballpark forced him to tailor his game and, wisely, he did.

"When I first saw Forbes Field, I said, 'Forget home runs,'" Clemente said. "I was strong, but nobody was that strong. I became a line-drive hitter."

As the spring remained uncommonly cool, Clemente's line drives—in the vernacular, "frozen ropes"—became less frequent. His head bobbed wildly at the plate, and he became susceptible to off-speed pitching. And the base on balls was unacceptable to anyone who had grown up swinging at so large a target as a soup can. Clemente walked only an average of once each eighteen times at bat, his competitive temperament fiery, his batting stroke unfettered and unconscionable. The pitched ball was meant to be struck, not ignored. He swung with abandon, striking out an average of once each eight times at bat.

On May 26 against the Phillies in Pittsburgh, both the Pirates and Clemente hit rock bottom. Early in the game, Clemente badly sprained his right ankle. In the ninth inning of a 4–4 game, with Saffell on third and young Gene Freese at first, Mejias singled up the middle. Saffell crossed the plate with the apparent winning run. Fans poured onto the field as Freese swerved off the basepath. Phil infielder Roy Smalley retrieved the ball and tagged second base. Freese was out; the run didn't count. The Phils won the game in the eleventh inning. Such were the 1955 Pittsburgh Pirates. They fired the fans' imagination with five- and six-game winning streaks; then doused it by falling into prolonged, inexplicable slumps.

If Clemente jeopardized his job at the plate, he sustained it in the field, quickly mastering the right-field fence at Forbes Field, which spit line drives at a hundred different angles only to softly embrace the odd baseball and allow it to drop gently to the ground. In his first fifty games, Clemente had ten assists, gunning down four runners in a five-game stretch.

His remarkable catches made him the darling of Pittsburgh fans, long thirsting for mere competence, and a bit undone in the presence of artistry.

"All I thought about was the batter and myself," Clemente said. "I knew if I could not play right field well, I might not play regularly. I didn't like that much."

Summer consumed spring. Humphrey Pennyworth fell before the gentle but determined ministrations of Joe Palooka; the national debt rose to $269,756,502,965 and change; lovable Ike continued to warn against America becoming involved in an Asian land war; cigarette packages held no warning that the contents might be injurious, and Roberto Clemente flailed away, increasingly frustrated by a lack of contact with both the pitched ball and his white teammates.

Silent, fired by an ambition peculiar to people who have never owned more than one pair of shoes, he viewed the malice sent his way with wonderment. "He was so emotional, so intense, so sensitive. He didn't understand a lot of things," Brown said.

One of the things Clemente didn't understand was his teammates, who played . . . performed . . . appeared each day. The less he understood their jibes, the more he withdrew, constantly asking his only confidants, Mejias and the postal worker, Phil Dorsey, "Why? I never hurt anyone in my whole life."

When his ailing back restricted him, Clemente didn't play, although his absences from the lineup were brief. Still, to absent oneself from the field of battle was not adhering to the baseball tenet that demanded a player rub dirt on his wounds and "hang it out," a term sexual in connotation and a red badge of courage often worn in lieu of common sense and/or talent.

"He could've been hypocritical and gone out and played," said Nelson King, a pitcher for the 1955 Pirates. "But no one then seemed to realize the sensitivity he had for his body. He looked at it the way a mechanic looks at a racing car. If it wasn't right, he wanted to tune it. Some guys used to ridicule him because he didn't play every day, but most of them were playing every day so people would say, 'Gee, that guy has balls.' They were doing it because they were afraid of criticism if they didn't. The only thing that dictated what Clemente did was what he felt was right."

King is not a stranger to struggle. A bony right-hander, he persevered to record a 7–5 career record in four years in the majors before his arm failed. After finding no particular satisfaction in the business world, he turned to broadcasting at a tiny radio station in Arnold Palmer's hometown of Latrobe, Pennsylvania, and put in a long apprenticeship before becoming a member of the Pirates' radio and television broadcast team.

"I know Roberto was hurt deeply by the criticism he took the first years here," said King, a bright, sensitive man. "He was withdrawn partly because of the language. He'd only ever been out of Puerto Rico one other time. Everything here was confusing to him."

Nothing confused Clemente more than the press. During spring training in Fort Myers, Florida, a sportswriter referred to him in print as "the Puerto Rican hot dog." In baseballese, a peculiar language at best, a "hot dog" is a player the fans consider colorful, and the other players, and reporters, consider untoward. What to San Juan softball fans had been exciting and innovative was lacking in sophistication to a faction of the American sporting press. "Why the hell they picked on a kid who hadn't ever played before is beyond me," sighed Joe L. Brown.

"The trouble was that he was driven, and anyone who was different was automatically wrong."

Clemente was, of course, different. He didn't use the word "you-uns" when engaged in a conversation involving more than one other person, a verbal idiosyncrasy peculiar to Pittsburgh. To be sure, he ravaged the English language; the writers who covered the Pirates did likewise to his stiff-necked pride. He was quoted phonetically and issued forth sounding like a Bavarian: "I no play so gut yet. . . . Me like hot weather. I no run fast cold weather." Although none of them realized it, the Pittsburgh writers were sowing the seeds of a feud so enduring that Clemente came to nurture and relish it.

"He couldn't understand why they called him 'Puerto Rican hot dog,'" said Dorsey. "He was proud of being Puerto Rican."

Phil Dorsey is a black man. He's rotund, amiable, and as suspicious of motive as any black man who ever reached middle age. A BAR man in Korea, he remained on reserve duty after the peace-keeping gesture and served in a Pittsburgh unit with Bob Friend, a Pirate pitcher. The morning Roberto Clemente came to Pittsburgh, Friend introduced him to Phil Dorsey. Young Don Quixote, who would tilt with every windmill baseball had to offer in the next eighteen years, had found the perfect Sancho Panza. Dorsey was also single, and eight years older. Born and raised there, he knew the city. He understood how Pittsburgh was happy with its blacks as long as they remained in The Hill under the shepherding of black ward heelers loyal to Mayor David Lawrence's political machine, which ran the town with a control equal to that which Chicago has experienced under Mayor Richard Daley. And Phil Dorsey had qualities unique to becoming Roberto Clemente's friend. He liked to shoot pool, watch swashbuckling movies, play poker, and sleep. And he regarded loyalty as the chief virtue of man. Phil Dorsey became Roberto Clemente's man for all seasons—chauffeur, valet, corresponding secretary, masseur, and alarm clock. When people commented on Dorsey's sundry chores in behalf of the ballplayer, Clemente would say stiffly, "Phil is not my chauffeur . . . Phil is my friend."

And so Dorsey was. They would split a hundred pennies and play poker. "He usually wound up with all my pennies," Dorsey said. They would shoot pool, Clemente's skill occasionally attracting a small-time hustler, who was made to feel welcome. "They didn't invent pool in Pittsburgh," Clemente would grin at Dorsey. The slim, younger man and his stocky sidekick made weekly runs to the Chinatown Inn and watched Errol Flynn flicker across a drive-in movie screen, a band of pirates helpless before his omnipresent sword. Dorsey slid easily into the role of batman-adviser.

"He was shy . . . he had a thing about not forcing himself on people," Dorsey said. "He would tell strangers, 'No, he is Roberto Clemente. My name is Dorsey.' But with me, he wasn't shy. He loved to argue, and he'd get mad when you gave in. He'd say, 'If you believe that, you should keep arguing for it.'"

Bolstered by Dorsey's unflagging friendship, Clemente quit turning to autograph-seekers for personal contact, as he did the night he spent forty dollars on dinner for the family of a fan who had stopped him to say, "I just wanted to tell you you are a helluva ballplayer," or the night he drove a girl in a wheelchair and her mother thirty miles after they missed their bus while waiting for him to sign a scorecard. "Don't ever lie to me and we'll always be friends," Clemente told Dorsey.

Their friendship was assured the day Dorsey found Clemente a place where he could sleep without interruption. Roberto Clemente looked upon sleep in the manner young priests view the cardinal's ring. He gloried in its restorative powers and chafed mightily in its absence. He forever pleaded insomnia, but once asleep he was an incarnate Rip Van Winkle. When he first came to Pittsburgh, Clemente resided in Webster Hall, a slowly deteriorating hotel perhaps a four-wood shot from Forbes Field, where "Please Do Not Disturb" signs were generally ignored.

Shortly, he and Mejias moved to an apartment building that turned out to be no less busy than the hotel. Men came and went at all hours of the night, noted Clemente, capable of being disturbed by a key turning in a lock. "Who are all these guys?" Clemente complained to his teammate. "What are they doing?" What they were doing, Dorsey informed him later, was transacting the world's oldest form of commerce.

A brothel was no more restful than a hotel. "Phil, I got to get out of here. I can't get any sleep," Clemente said, moving again, this time to the tranquil home of a Jewish couple. Still, what he considered to be a minimum quota of rest eluded him. Dorsey would place the ballplayer's telephone on a pillow, which he then placed in a closet. "Phil, the telephone is ringing," a groggy Clemente would announce, his nap interrupted. "I'd go to the closet, and the phone would be ringing," said Dorsey, who came to be a human alarm clock. "When he had to be someplace, I'd go by his apartment and wake him up. I can still hear him saying, 'Phil . . . five more minutes, Phil!'"

Clemente spent a lifetime seeking those "five more minutes." Such were his dreams that he memorized hotel room layouts because a particularly severe nightmare caused him to walk in his sleep, "and I didn't want to walk out the window." Once he confided to Dorsey, "If I could sleep, I would hit .400."

Lacking the required solitude, Clemente still led the Pirates in hitting in June of 1955. Haney, resigned to the fact that with no apparent difficulty the Pirates would descend into last place in the eight-team National League for the fourth straight year, was satisfied. Clemente was not. As the Pirates sought their natural level, he seethed at both the team's inadequacies and his own. "He was only twenty, and he was sensitive to the general conditions," Brown said. "He was stimulated by challenge, and we weren't competitive."

Clemente vented his rage in a singular but costly fashion, destroying the team's plastic batting helmets. The new headgear were considered unfashionable but not intolerable by his teammates; to Clemente they became red flags. In moments of frustration, he smashed them with his bat, splintered them against the dugout walls and, when unusually exasperated, leaped upon them with both feet. When the number of unusable helmets reached twenty-two by actual count, even the patience that had stood Haney so well in his time of trial wore thin. "I don't mind you tearing up your own clothes if you want to," the little manager told his young charge, "but if you're going to destroy club property, you're going to pay for it."

Economically sanctioned, Clemente was properly repentant. "Haney, he tells me it cost $10 for each helmet, that's $220," Clemente said. "I do not make so much money. I stop breaking the hats."

Had some of the Pirate heads remained in the helmets, evidence insists Clemente would've gladly accepted the $10 tariff necessary to their destruction. Adam was probably no more surprised at encountering the serpent in the garden than Roberto Clemente was at meeting blatant racial prejudice. Not only did it tear at his pride, it affronted his sense of every man's worth. "What difference does it make what color a man is?" he would inquire of Dorsey, who must have wanted to smile at the incredulity in Clemente's voice and cry over the innocence of such an inquiry.

Most of the 1955 Pirates groused over Clemente's preoccupation with his back, the shrill sound of his complaints. Some merely disliked him because he was black. Jackie Robinson's penetration of the color barrier in the majors had occurred only eight years before. Blacks were still relatively new to baseball, and baseball was still skeptical of them. Certainly one was to be suspicious of a colored boy who didn't automatically move to the back of the bus and spoke a language with no equivalent of "Yassuh, boss."

Two years before, Pete Zorilla had warned Clemente he would no longer be playing in a country where the indignities befalling a man because of the color of his skin were subtle. "You can't change things there," cautioned Zorilla, knowing that the proud young man who glistened in the sunlight and didn't know there was such a word as "lynching" would try to change them. "Those people have lived that way two hundred years. You are going to play ball. That's all."

Sound advice, perhaps. And ironical. Zorilla is a fair-skinned Puerto Rican. Racial prejudice is not rampant on the island. See a brown person, his skin says his antecedents probably came from the mountainous interior of Puerto Rico. The island's blacks are indigenous to the coasts, some of them no doubt on the beach in 1493 to greet Columbus and his Spaniards, who brought with them social domination.

Pete Zorilla owned a baseball team; he is the color of coffee liberally laced with cream. Melchor Clemente cut cane; he is the color of coffee with no cream. When Roberto Clemente strolled through the exclusive Rio Piedras suburb in which he lived, he did not see a skin blacker than his own. There has never been a man as dark as he was to govern Puerto Rico. "Our prejudices are subtle," leers a Puerto Rican.

A teacher who held Clemente in abiding affection, Mabel Caceres, says without hesitation or malice, "Roberto was very handsome for a black man." Maria Rodriguez, the secretary of the church in which Clemente was baptized and married, a gentle, gracious woman in her seventies, says almost reverently, "Roberto's face was black, but his soul was as white as an Ingles." María Rodriguez and Mabel Caceres would not draw a glance if they walked into the Birmingham Cotillion.

Surrounded by such a subtle bigotry, Clemente came to Pittsburgh naïve in the ways of racial confrontation. That naïveté did not long survive. In Montgomery, Alabama, that winter, a department store clerk named Rosa Parks dropped wearily into a seat in the middle of a bus. Her feet ached. The bus driver ordered her to surrender her seat to a white man. She thought about her sore feet. She told the driver to go to hell. She was promptly arrested. Six hours later a young minister new to the city, Martin Luther King, Jr., organized a bus boycott, and Jim Crow started to die. In Pittsburgh, Clemente was discovering him for the first time.

"I don't believe in color; I believe in people," he insisted. "I always respect everyone, and thanks to God my mother and my father taught me never to hate, never to dislike someone because of their color. I didn't even know about this stuff when I get here."

Curt Roberts knew about it. He, Clemente, and Mejias were the only men of color on the 1955 Pirate club. The stumpy second baseman, a weak hitter from Oakland, California, explained the facts of major league life to Clemente, i.e., indignant outbursts over racial inequality were not tolerated by anyone hitting under .350. "Keep your mouth shut, you can't change anything," warned Roberts.

"I don't care," Clemente's tenor rang with outraged pride. "I don't want to be put in the shithouse because I am Puerto Rican. I don't stand for disliking people because of their color. If that is the case, I don't want to be living. I am a 'double-nigger' . . . for my skin and my heritage."

Such an outburst was melodramatically Clemente. That was precisely the case; he did not perish. Neither did he yield. In the dugout, he heard his teammates slur opposing blacks. Often he would move to the far end of the dugout to escape the cruel bench-jockeying; often he would not. "Mejias and me stood up lots of times," he said. "A lot of the players didn't like us because we were not white. They made remarks about the colored fellows on the other teams."

Bench-jockeying is popularly conceived as cute by-play; often it is vicious; gut-shooting where an opponent may be most vulnerable. There are no restrictions; the most personal weaknesses are fair game. In 1955, the word "nigger" had yet to become socially unacceptable, and Clemente heard it over and over. "Sometimes I acted like I didn't hear it," he said. "But I heard it. I heard it."

His pride was honed on such words, and it was only a matter of time until it forced him to retaliate. Returning to the dugout one night, the strikeout victim of a white pitcher, he trailed racial insults behind him. "I call him names," Clemente admitted. "The manager said, 'You should not talk like that.' I say, 'Why?' The manager say, 'You are Puerto Rican.' I say, 'So what? They are allowed to call me black, I cannot call them white? I don't understand.'" He never did, really. On the day Martin Luther King, Jr., was assassinated, a poll was taken by team officials to determine if the Pirates were willing to play that night. "If you have to ask, we do not have a great country," Clemente said softly. Still a naïve manchild in the land of fallen promise.

The anxieties of his rookie year extracted their pound of flesh. Clemente's average slid steadily down through late summer, and he finished his rookie season at .255. But 39 of his 121 hits were for extra bases, and the Pirates improved slightly, losing only 94 games. Fred Haney was somewhat buoyed by his club's refusal to meet the 100-loss minimum of the past 3 seasons and was shocked to learn that he had been fired. Totally disillusioned, 74-year-old Branch Rickey retired in favor of Joe L. Brown days after the 1955 season ended.

The new Pirate manager was Bobby Bragan, a delightfully uninhibited Texan known to take a nap in the third-base coaching box when displeased by an umpire's decision. He would be driven to further unusual acts by the 1956 Pirates.

In defiance of a hallowed baseball tradition, the Pirates were weak down the middle when Brown and Bragan replaced Rickey and Haney. But a key trade was engineered, and the Pirate farm system produced a pearl. Bobby Del Greco and his superlative glove were shipped to St. Louis for bespectacled Bill Virdon. Brown's first major deal was a smash. The 1955 Rookie of the Year, Virdon would hit .319 in 1956 and narrowly miss winning the batting title; Del Greco would bounce around to teams needing a golden glove and a rubber bat. Ironically, Virdon later managed the Pirates and employed a batting-practice pitcher named Bobby Del Greco.

If Virdon's bat was a welcome addition, so in late

spring was the peerless glove of young Bill Mazeroski. Suddenly the Pirates were no longer "weak down the pipe."

Bragan shook up the Pirates lightly, replacing players, loosening the cliques. A big power-hitting first baseman, Dale Long, helped Clemente discover some rapport with his teammates. "He was very helpful to Roberto," said a 1956 Pirate. "He was sympathetic, and he could kid him the right way, get him to open up."

During the off-season, Clemente's back trouble had become more troublesome, and Luisa Clemente renewed her vision of an engineer in the family. Clemente bought his parents a $12,500 house and played sparingly in the winter league. "My mother wanted me to go back to school," he said. "The people in Puerto Rico want me to play, but I say I am hurt. Finally, I tell my mother and father, 'I will try it one more year. If I still hurt, then I quit.'"

It was an idle threat. Ever the free swinger—he walked an average of only once each forty-three at-bats—Clemente made increasingly better contact in 1956, spilling wicked line drives all over National League parks. More familiar with the city, his lifestyle relaxed. "He began to get used to things, people," Phil Dorsey said. Now, Clemente fully understood when Errol Flynn informed a buccaneer captain, "You'll taste my steel, scoundrel."

Virdon, an intense, mentally tough man, noticed the increasing confidence immediately. They were as diametrically different as two personalities could possibly be.

Virdon was somber and steady; white, out of the American heartland and held firmly by its work ethic; a success in spite of a lack of superior gifts. Clemente, running passionately up and down the emotional scale, was a bundle of nerve ends; black; out of a far-off American possession and held firmly by its honor ethic; extraordinarily gifted.

"It was obvious he didn't doubt his ability to play the game," said Virdon. "He didn't brag, but he said things that indicated his confidence. Most people who are good know it. There are two kinds of confidence in baseball. I had one kind, he had the other. I didn't know if I could play in the big leagues. I struggled for five years in the minors. When you struggle, you have to be concerned. He hardly played in the minors. If I hadn't stayed here, I could've accepted that. He knew he was going to make it; he didn't even think about not making it."

During the 1956 season, Clemente made it. He hit .311, fielded incredibly, threw as he always had, and only occasionally drove Bragan to distraction, as he did in a game when, after doubling three times, he bunted with the tying run at second and two out in the ninth. Blithely, he offered an explanation for the foolish tactic to his livid manager. "How could you do something as dumb as that?" Bragan inquired. "The law of averages was against another double," Clemente explained breezily. Later in the season, again with two out in the ninth, he ran through third-base coach Bragan's signal to hold up. "I say to Bobby, 'Get out of the way and I score.' If I score, the game is over, we no have to play any more tonight; if I don't, the score is still tied." A manager accused of operating mechanically, Bragan could only laugh, "I've often felt like using a ballplayer's head for fungo practice."

Under Bragan, there was less clubhouse gossip of Clemente's malingering. Clemente played in all but seven games. The 1956 Pirates were trying to crack an old mold, and they were a maddening crew. Bob Friend's pitching and Virdon's hitting carried the club to respectability in the first month, during which Bragan grabbed complete control of the club. In one game he fined Clemente for missing a bunt sign and Dale Long for cutting off a throw to the plate. The players reacted differently to the twenty-five-dollar assessment. Clemente did not say a word; Long argued it would make him a better player. He was right. Immediately, he went on a home-run binge unexcelled in baseball history, hitting one a day for eight straight days and igniting the Pirates.

On June 13, the ragtag Pittsburgh Pirates, antecedents of the New York Mets of the 1960s, were in first place, and Roberto Clemente was the third-leading hitter in the league with a .357 average.

Five days later, the impossible dream began to die. The Pirates fell out of the lead and continued to sag the remainder of the summer. Virdon hit .319, Clemente .311. Friend pitched well but finished 17–17; and in a classic example of nonsupport, a young hurler named Ron Kline was 14–18 with a respectable 3.38 earned-run average. In his eighteen losses, the Pirates provided Kline with twenty-one runs.

Bragan went to remarkable lengths to stop the Pirates' steady skid. He baited umpires unmercifully. He juggled the lineup daily, often having the pitcher bat eighth or sixth. He pleaded and cajoled and ranted. The nucleus for a winner was there; the experience wasn't. One night, with the Pirates a run down in the ninth, no one on, and two out, Clemente bunted into an easy out. "How could you do that?" an incredulous Bragan screamed. "Boss, me no feel like a home run," the manager was informed.

The Pirates slid clear to seventh place and ironically decided a two-team pennant chase between Milwaukee and Brooklyn—on the last Saturday of the year losing a doubleheader to the Dodgers that set off a celebration in Flatbush.

Still, these were not the old Pittsburgh Pirates. They were building around an embryo superstar. Clemente played in 147 games, and the charge of malingering that enraged him had been dispelled. One year and a new manager later it would be revived. In the newspapers.

Chapter 7

DAMN PRESS!

To the reporter, the baseball player is golden, eternal youth. He is too young, too muscular, too handsome, too self-assured, too full of his own importance, and he makes too much money. The player is, in short, what the reporter is not, and this both saddens and irritates the reporter.

At 2:00 A.M., when the reporter is munching the olive in his seventh martini in a lonely hotel bar, he is certain beyond doubt that the player is upstairs locked in passionate embrace with the pretty young girl who had smiled pleasantly at the reporter earlier in the day. In a moment of truth-seeking, the reporter asks himself: What is the real worth of a man who spends his time playing a child's game? Truth-seeking stops short of the obvious: What is the real worth of men who chronicle children's games?

To the baseball player, the reporter is too guileful, too secure, too curious, too well-educated, and he makes too much money. The reporter is, in short, what the player is not, and this both saddens and irritates the player.

At 2:00 A.M., when the snoring of a roommate causes the player to toss fitfully and contemplate the evils of curfew, he is certain beyond doubt that the reporter is downstairs in the bar, stirring with whispered lies the pretty young girl who had smiled pleasantly at the player earlier in the day. In a moment of truth-seeking, the player asks himself: What is the real worth of a man who describes the occurrences of a child's game? Truth-seeking stops short of the obvious: What is the real worth of a man who plays such a game for a living?

The baseball player and the reporter are natural enemies, and as such, in an honorable state of grace that they never seem to recognize. "Joe is O.K., for a player (reporter)," they assure colleagues, made uneasy by the lack of a middle ground between them. The player is sure the writer is living off the sweat of his brow; the writer is not sure it does not work the other way around. Sadly, neither ever realize the simple logic of an equation that states inarguably: The ballplayer profits by the interest in his game generated by the reporter, whose accounts of games sell more newspapers, which in turn increases reporters' salaries.

Consequently, the player regards the reporter as a useless hanger-on whose interest in him wanes save for those occasions when the player is having breakfast on the road with a "niece" from Boston; and the reporter's definition of the player smacks with a brevity not often seen in his prose, to wit, "I'll still be eating the postgame buffet when you are a sore-armed, used-car salesman in Joplin."

This is all well and good for both the reporter and player, for the ethics of their respective trades run at cross purposes. The player seeks an image the public accepts; the reporter of integrity must construct such an image of the player as he sees. This, of course, frequently leads to young, muscular players punching old, flaccid reporters, but sports journalists readily accept the hazards of their calling, a black eye produced by a player's fist being visual proof of reportorial honor.

Roberto Clemente did not punch Les Biederman, or Jack Hernon, or Chilly Doyle, or George Kiseda, or Chet Smith, or Al Abrams, or Roy McHugh, or Bill Christine, or Charley Feeney, or Bob Smizik. Or any other reporter to cover the Pirates during his career. Evidence suggests that, had he foreseen an untimely death, Clemente surely would have corrected such an oversight.

Like most players, Clemente did not read newspapers; but like most players, he had many friends who did, and they loyally kept him informed of what was being written. Through their devotion, by the time Clemente had attained his majority, he was daily and feverishly charging the news media with: implying he was a malingerer, accusing him of receiving preferential treatment, ridiculing his use of the English language and his style of play, racial bias, ignoring him, unjustly denying him a Most Valuable Player award, and other crimes against humanity too numerous to mention.

Every day of his professional life, Clemente sat in judgment on the news media. The verdict (guilty) and the sentence (his enmity) were unchanging. The press, he believed, portrayed him as a comic figure. He would tell reporters, "My bad shoulder feels good, but my good shoulder feels bad." The words were humorous, but the intent behind them was not, and to appear publicly cast as a buffoon rubbed Clemente's pride raw. Still, it is reasonable to conclude that he cherished his feud with the press; made it do his bidding; and drew forth from it inspiration.

"If I would be happy, I would be a bad player," he once admitted. "With me, when I get mad it puts energy into my body."

His body was eternally charged from the moment he saw himself referred to in cold, unmistakable type as "the Puerto Rican hot dog." It mattered not a whit that the local press treated him with deference, was more often than not servile, and criticized him rarely and with claws sheathed, in the manner of a kitten punishing a ball of yarn. He resolutely fueled himself on imaginary adverse criticism when the documented stuff could not be found. Every reporter new to Clemente paid for the original sin of some unknown colleague who had laid bare the pride of a nineteen-year-old.

A small, mild reporter named Roy McHugh recalled his first interview with Clemente, who on this day had struck a prodigious home run. "That the longest home run you ever hit?" McHugh inquired innocently. "I'm tired of that stuff," Clemente roared, black eyes blazing. "You guys never give me any credit."

Years later, as a nervous novice, I approached Clemente for the very first time. "Stay away from that son-of-a-bitch when you can," a coworker had advised. I dismissed his advice as cynical. Man and boy, I had long marveled at Clemente's talent and the effortless grace with which he displayed it. I was his fan. Virginally, I thought, "Could any man mistreat his fan?" Ho, ho, ho. He fired as soon as he saw the whites of my eyes. "You reporters are all the same," he screeched somewhere in the middle of the amenities.

The charge this day was racial prejudice. I was informed that I was a bigot. I had been raised in an integrated neighborhood, which at that moment the federal bureaucracy was defining as "culturally deprived." The inseparable pal of my youth was a kid blacker than Clemente. Fear battled ravished innocence and lost.

"You don't know me worth a damn," I sputtered, my Adam's apple sawing through the knot in my tie. For a half hour we talked, rising voices occasionally deflecting into the deepest recesses of the dank, near-empty Pirate clubhouse. We parted with a noisy, undeclared truce; me sensing correctly that my youth or outraged indignity, or some combination thereof, would leave us amicable sparring partners in the years to come.

As this is written, I empathize with his view of the press, for all of its obvious flaws. My instincts tell me he was misunderstood, victimized by reporters who somehow lacked the sensitivity to deal with him justly. This is, of course, one part ego trip, one part fantasy. There is no hard evidence that he was ever abused by the press; likewise there is no hard evidence that its members ever perspired in seeking the man inside the flannel suit. Perhaps the truth lies with the reporters who built his image, myself included, and then wrote at his death that he was among the most misunderstood of men.

Les Biederman of the afternoon Pittsburgh *Press* covered Clemente's career the longest. Methodically and mechanically, Biederman wrote baseball from 1938 until the conclusion of spring training thirty-one years later. He was the gentlest of critics. On one occasion, a Pirate pitcher named Bob Veale complained to a wire service reporter named Ira Miller that he was being neglected. Miller wrote the juicy story, and later said Biederman sought to have him barred from the Forbes Field press box shortly after its publication. Reporters seeking follow-up stories were told by Veale: "Mr. Biederman says I shouldn't say anything."

Essentially a man whose personal wit was not reflected in his copy, Biederman's prose was routine and uninflammatory. He wrote regularly for *The Sporting News*, a national baseball weekly once indicted as "a trade paper of inestimable value to perusers of minor league box scores and journalism instructors in need of examples of how not to write sports." As Clemente became increasingly aware of a lack of national recognition, despite increasingly impressive credentials, he pointed a quivering finger at Biederman.

At the sight of Jack Hernon, who covered the Pirates for the morning *Post-Gazette*, Clemente merely quivered. A hugely agreeable man, Hernon loved the Pirates unabashedly. But their ineptitude would occasionally drive him to the typewriter a study in frustration, and he would, individually and collectively, flay them in exasperation for their failures. Hernon covered the majority of Clemente's career before dying of cancer, but for reasons known only to the reporter and the player, the two men did not speak the final year of Hernon's life.

Not until 1958, when George Kiseda became the baseball writer for the Pittsburgh *Sun-Telegraph*, a Hearst paper justifiedly in its death throes at the time, did anyone write meaningfully of Roberto Clemente the human being. Kiseda wrote flowing features about him, apparently overcoming the language barrier that had impeded Biederman, Hernon, and Kiseda's successor, Chilly Doyle. A lovable eccentric who lived within sight of Forbes Field, Doyle often telephoned the Pirate offices to inquire of the weather at the ballpark. Once he drove a new automobile to Philadelphia and returned by train to Pittsburgh, reporting the car's theft upon arrival. Doyle—who once stood in the locomotive of a train and asked the engineer, "Which way to the dining car?"—did not write in-depth pieces on Clemente.

Kiseda did, unaware of Biederman's observation that Clemente "had an odd way of speaking." However, Kiseda, a talent far superior to his competition, covered the Pirates for only one season before the *Sun-Telegraph* did the honorable thing and ceased publication. Kiseda's affinity for the black athlete was and remains a professional millstone. He once caused a national commotion by pointing out that the Army football team was shortly scheduled to play Tulane in a segregated stadium. For this, Kiseda earned the disfavor of his publisher and the respect of his contemporaries. Had he been able to continue writing about Clemente, the player might have been less irksome to the press.

During Clemente's entire career, the sports editor and columnist of the Pittsburgh *Post-Gazette* was Al Abrams, once described as "the most beloved sports writer in America." Abrams and Clemente got on well. A wry Lebanese who loves good food almost as well as good conversation, Abrams for forty years took a paternal interest in Pittsburgh athletes, Clemente among them. "Roberto could communicate with Al," Phil Dorsey said. Abrams didn't quote Clemente phonetically, as did Biederman, who would later say, "Clemente was always unsure of himself because he didn't speak well. His language didn't improve much from his first year." Biederman's phonetic quotes grated on Clemente. "I never talk like that; they just want to sell newspapers. Anytime a fellow comes from Puerto Rico, they want to create an image. They say, 'Hey, he talks funny.' But they go to Puerto Rico, they don't talk like us. I don't have a master's degree, but I'm not a dumbhead and I don't want any bullshit from anyone."

Abrams, whose daily column was often given over to tidbits of information on the city's superfans and bursts of praise for its athletes, never seriously strained his relationship with Clemente, nor did he probe the subject deeply.

Abrams' counterpart on the afternoon *Press* was Chet Smith, a witty, irreverent writer who once said of the professional basketball championship, "If they were playing it in my backyard, I'd pull down the shades." He was prevented from painting a broad word-picture of Clemente by habit of writing as critic rather than reporter, and did not often stoop to discussion with his subjects.

Smith was succeeded as sports editor by Biederman, who continued to cover baseball without revealing any insight into Clemente, who continued to thrive on imaginary rebuke. Hernon was succeeded by Charley Feeney, an amiable fast-talking New Yorker who prides himself on hard-boiled baseball reporting.

Feeney's arrival and Biederman's retirement signaled more coverage of Clemente, who in time came to sustain his feud with the press. "Oh, I am fine," he would mock writers inquiring after his health. Biederman was replaced on the baseball beat by Bill Christine, a lanky, industrious nomad who had wandered about the country leaving newspaper strikes in his wake. But, after working in East St. Louis, Baltimore, and Louisville, Christine was inspired by his first major beat. The scene was fresh; Feeney's steady competition an incentive. Christine sought out Clemente. Was he a malingerer? Was he detrimental to the team? A fine if dispassionate reporter, Christine sparked renewed interest in a truly ignored superstar. The competition between Christine and Feeney brought Clemente into sharper public focus, and encouraged more visiting writers to air their views on the stormy Pirate star.

Nevertheless, the most incisive reporting done on Clemente was that of Roy McHugh, Biederman's successor as sports editor and surely the city's most able newspaperman. A quiet Iowan with a huge affection for words and a surgical deftness in their use, McHugh wrote of Clemente with a eunuch's impersonal touch, but his stories were revealing and often softly satirical. It was McHugh who theorized that Clemente's antagonism toward the press was self-serving. "Roberto Clemente's revving himself up to lead the National League in batting again," observed McHugh.

And so it seems in retrospect that Clemente had long been guilty of honing his competitive fire on the hide of a news media baffled by his antipathy. "Almost every day, reading between the lines of the newspapers, Clemente sees insinuations that his aching left shoulder doesn't really ache, that it's just an excuse to loaf through spring training," McHugh wrote. "He hears reports that on television and radio, character assassins have portrayed him as the opposite of a team player. As the season approaches, he is working himself into a lather."

If Ted Williams had thrived on a hostile press—which so embittered him that on his final day as a player he forsook nostalgia to assail "the knights of the keyboard"— Clemente was no less inspired by pussycat media. Periodically, like a geyser, he would erupt over some slight, real or fancied. To write of his injuries, he suspected, was to accuse him of, in baseballese, "jaking"; not to write of them was to doubt they were genuine. The writers, he was to insist, were ruining his image, ably assisted by the sportscasters.

When a young Pittsburgh sportscaster named Dick Stockton dominated the ratings through the simple device of airing his personal opinions, Clemente's criticism of the media reached a crescendo. Prior to Stockton's arrival, Pittsburgh sportscasters almost nightly offered Clemente bouquets, their occasional brickbat encased in velvet and handed over rather than thrown. But when Stockton implied that Clemente was not a team player—"a team player" not being defined—the Pirate outfielder exploded.

"You say maybe I no a team player," Clemente raged at a group of newsmen prior to an exhibition game in Florida. "I win four batting titles. I kill myself in the outfield. I try to catch everything that stays in the park. I play when I am hurt.

"What more do you writers want from me? Did any ballplayer come up to you and say that I am not a team player? Who say that? The writers, right? Well, I tell you one thing, the more I stay away from writers the better I am. You know why? Because they are trying to create a bad image for me. You know what they have against me? Because I am black and Puerto Rican. I am proud to be Puerto Rican."

Refreshed by a breath, and perhaps inspired by having produced a single in seventeen previous at-bats in the spring, Clemente continued, quickly becoming a soprano. "Did you ever see me loaf on the field? I break my ass out there. Even Harry Walker [one of two Pirate managers with whom Clemente was to have a love-hate relationship] say to me, 'Roberto, why you break your ass out there? Look at what the other fellows do, how they play. Take it easy.'"

Later, Clemente would ask, "Why that son-of-a-bitch say those things about me? Why he hurt my family? The year I come to this town I hurt my back, but I do my best. They call me a goldbrick, a mama's boy, a rotten fellow. I never do anything to that Stockton. He come in this clubhouse, I tell you, I kill him."

What brought such fury to a player who obviously found a near-idolatrous press lacking in sufficient compassion for him? Was it really a need for a combination whipping boy-catalyst? Was his ego insatiable? Why Clemente battled the press is easily understood. A baseball player's failures are highly visible and starkly recorded in the newspapers for the edification of a public apt to respond with such ballyard endearments as, "Ya bum, ya." What was puzzling was why Clemente fought the war so zealously, never hinted interest in a truce—unconditional surrender, really—that could have been his at a nod of the head.

Perhaps, as McHugh had written, the press fueled his competitive drive. "I get sick and tired of people saying, 'Clemente is all for himself.' If I hit .350, they say I should hit .351. Every year I hit better than four hundred players in this league, but still they write Clemente is no good. He no hit in the clutch. I would like to see one player who hit more than me in the clutch." Implied in such a statement was the obvious: I'll show them.

Or perhaps it was his admittedly healthy ego, pricked by reports that the injuries that kept him off the field were products of his imagination. "The only thing that amazed me was this thing about not playing," he said. "It amazed me because when I am hurt, I play. A lot of the fellows don't play when they have a cold."

Probably the best explanation for Clemente's tilts with the Fourth Estate came from its failure to hail him as the greatest player of his day. Not one of the greatest; *the* greatest. "Why they always write, 'Clemente is one of the best, but . . .'" he would ask, furious at the minutest qualifications of his ability. "Why always 'one of the best'? Why always 'but . . .'?" Later, he would win the 1966 MVP award only to ask leeringly, "What kind of a 'but' they have now?"

If he was acknowledged as the greatest—greater than Mays or Aaron or Mantle—not only Roberto Clemente would profit. Kids seeking to emulate his success would emerge from the barrios, new Roberto Clementes to further enhance the island's prestige. And the original model? He would have helped prove that "Puerto Ricans are as good as anybody."

"To the people in the Caribbean . . . it is like you have Babe Ruth here," Clemente said, seeking at once to retain modesty and spread truth. "You have an image. That is why I compare myself to Mickey Mantle. I am not jealous of Mantle, but to people in my home, the image I have is all about injuries, no matter what I say. Whenever the press talk about me, it is always the same thing: injuries. If they want to talk about injuries, they should send me to Vietnam. People don't believe Roberto Clemente when he say he is hurt. But when Mickey Mantle say his leg is hurt, it is O.K. I have my followers. To me, I don't want to accomplish something so I can be able to say, 'Hey, look at me, look at what I did.' I want to accomplish something for life."

Like most athletes—and politicians and mothers of sons who rob banks—Clemente never came to understand a reporter's role. "If I was a writer, the first thing I would try to do is have good relations with the players," he said. "I never criticize a writer when I think he is sincere about his writing."

The writers, Clemente suspected, doubted his sincerity. Mantle overcame conspicuous injuries—hip abscesses, osteomyelitis, etc.—and was deified for his courage. Clemente's injuries were mysterious and fugitive—wayward discs, insomnia, floating bone chips—and he believed he was being crucified for crying out that, by God, he was hurting. "Mickey Mantle is God," he complained, "but if a Latin or a black is sick, they say it is in his head."

As Clemente became more irascible to reporters and got to know them better, he rated them by city. In Chicago were the fearful. "They are afraid of me," he once giggled of the men who covered the Cubs. There was no malice in his heart, for if he sought to punish writers who had trampled on his sensitivities, he could still give away a treasured personal trophy to a sportscaster. In Philadelphia were the fearless: tenacious reporters beyond badgering, perhaps the cream of the nation's sportswriters. They asked interesting, penetrating questions that at once both exasperated and amused Clemente. But he treated them civilly, and nowhere more than in Philly was he questioned by the news media.

If the Philadelphia writers eagerly sought out Clemente, the San Francisco writers treated him deferentially and were properly humble, giving evidence to an earlier charge by Jim Brosnan that they "covered the San Francisco baseball scene with all the aplomb of a three-year-old fingerpainting on the wall."

Elsewhere, Clemente's reputation as a fire-eater brought him, as the phrase goes, no ink. Some of this lack of recognition stemmed from his often boorish treatment of honest newspapermen.

"I always had to stand there and listen to his five-minute denunciation of sportswriters," McHugh said. "I got tired of it. He'd start yelling, and everyone would turn around and look at you. It wasn't that you were afraid of him, you just didn't want to be embarrassed. It got so tiresome, I avoided him unless I had to talk to him."

Finally, Clemente's tirades attracted national notice, and McHugh returned to a subject he admittedly found interesting. "Maybe he kept on hollering because he got some attention," the writer theorized.

To a man, Pittsburgh reporters felt, as McHugh did, that Clemente "got an idolatrous press. He seemed paranoid about the press. He expected superlatives."

An older though unmellowed Clemente was generally liked by those who recorded his successes and odd failures. "One thing stood out," said Ira Miller of United Press International, "through all the outbursts and the arguments and controversies, it was almost impossible not to like the guy. I can remember the first time as a rookie that I had to interview him. He was polite and pleasant, as though he sensed my anxiety and was trying to make it easier for me. If the question was particularly penetrating, he might sit there for a moment with that quizzical, little-boy look on his face. But always there was an answer, and always it came from the heart."

Biederman and Hernon were products of a school of journalism that ignored controversy, at least until the third fingernail was extracted. Hernon wrote innocuously, but held strong personal opinions.

"Clemente's a hypochondriac . . . always was," he assured a colleague. "He can't hit in the clutch; it's a proven statistic. He's always making excuses for something."

In time, Clemente attempted to disregard the press. "I don't have to worry about what the writers say about me any more," he would say. "The fans have seen me play . . . they know the truth. If I listen to the writers, I don't know what kind of a player I am. No matter what I do, it is no good.

"I must be the worst ballplayer ever."

Chapter 8

THE PROMISED LAND

What price pennant?

Power, speed, pitching, defense? All of these. And more. Luck. The brash confidence of youth. The old folks who settle a team during those dark July losing streaks when the kids begin to bicker and have trouble swallowing and lose their brashness. A superman: the guy everyone instinctively glances at in the dugout in the ninth when someone blurts out, "Goddamnit, we got to make a move." A clubhouse camaraderie that absorbs and smooths personality conflicts, beats back fatigue, dispels doubt. A steady tactician at the controls for those mean, gritty games that want, demand, just the right strategy at just the right moment. All of these.

The Pittsburgh Pirates of 1957 seemingly could pay that price. As it turned out, they could not. It would take three years for them to acquire those necessary ingredients, or for those ingredients to evolve. They were a curious crew, the Pirates of 1957 and 1958 and 1959, their effectiveness tied by some invisible string to the physical and psychological well-being of a brilliant young outfielder, a burgeoning superman who had created a tempest in their midst.

When Roberto Clemente was well and playing daily—not plagued by the ills his teammates considered largely imaginary—the Pirates swashbuckled about the National League; when he was not, they seemed to stand trembling at the end of the plank. In reality, both the Pirates and Roberto Clemente were inching up the mountain.

To be sure, the Pirates had plummeted from first to seventh place during the 1956 season, but in the sweet spring of the year, when all teams are contenders, the 1957 Pirates spoke glowingly of their pennant hopes. Brown had attacked the reconstruction with an energy Rickey had been unable to muster. Dick Groat, a prematurely balding All-America basketball player, had roared off the Duke campus to join with Bill Mazeroski and immeasurably strengthen the heart of the infield. Virdon had chased Milwaukee's Henry Aaron to a batting title. The Pirate pitchers were young, strong, talented, and flushed with potential. And Bobby Bragan's managerial talents were not yet suspect.

"Bragan knew as much baseball as any manager in the game," said a 1956 Pirate. "He made moves ahead of other managers, was deeper into the strategy of the game. But we were tools to him, not people."

Roberto Clemente was an unworkable tool. He had endured an aching back throughout 1956; he could not in

1957, even though he was taught how to manipulate a wandering disc back into place. "It's like an automobile with the rear wheels out of line," he explained. "It isn't going to run right until the wheels get straightened out."

They never did, really, and the Pirates also fell out of alignment. Strong hitting by Groat and Thomas could not compensate for a laboring Clemente and inconsistent pitching. And again there were grumblings in the Pirate clubhouse. Clemente was a goldbrick. Clemente was a crybaby. And that worst of all baseball accusations, he was "jaking it."

The Pirates crumpled early-on, losing twenty-one of their first twenty-nine and settling comfortably into their role as the National League in-joke. Clemente played with his back in a brace. To swing a bat was painful; to run, agonizing. He was out of the lineup days at a clip, and Bragan left the impression that he felt Clemente's problems were mental rather than lumbar, although there was no open breach. "Bragan know I like to play . . . that I get sick when I see somebody play and I cannot," Clemente insisted.

Other Pirates succumbed to injury or indifference. Thomas was benched and complained to Brown. The next day Bragan told a clubhouse meeting, "I don't take orders from anybody . . . including Joe Brown. Do you understand that, Frank Thomas?"

As the Pirates threatened to become the tenth Pittsburgh team in twelve years to finish last or next to last, the front office located the site of Clemente's back problems. It was in his throat. "Have your tonsils out," he was told. "It is my back that hurts," he explained. The tonsils were removed, but in July Clemente went off to visit the Logan College of Chiropractic in St. Louis, where a doctor informed him that, among other things wrong with him: One of his legs was shorter than the other, one was heavier than the other, his spine was irritated and, in general, his sacroiliac area was a mess.

Meanwhile, Bragan was at wit's end—well, not quite— managing a last-place club that owned four .300 hitters. His patience gave out one afternoon in Cincinnati. Suspecting Reds' pitcher Raul Sanchez of throwing spitballs, Bragan dispatched two Pirates to the mound carrying a bucket of water. "You want to wet the damn ball, here," the stunned Sanchez was told. Bragan was ejected for the fourth time that season and fined fifty dollars. The next fine was his last in Pittsburgh.

On the final night of July, he critiqued a decision by umpire Stan Landes, using the classical form, thumb to nose, four fingers waggling. He was thrown out of the game, but returned moments later carrying a bottle of orange soda, which he offered to plate umpire Frank Dascoli and his colleagues. Enraged, they shooed him off the field. Bragan was fined a hundred dollars, which didn't hurt nearly as badly as Brown's blunt comment four days later when Bragan became unemployed "for the good of the team."

The manager's job was offered to superscout Clyde Sukeforth, who studied the situation briefly and demurred. Joe Brown turned next to an engaging Irishman, Danny Murtaugh, who looked like, and was, a hard-nosed elf. A tobacco juice-spitting second baseman of modest credentials, Murtaugh became "interim" manager.

Nothing clears the air so cleanly in baseball as a dismissed manager. The Pirates played .500 ball the remainder of the season, beating the New York Giants the last two days to tie Chicago for last place. An aching Roberto Clemente played in only 111 games, drove in only 30 runs, and batted only .253. He and his team were united in misery.

When the 1957 season ended, Clemente rested briefly in the new house in the Barrio San Anton and then returned to fulfill his obligation to American society. Six months later he walked straight and tall out of the main gate of the Parris Island, South Carolina, Marine Corps Recruit Depot. The wandering spinal disc had found a comfortable home during his tour as a reservist, and the Pittsburgh Pirates were equally healthy. This year they would put the league to the sword.

Where Bragan had been mechanical, Murtaugh was daring. The Pirates would run, he said. They would pay attention to the game's fundamentals, he said. They would hustle, he said. And, lo and behold, they did, breathing fresh life into the baseball manager's oldest clichés. Throughout midsummer, they lay just off the league lead. Murtaugh spit tobacco juice on his players' shoes and applied the lash. They responded, and Clemente played every day, batting almost .400. In a pivotal two-game set with the now San Francisco Giants in late May, the league quit laughing at the Pirates.

Early in the season, Giant pitcher Reuben Gomez had put Pirate catcher Hank Foiles on the disabled list by hitting him with a pitch. On May 24, Gomez hit Mazeroski on the arm. Murtaugh gave Pirate pitcher Vernon Law his instructions the next inning. "Hit him [Gomez] on his right knee," the manager ordered the devout Law, a handsome deacon in the Mormon Church whose chiseled features bespoke piety. "The good book says to turn the other cheek, skip." Murtaugh let fly a stream of tobacco juice. "It'll cost you a hundred if you don't."

Law decked Gomez with his first pitch. "He who lives by the sword shall perish by the sword," Law explained later. As the plate umpire warned Law about the consequences of further beanballs, Murtaugh leaped from the dugout and rushed the bat-wielding Gomez. The Giants' Orlando Cepeda ran to intercept the chunky Pirate manager and was felled by teammate Willie Mays' flying tackle.

Peace was restored (fans later raised a hundred dollars to pay Murtaugh's fine), but two simple truths had been revealed by the incident. The clowns who had not seen the first division for a solid decade were no longer amusing, and the fire that must course through a champion ran in the Pirate veins. A part of the pennant price had been paid.

But only a part. The summer of 1958 was wanton and wild in the National League. Eight teams were separated by as many games late in the year. The Pirates were one of them, rising and falling with Clemente. His average dropped a hundred points by midseason, and the Pirates lost seventeen of twenty-two. Two kid pitchers, George Witt and Curt Raydon, and a brash rookie who had hit sixty-six home runs the previous year in the Western

League were added to the roster. The young slugger signed his autographs "Dick Stuart, '66.'" At first base he became known as "Dr. Strangeglove," and when the Pirate bus went past a junkyard it was *de rigueur* for someone to say, "Stop, we'll get Stuart a new glove." But he hit sixteen home runs before the season ended and took up the slack for a faltering Clemente.

Then in August, Clemente went on a tear behind the pitching of Bob Friend and Witt, the league's earned-run average leader. The Pirates won twenty-two of thirty-one, whipping the Giants three straight and climbing into second place with a lofty 84–65 record. Unfortunately, there was no one to chase to the wire. The indefatigable Braves won the next day to clinch the pennant.

But surely the stage was set, the price had been paid. These were the new and wondrous Pirates, who had won more games than any Pittsburgh team in 20 years. Frank Thomas had hit 35 home runs and had 109 rbi's; Friend won 22 games; Raydon and Witt, the kids, claimed 17 victories between them and spoke of fine promise; Bob Skinner batted .321, Groat an even .300, and Mazeroski had hit 19 home runs. And the clubhouse was a warm, friendly respite from the tension of the field. The conversation centered on sex and high prices and politics and sex; Roberto Clemente's ailments were passé in 1958. He played in 140 games, hit a solid .289, threw and fielded better than any right fielder in the league, and was obviously the superman a winner needed.

In the National League's morgue, the Pirates had drawn 1,310,000 fans. They had patiently awaited a pennant for

31 years and certainly it could now be seen, just there over the calendar's horizon.

But the price was not yet right for the 1959 Pirates, nor for their phenom, Roberto Clemente. Less than thirty days into the season, he was hit on the elbow with a pitch and did not return from the disabled list until July 5. Even then he said his arm "hung straight down to the ground." By then, the dream was ashes. Witt's right elbow became inflamed; Raydon's touch disappeared as if by magic, and he was optioned to the minors, never to return. Friend staggered en route to losing nineteen games. A major trade was slow in bearing fruit. During the off-season, Thomas had been shipped to Cincinnati for third baseman Don Hoak, catcher Smokey Burgess, and left-hander Harvey Haddix. They helped. But not enough. In July, bone chips sloshing around in his right elbow and his back tormenting him again, Clemente could not throw, and he was hitting .176. All he could do was field. And run. One night he scored from first base on a single as Cincinnati outfielder Wally Post leisurely returned the ball to the infield.

It was one of the few bright spots of a season that in reality probably died on May 12, when Haddix pitched the greatest twelve innings in baseball history and was beaten. On a muggy night in Milwaukee, the sweat flowing freely down his gamin-sad face, Haddix did not pitch from the stretch for twelve innings. The Braves' Lou Burdette labored, giving up twelve hits but no runs. Haddix fell behind on the count to only two of the first thirty-six Braves he faced; Burdette battled control problems.

Pirate infielders flawlessly handled their first twelve

chances, but Don Hoak fumbled No. 13, a bouncer by Felix Mantilla that opened the thirteenth inning. Eddie Mathews sacrificed, and Haddix purposely walked Henry Aaron to set up the double play. Haddix threw a slider to the next hitter, Joe Adcock. Twice, Adcock had gone down swinging on a slider. This one was too high, too ripe. Haddix knew it the moment he released the ball. The bat rang, a towering fly arched toward the fence in right-center. Clemente's substitute, Joe Christopher, wheeled and raced back into the shadows, pressing his shoulder blades deep into the fence. Adcock's fly ball cleared the fence by a foot. The heart quit beating in the 1959 Pittsburgh Pirates. They never quivered again, struck by a rash of injuries so persistent that both catchers, Hank Foiles and Burgess were lost in a single game in July.

And Danny Murtaugh's bench chafed Clemente worse than those run by Max Macon or Pete Zorilla. Feisty and aggressive and frustrated, Murtaugh tired of seeing all that talent sitting ten feet away. "You're faking the goddamn injury," he bellowed one night. "Take off the uniform."

"No one takes off my uniform while I am playing for the Pirates," Clemente retorted. Their conflict would smolder for years and never really die, but after returning to the roster in July, Clemente missed just two more games the rest of the way.

The Pirates won seven of their first eight games after he returned to the lineup; Elroy Face, the tiny, taciturn relief pitcher who was the talk of baseball for winning eighteen straight games, continued to carry the club, and Clemente inched his average up to a respectable .296.

But the Pirates, rated no worse than five to one to win the pennant, finished fourth with a 78–76 record and disappointed a city that had waited so long.

Clemente missed forty-seven games. He was a five-year veteran, but when people spoke of him, they used the term "potential," or the other, hated, term, "injury-prone." And always the "but." Clemente had a howitzer for an arm . . . but; Clemente hits the ball harder than anyone . . . but

"In the 1960s," wrote one observer, "there will be no 'buts.'" Still, friction returned to the Pirate clubhouse, set off again by the frustrations of the 1959 season. Elroy Face was occasionally unable to comb his hair after pitching almost daily; Mazeroski played with painful pulled leg muscles; it would have taken a drayhorse to get the fiery Hoak off the field. "Clemente loosened up a little from his first two years, but he didn't have many friends on the ballclub," said a teammate. "He wasn't the only one hurt. And he always talked about it. Some of us got tired listening."

Baseball remained Clemente's lone serious pursuit. He played summer and winter, supporting his parents and any and all needy relatives; the Jibaro in him demanded it. He was a man engaged in lonely pursuits, fashioning pottery, building lamps, carving wood when not playing baseball. The quiet boy of Carolina had become a brooding man, hiding silently behind his pride and his dignity.

Somehow, and he did not know exactly how, he had acquired a reputation. All of his life, he had wanted to "run fast, hit the ball hard, play as hard as I can." They dipped lightly into baseball's sea of clichés and branded

1. Triple-exposed, the Clemente swing was not unlike the man himself: tight, forceful, effective, abandoned to the pursuit of perfection.

ADIOS AMIGO ROBERTO

2. Atop the highest of the seven hills that encircle Pittsburgh, a neon sign that usually heralds the virtue of a local beer says it for everyone in a grieving town.

3. An exhausted crew of U. S. Navy divers grabs a breather in the final hours of a fruitless search for Clemente's body. Ironically, the only trace of Clemente, his briefcase, was washed onto a garbage dump just yards from the divers' barracks.

4. Transistorized hope is like any other, a lifeline, and friends and relatives cling to it in Clemente's living room during the search.

5. One couple's castle, sixteen days before it became a public curiosity that forced the widowed Vera to leave it.

6. Daddy Sugar, as he reigned over Don Pepito Rubert's cane fields, where Melchor Clemente painstakingly instilled the virtue or vice of pride in his son, Roberto.

7. The uniform number was retained; but the smile soon faded when Clemente discovered his first year as a pro would be spent, as Santurce owner Pete Zorilla put it, "learning to wear the uniform."

8. The suspicion in Clemente's eyes was later justified when it became apparent he had been secreted off to Montreal, to be hidden there by the "deceitful" Dodgers.

9. The sweetest of waltzes came on the day Clemente the rookie crashed the Pirate lineup and managed to evade pitcher Johnny Podres to score his first major league run against . . . yeah . . . the Dodgers.

10. An uncomfortable stranger in paradise and his closest friends. "What is a nigger? ... Who is 'buddy'?"

11. In the grandstand, Clemente had no enemies, only admirers, and there he looked for absolution.

12. A grin begins to emerge as Clemente—on the way to victory over the Yankees—crosses the plate in the final game of the 1960 World Series.

13. Home is the hunter after winning the National League batting title in 1961. Luisa Clemente no longer wants an engineer in the family.

14. A greater outfield no manager could want: Clemente, Mays, Aaron. In the 1961 All-Star Game, Clemente got the big hits and Mays the ink, and the smile evaporated into bitterness.

15. The calm before the storm came on the opening day of spring training in 1965 and, like most of Roberto Clemente's relationships, the one with manager Harry Walker was tumultuous.

16. A man who had known pain himself brought comfort and diversion to Pittsburgh's Children's Hospital . . . many, many times.

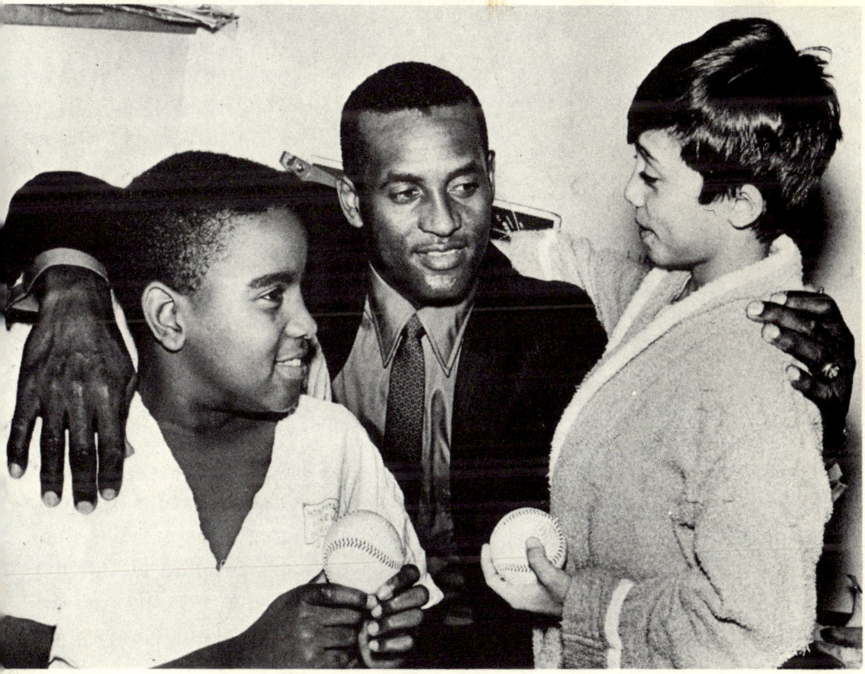

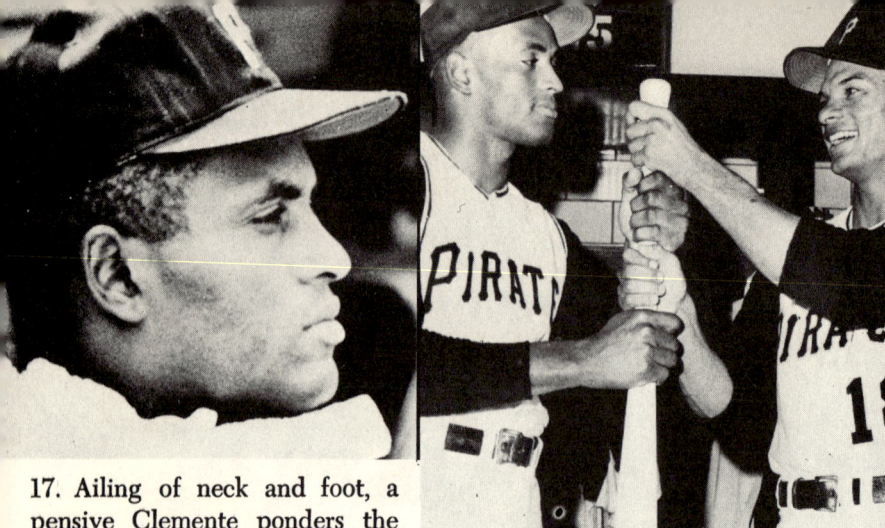

17. Ailing of neck and foot, a pensive Clemente ponders the nature of the fates who would visit crippling injury on an honest man at a time when his team was busy falling behind in the great pennant chase of 1966.

18. Matty Alou held onto top spot and eked out his instructor-predecessor to claim the 1966 batting championship.

19. After umpire Stan Landes agreed he had safely stolen second base, Clemente takes a pause that was obviously refreshing while St. Louis manager Red Schoendienst comforts his indignant second baseman, Julian Javier. A similar Clemente pose would be adopted at the conclusion of the 1967 season—"my greatest year but my biggest disappointment"—when Roberto blasted some of his teammates after the Pirates finished sixth.

him. "Clemente doesn't come to play," they said. He was hurting; a crowning forest fire of pain in his back, bone chips knifing into the tender tissue of his elbow. "Hypochondriac," they snickered.

They? His teammates, the press, but, mostly, the devils that drove Clemente toward greatness, the silent voices pursuing him through sleepless nights, goading him to reach higher, run faster, hit the ball harder, play as if he were possessed.

For five years he had been, by any standard, a good major league baseball player. But "good" was nowhere near sufficient. Greatness was his goal. Acknowledgment that no one played this game better. It would elude him for years, even in 1960, when "they" would steal from him the prize he sought above all others.

The 1960 season. The melding of a baseball team and a city that had awaited it thirty-three years and came to embrace it unashamedly. An affair of the heart between a team that could meet any demands and a town that wailed at its defeats and, literally, danced in the streets at its triumphs. The 1960 Pirates, the "unforgettable Pittsburgh Pirates," as immortalized on a long-playing phonograph record and viewed as "destiny's darlings" by no less an authoritarian than celebrated sportswriter Red Smith. The 1960 Pirates, the beloved Bucs, were a team for all time; all grit and hustle and daring. They snatched gut-wrenching victories from the brink of defeat. And they brought credibility to the basest of all baseball clichés—the one about "the game never being over until the last man is out in the ninth." Twenty-one of the Pirate victories of 1960 came in the ninth inning, twelve after two were out.

They were the embodiment of Don Hoak, the third baseman who had come from Cincinnati and points east and west. Ex-boxer, stevedore, hobo. "Hoak's 0–15, lifetime," Gil Hodges had said of his ex-Dodger teammate's fistic battles.

But Hoak was dubbed "the Tiger," and no man carried a more meaningful *nom de guerre*, for he was the inspiration for a spirited, unsinkable band. He was outrageously bold; so were they all. Once, in front of a large group of people that included her husband, he suggested to a beautiful redhead that they consummate their five-minute friendship in a nearby swimming pool. On another occasion, he lost a radio show sponsored by a local beer company because, accompanied by company executives, he loudly informed a bartender, "I wouldn't be caught dead drinking that crap."

When reserve outfielder Gino Cimoli began swaggering into hotel lobbies in July and announcing, "the big, bad Buccos are in town," he was bearing a bravado instilled in the entire club by Hoak.

No city could fail to love such a crew, and Pittsburgh didn't. A war cry sprang up: "Beat 'em, Bucs." A song was written, and a Dixieland band played it unceasingly between trumpet blasts and cries of "Charge" as the Pirates came thundering down in the gloaming of a game.

They were virtually unbeatable at home, winning 52 and losing only 25, as 1,705,828 fans overran old Forbes Field. "Beat 'em, Bucs" leaped forth from half the solid surfaces in Pittsburgh. People painted it on dozens of homes, chalked it on the sidewalks, and one young loyalist had it etched into his crewcut. U. S. Steel and the city's only map company printed it on their invoices. "Beat 'em, Bucs."

And they did. No game was irretrievable. In June, down 5-0 with two out in the ninth and Cincinnati pitcher Sherman Jones working easily on a three-hitter, they ran off six quick runs. Their triumphs came like thunderclaps, and people took to ignoring radio broadcasts until the eighth inning, when the Pirates would unfailingly make the sky fall on the National League.

Roberto Clemente, a hero among heroes, ended the month of May leading the National League with a .353 average. He fielded like Merlin and threw like Zeus, cutting down nineteen base-runners. "They" forgot about his injuries. In a game at Forbes Field, Willie Mays ripped a liner down the right-field line. "I must catch it . . . I must catch it," Clemente told himself. He made the catch and hit a concrete abutment without breaking stride. Blood spurted wildly from a slashed jawbone; he held the ball to preserve a shutout for Vinegar Bend Mizell. When he went into the hospital to have his chin stitched up, the Pirates had a seven-game lead over Milwaukee; when he came out five days later, the lead was down to two games. Murtaugh put him back in the lineup immediately. "Sometimes I thought Murtaugh didn't believe me when I said I was hurt," Clemente said.

"Consistency" and "amiability" were the Pirate bywords of 1960. The team never lost more than four in a row. When they were en route to winning eleven straight, Clemente became superstitious and would not change his sweatshirt. "About the tenth day, he was in trouble," laughed Mazeroski. Every day is fun day when you're running wide open and winning the tough ones. "To win, you must play as a family," Clemente said. "We played as a family."

The Mafia wasn't as united as the Pirates beat back runs by Milwaukee, then St. Louis. Clemente homered and singled on July 25 in a victory over the Cardinals, and the Pirates were never headed again. When they faltered, losing four in a row before going on a trip to the West Coast—and if they were going to come unglued, this would have been the moment—Clemente pulled them together. He hit home runs on three straight days, and the Pirates put together a four-game skein and began swaggering anew.

On September 25 in Milwaukee, where they had fallen apart the year before, the Pirates clinched the 1960 pennant. Chicago's Glen Hobbie shut out St. Louis to eliminate the Cards, and when the score appeared on the board at Milwaukee County Stadium, Clemente was in the on-deck circle. Hearing a buzz from the dugout, he turned to Dick Stuart. "We win it?" Stuart's huge grin was all the answer he needed. Clemente went to the plate, ripped a ringing double, and minutes later ignored a stop sign at third base to score in the proverbial cloud of dust. "Stop at third?" he asked later. "I want to get on the bench and talk about the pennant."

Pittsburgh had its first championship in thirty-three years. A drunk commandeered a streetcar and joyously wheeled it around the city for two hours before smilingly submitting to arrest. A hundred thousand wild-eyed fans met the returning flight from Milwaukee, and there was an enormous victory parade through downtown. But the city was saving its celebration for a World Series triumph over the New York Yankees of Mantle and Maris and Ford. That it would come, they had no doubts. These were the big, bad Buccos, and in a triumph of loyalty over logic, no one in Pittsburgh doubted their destiny.

But Clemente went into the Series fretting. In St. Louis at midseason, Stan Musial had told him, "If you don't win the MVP award this year, you never will." By August, Clemente knew he would not win it; that Dick Groat had a lock on it. A Los Angeles sportswriter showed Clemente a letter he had received from a Pittsburgh writer soliciting a vote for Groat, who led the league in hitting with a .325 average but missed the final month of the year with a broken wrist. Clemente still fumed as the World Series opened, the Pirates facing the Yankees, as they had in 1927 when legend had it that the Bucs folded after being awed by watching Ruth and Gehrig and Lazzeri take batting practice.

These Yankees were also awesome. And they had a book on Clemente. It said, loosely translated, "Stick it in his ear." "It makes me very mad," said Clemente, "so I try to hit the ball over the fence. That's no good, because they pitch me outside and I can't pull it. I had to remember to hit to right field." He did, getting nine hits and hitting safely in all seven games.

After six games, the series had progressed to a stalemate. The Yankees bombarded the Pirates three times, 16–3, 10–0, and 12–0, winning all the laughers. But in the mean, no-quarter games, the Pirates ignored the psychological implications and, in the vernacular, hung tough. They won 6–4, Clemente delivering a key hit; 3–2; and 5–2. So it came to crunch before 36,683 believers at Forbes Field on a lovely fall day.

Neither team seemed interested in the final victory. The Pirates led, 4–0; the Yanks led, 5–4, and then 7–4 into the bottom of the eighth. Need anything more be said? These were the unsinkable Pirates, the eighth and ninth innings belonged to them the way France belonged to Napoleon, the way Harvard belonged to the Ivy League, the way Jiggs belonged to Maggie. "Beat 'em, Bucs" had become a plea, and the Pirates answered it. Cimoli singled. Bill Virdon hit a perfect double-play ball to Yankee shortstop Tony Kubek, only the ball leaped off the alabaster infield and struck Kubek in the Adam's apple. Groat, his timing shot by the month-long layoff, singled for only his fifth hit of the Series, scoring Cimoli and knocking tiny Bobby Shantz out of the game. Jim Coates came on and got two outs, and it all came down to Roberto Clemente.

"Outside, keep it outside," Coates told himself. "He'll swing at anything." Clemente fouled off three straight pitches before topping the fourth one to the right of Yankee first baseman Bill Skowron. The inning seemed over, only Coates hesitated, fatally. Clemente's dash beat him to first base, Skowron forced to hold the ball fifteen feet from the bag. Virdon scored and Hal Smith followed with a three-run homer that gave the Pirates a 9–7 lead.

The Yankees wouldn't die, scoring twice. The game went into the bottom of the ninth deadlocked. It stayed that way for exactly two pitches. Bill Mazeroski hit reliever Ralph Terry's second fast ball 406 feet into the maple trees that framed the picturesque left-field wall. Pittsburgh erupted.

Mayor Joseph Barr leaped to his feet as the capless Mazeroski danced and pranced and threw himself into the air as he circled the bases. Barr's elbow struck his wife, Alice, almost knocking her cold. In the wild, wild clubhouse, Cimoli swaggered around, naked save a cigar stuck precariously in the far corner of a huge grin. "They set all the records, but we won the games, baby. We won the games," he crowed. Stuart poured beer after beer on the mayor's head. It would've taken a jaw broken in five places to wipe the smile off the red face of Murtaugh, who later told his wife, Kate, "If you had been standing on one side of me and Maz on the other, and I hadda kiss one of you, it wouldn't have been you."

Twenty blocks away in the downtown area, people had abandoned their cars and swarmed into the swinging streets. In three hours there wasn't a drop of liquor left in any downtown bar. Police pleaded with people to quit coming into downtown. They came like the tide, leaving their automobiles on the twelve bridges leading into downtown. Before it was over, at dawn, the police estimated that a million people had been in town during the night. Hundreds didn't leave until the following afternoon.

But at least two celebrants were restrained. In Torreon, Mexico, a house painter named Antonio Duenas walked glumly into a bar. "The Yankees gave it away," he said. The bartender—a Pirate fan—shot him dead.

And while the corks ricocheted around the Pirate clubhouse, Roberto Clemente dressed quietly, interrupted Murtaugh's gaiety to ask if he could take his glove as a remembrance, and left. There are pictures of an ecstatic Clemente lifting Hal Smith clear off his feet after the home run that had given Pittsburgh a 9–7 edge. But now Clemente abandoned the revelry to walk the streets for hours with the Pirate fans.

"I feel like one of them," he replied. "I never see anything like them." Days later, when he was criticized for prematurely leaving his teammates, Clemente did not understand. "I want to be with the people who pay my salary. I shake hands with my players and everything, show them how happy I was. But I have no words to say how I feel when I went outside with the fans."

Whether or not those fans felt Clemente was the most valuable Pirate is as unimportant, really, as the MVP award itself. Untrue? Who was the National League's most valuable player in 1970? Last year? Later, Clemente would play down the award. "It doesn't matter," he said in his last few years, but he never looked at you when he said it, always turning away from the lie.

Dick Groat was the 1960 winner, followed in the Baseball Writers Association of America voting by Don Hoak, Willie Mays, Ernie Banks, Lindy McDaniel, Ken Boyer, Pirate pitcher Vernon Law and, eighth and furious, Roberto Clemente.

"If I am not the most valuable, why it is me they throw at all year?" he asked, enraged. The bitterness he felt would linger for years; forever, really. When his 1960 World Series ring came, he put it in his trophy case and never wore it.

Clemente felt, to the core of his being, that Groat had received the award because he was white, got along with the writers, and had the good fortune of being born and raised in Pittsburgh. The writers had dishonored him, and in so doing had dishonored his island and his people. He would never forget it. "Roberto changed after that," said a 1960 Pirate. "He was no longer a kid. He got inside himself."

Clemente accused a Pittsburgh sportswriter of campaigning for Groat, and an unimpeachable source says the charge was true. "A writer in Los Angeles showed me a letter from this Pittsburgh writer—and I'm not going to tell you who," Clemente said. "This L.A. writer said, 'I cannot vote for you.' I told him, 'You live in a democracy. You should not let anyone tell you how to vote.'

"I always talked about democracy when I was a kid. I got a taste of democracy then."

Later, Clemente amended his remarks. "I never say Groat should not win it," he said. "I feel I should not be close to tenth. I led the club in rbi's with ninety-four. I hit twenty home runs [sixteen, actually]. But in the Series, you need a magnifying glass to see my name in the papers."

At least one of the Pirate regulars of 1960 thought that the writers had done well in their balloting. "There were two or three more valuable guys on the club," he said. "Clemente drove in ninety-four runs, hit .314, but Groat, Hoak, and Bob Skinner were more important to us that year. Day in and day out, they drove in the important runs. I'm not prejudiced, and I might be wrong, but I think the other three made the bigger plays. And Clemente wasn't always in the lineup."

In 1960, "they" had won. In 1961, and in the years to follow, Roberto Clemente would win.

Chapter 9

FAT CITY . . . MOSTLY

Tap City. We've all been there at one time or another. Tap City? That mythical locale where life always runs uphill and the wind is always in your face, and if it rained pennies from heaven, your bucket would spring a leak. Tap City. Abe doesn't want to go to the play; Mary insists. Tap City. Samson forgets to lock up the scissors. Tap City. You're a leg man and some French fop invents the maxi. Tap City.

On the other side of life's ledger, there's another such mythical locale. Fat City. You notice her mother has a mustache, so you don't propose. Fat City. The place where the sun always shines and they never audit income tax returns and when you fall in the proverbial bucket, you always come up smelling like the proverbial rose.

When it rains pennies from heaven in Fat City, you're always carrying a five-pound magnet.

Roberto Clemente resided in both places during the years 1961 through 1965—dependent, of course, on his physical condition, which strayed between "resting comfortably" and "critical." In those five years, he agonized more than any mortal man should, and for the most part the world excused his agony as mere hypochondria. Engaged in relentless warfare with two managers, at least one umpire, a battalion of doctors, and a world that wouldn't—no matter the length of his discourse—acknowledge his pain, he managed little more than acquiring three National League batting championships and a small portion of the credit he had long and futilely sought.

But no part of his anatomy was spared, and he suffered from his head (tension headaches) to his feet (strained insteps). Through it all he grimaced and prevailed, also acquiring the undying loyalty of the Pittsburgh fans despite the Pirates' failure to repeat their 1960 conquest. Along the way, he played in each All-Star Game; was suspended for ten days; once more finished a light-year away from an MVP award he felt he might have rightfully earned; managed to attract malaria and a typhoid infection at almost the same instant; got married; and threatened, for the first time but not the last, to retire prematurely. Clemente, in fact, ran between Fat City and Tap City like a streetcar.

Psychologically tuned by his failure to win the 1960 MVP award, Clemente attacked the 1961 season with a ferocity the rest of the Pirates were unable to muster. In the spring, when he switched from his usual thirty-one-ounce bat to a much heavier bludgeon, Pirate batting instructor George Sisler suggested that Clemente might well win the batting title. Clemente's arched eyebrows considered the suggestion unnecessary, even impertinent. He lacked real power and admired Dick Stuart's, but he would retain his own slashing style. "I tell you, I could make two hundred thousand dollars a year with Stuart's power and my brains," he sighed.

Stuart's brain, in fact, became the subject of considerable conjecture in the first rocky month of the 1961 baseball season. While a Russian named Gagarin was making history's quickest trip around the globe, John F. Kennedy threw the switch on the Bay of Pigs, a fiasco that accomplished nothing save turning a Cuban beach blood-red. Across the world, the Congo had become the world's largest outdoor slaughterhouse. Homo sapiens was hard at work committing suicide on varied fronts. Meanwhile, Stuart was the focal point of a baseball team engaged in similar activity. At the time, Roberto Clemente was taking the first cautious steps of a genuine superman. In May, Stuart was benched, and he marched angrily from the dugout. Murtaugh located him in the clubhouse, about to mail a letter. "That stamp'll cost you fifty dollars," Murtaugh growled. In short order, Stuart had been chewed out twice by Don Hoak—"if you don't want to give us the full ninety feet, stay home"—and had almost come to blows with Bob Friend over what the veteran pitcher felt was lackadaisical fielding.

Clemente soared; the Pirates plummeted like a gut-shot duck. On June 23 in Philadelphia, they built an 11-2 lead into the eighth inning. Aided by four errors, they lost,

12–11, suffering their thirty-eighth defeat in seventy games and falling to fourth place, seven games arrears of Cincinnati. Clemente had stomach trouble and a .332 batting average.

Pitchers Vernon Law and George Witt had been sidelined by injuries before the All-Star break and the Pirates were lackluster, with the exception of Clemente, who continued to bemoan his fate of 1960 and thereby create rumors that the club was plagued with that worst of all baseball infirmities, dissension.

"You'll have to take my word for it, but there isn't any," insisted Danny Murtaugh. "The only one disgruntled is Roberto, and it hasn't affected his play." Obviously it hadn't, perhaps because for the first time in his career, his teammates were treating him with affection. In the spring—a few Pirates possibly motivated by sadistic traits —they began openly calling him "No Votes." Roberto Clemente was being needled, not surreptitiously but gleefully. A small crack appeared in the wall he had built around himself.

The Pittsburgh fans lavished affection on Clemente in 1961, recognizing, if the writers hadn't, that he had been treated shabbily. "They had begun pulling for him when he was younger, and as he became greater, they loved him more," theorized General Manager Joe L. Brown. "He proved they were right to have given him their affection. They began saying, 'I knew a long time ago he was great.'"

Pirate manager Murtaugh, against his nature and for the last time, also tried to smooth the feathers ruffled the year before. Murtaugh had come out of a hard town,

Chester, Pennsylvania, in a hard time, the post-Depression, "Hey-buddy-you-got-a-dime?" years. As a journeyman second baseman, he had survived a brief major league career on moxie rather than natural ability, standing his ground on the pivot, moving the runners up, keeping his nose clean. He defended his job with grit and hustle and obvious desire . . . and played when he was hurting.

No two personalities could've been more diverse than the feisty, tough little Irishman and his sensitive superstar. Murtaugh was a quiet man of genuine dry wit, outgoing. He had been scarred a dozen times by biting spikes without a public wail. He was dedicated to both the game that had taken him out of a Chester mill and its command that the good baseball player is the one who "wouldn't say 'shit' if he had a mouthful."

Clemente's humor was no less wry than Murtaugh's, but it was submerged by the intensity that he brought to all things in life. Living, Melchor Clemente had taught him, was serious business. Clemente was suspicious, driven, and, true to the Latin psyche, saw no grays in life. There was truth, all-pervasive, demanding; there were lies. There was black and there was white, and there was nothing in between.

Did he hurt? Yes, right here, and here. In detail. Was he bitter at the 1960 MVP voting? Damn right. No evasions. That is the Latin way. No compromise, no shaded truths to salvage another's ego or pride. How are you? Very good . . . very bad. Not pretty good or O.K. or fair.

"I say what I feel," Clemente said over and over. And

he never said less, even when it would have been less painful or far more popular—as it would have years later, when he laid harsh invective on Murtaugh.

But this was 1961. All-Star Game time. One of the big events in Clemente's career. And an attempt at compromise by Danny Murtaugh, who managed the National Leaguers. "The players knew I was most valuable last year," Clemente said before the game at San Francisco's biggest wind tunnel, Candlestick Park. "Then this year they voted me on the All-Star team. I am feeling very good and I will not let them down."

Aided by Murtaugh—who played him the entire game even though Henry Aaron sat on the bench—Clemente didn't. In his first at-bat, he tripled home a run off Whitey Ford; in his second, he hammered a four-hundred-foot, run-scoring drive that Mickey Mantle ran to earth in deepest right-center field. But the Nationals couldn't hold a 3–1 lead in the ninth, and the game went into the last of the tenth with the Americans up by a run, 4–3.

Pinch-hitter Aaron started a rally by singling off Hoyt Wilhelm and going to second when one of Wilhelm's knuckleballs eluded the catcher. Willie Mays doubled Aaron home and, true to his word, Roberto Clemente slashed a game-winning single to right.

"What makes me feel most good is that Danny Murtaugh let me play the whole game," said a smiling Clemente, who would wear the 1961 All-Star ring and leave the Pirates' 1960 World Series ring in his trophy case. "He pay me a big compliment. I do not think I let him down."

Clemente didn't; the Pirates did, continuing to sag in midsummer. Even a field fight with the Phillies didn't create a spark, although there were, by actual count, seven brawls taking place at one time, and Murtaugh received a spike wound in the neck.

In early August, Clemente had 20 hits in 36 at-bats, and the race for the batting crown was all but over. So was the race for the pennant. The Pirates finished in sixth place in 1961 with a dismal 75-79 record. Clemente's .351 average was high in the majors; he had 201 hits, the first time he had breached the coveted 200 mark; his home runs (23) and doubles (30) were career highs, and he had a truce with Murtaugh and a respite from the stomach ache. The last two items quickly proved perishable.

For the first 10 days of 1962, Forbes Field again rocked with cries of "Beat 'em, Bucs." The Pirates opened with 10 wins in a row in spite of Clemente, who weighed 171 pounds. The doctors diagnosed his trouble as "a nervous stomach." By late May, he was hitting .256, but the Pirates were thriving despite, or perhaps because of, open warfare between Murtaugh and Clemente.

The manager was driven to distraction by the 1962 Pirates, a zany Jekyll-and-Hyde outfit. Clemente hit .312 that year, and the papers called it "a disappointing season": Groat hit .294 and was said to have enjoyed a fine year; a rookie, Donn Clendenon, and Bob Skinner both batted .302; Dick Stuart, finally humbled by the wrath of Pirate fans, slumped to .228 and Virdon to .247. Bob Friend won eighteen games; Vernon Law battled courageously against adhesions in his right shoulder. The Pirates streaked and sagged, taking ten straight, losing nine of the next ten.

In the eye of the confusion, with only the passion an Irishman and a Latin could bring to battle, Murtaugh and Clemente had at it. In St. Louis one June night, Clemente informed Murtaugh that the bone chips sawing away in his right elbow would prevent him from playing.

"You play," said the terse Murtaugh.

What followed was later recalled by Clemente in two versions. In the first, he remembered having "two stitches in my leg" when Cardinal pitcher Larry Jackson lined a ball to right that Clemente couldn't reach, Jackson winding up with a triple. In the second version, Clemente's elbow "was swollen like a softball" when Jackson took third on Clemente's woeful relay to the infield. "I couldn't throw any farther," Clemente explained in this version.

In either instance, the results were the same: Murtaugh's thinning, sandy hair stood on end.

"Take your uniform off and get out of here if you don't want to run," he roared when Clemente returned to the dugout. Clemente stiffened. There were more hot words before the Pirate half of the inning ended.

Later in the year, the Pirates dragging through one of their losing streaks, Murtaugh called a clubhouse meeting to air out the situation, which is what managers do when they can think of no course of action short of dynamiting the team bus and pleading just cause. Deciding, as was his wont, that discretion was not really the better part of valor, Clemente took the floor.

"We aren't trying . . . we aren't hustling," he beseeched. "We have a better ballclub than this."

Possibly seeking something to inspire the Pirates out of their doldrums, Murtaugh seized the moment.

"You really have a lot of appreciation for your teammates to say something like that," Murtaugh glowered, bidding his troops defend themselves. "Are you guys going to take that?"

Bill Virdon, austere, painstakingly honest, and blunt, looked up. "Clemente's all wet," he said.

"Maybe I was," Clemente would say later, "but I know we started winning after that."

And so the Pirates did, recording a 93–68 mark to finish a strong fourth, testimony that harmony may be an overrated virtue, at least in baseball. But before the year was out, Murtaugh vs. Clemente had become as routine as a four-round prelim. In Philadelphia one day, hobbling on an ankle with stitches in it, Clemente hit a liner to Phils' shortstop Reuben Amaro, who dropped it as Clemente staggered toward first. He was thrown out easily by Amaro. His ankle hurt, he said. He loafed, Murtaugh said.

"You're not hustling," Murtaugh yelled in the dugout. "Get out to right field."

"How am I going to hustle when I am hurt?"

The old argument persisted between the truth-loving ballplayer who suffered mysterious aches and the disbelieving old-school manager who could not comprehend leaving a game unless there was sufficient blood showing to make the paying customers uncomfortable.

"Get out there," Murtaugh insisted.

"I'm not going," Clemente insisted.

"If you don't, it will cost you $150."

"I'm not playing."

"Make it $250."

"I'm still not playing."

The impasse continued until Murtaugh gave up in exasperation, Clemente $650 the poorer for the argument.

"I stayed there on the bench," Clemente said. "I don't like to take no bullshit from managers. If they can't get the players to play for them, then they can't. Most managers know the game and have a certain number of good players. But it's getting them to want to play that counts."

It is easily conceivable that the 1963 Pirates and Clemente combined to lay the foundation for a heart problem that would force Murtaugh from his beloved game two years later, although Joe L. Brown's contribution cannot be overlooked.

When the 1962 campaign ended, Clemente returned to the Puerto Rican winter league to once more supplement his Pirate salary, now in the forty-thousand-dollar range. He needed the extra money, having adopted the children of a sister and a brother who had died, and having taken an interest in the study of chiropractic, with the ultimate aim of opening a large clinic to treat those of his countrymen who said "aagh!" when they bent from the waist.

When the 1962 season ended, Joe L. Brown did not seek to augment his income. He had a sick ballclub that needed attention, which loosely translated means that when the bus begins to break down it is not mandatory to shoot the driver. Brown traded for new parts.

Dick Groat went to St. Louis, Dick Stuart and his clanking glove to the Boston Red Sox, and Don Hoak to the Phillies.

Presto, disaster. The guy wearing the barrel at the conclusion of the 1963 season was Joe L. Brown, who gambled on Clemente taking up whatever slack would occur by replacing three fourths of the infield. Later, Brown would say, "This season was a nightmare."

While Groat was hitting .319 for St. Louis, new Pirate shortstop Dick Schofield was hitting .246; while Stuart was crashing 42 home runs for the Red Sox and leading the American League with 118 rbi's, Donn Clendenon was striking out at the same pace that had caused Stuart to be abandoned; while Hoak was belching flames on the revitalized Phillies, his sub, a $150,000 bonus baby named Bob Bailey, had been nicknamed "Beetle" by the club veterans who harassed him unmercifully.

The details of the year 1963 are gruesome. The Pirates, those wonderboys of just thirty-six months before, finished eighth, saved from last place only by the fact of expansion. But Roberto Clemente spent the season in Fat City. For the first time in memory, he professed no ailments; he was, in fact, in the pink save for insomnia, "which made me weak most of the season."

Yet, in such a glorious state of health, he managed his worst run-in with Murtaugh, was suspended for 10 days and fined $250, and blew the batting title by 6 points (.326 to .320) to Tommy Davis in the last 3 weeks. But, at 29, he suffered the slings of misfortune with more élan. The day the season ended, he bought his first Cadillac.

In May, however, Clemente almost was forced to miss a payment on his Pontiac. During a 1–0 defeat in Los Angeles on May 16, he was called out at first base on an outrageously incorrect decision. The following day's newspaper immortalized the umpire—photographs showing Clemente safe by a margin of not more than three feet. He was enraged.

Less than two weeks later, the thieves struck again. In the second inning of a game in Pittsburgh, Clendenon was called out on a questionable decision by umpire Bill Jackowski. An argument ensued, involving Murtaugh, Pirate first-base coach Ron Northey, and Jackowski. Outnumbered, Jackowski nevertheless prevailed.

In the fifth inning, with a man on first, Clemente grounded to short. He and the ball arrived in front of the umpire at the same instant. Jackowski jerked his thumb into the air.

Clemente suggested where Jackowski might next place his thumb and moved toward the umpire. Northey attempted to establish a zone of neutrality between the player and the arbiter. What happened next is unclear. Clemente said he "accidentally hit" Jackowski "with an open hand" and was "only trying to get away from the coach [Northey]."

National League president Warren Giles, whose most recent serious decision involved signing the official league ball, disagreed via telegram, in the third person. "Your actions were," his wire informed an indignant Clemente, "the most serious reported to our office in several years." The sentence was $250 and 10 days.

There was an appeal by mail. Clemente pleaded his innocence. "I come from a close family. My mother is very religious; my father is a fine man. I am not a violent man. I hit the ball and they threw to first for the double play. I argued. Everyone on the bench argued. I hear the fans scream and I turn and Murtaugh was arguing. Ron Northey say, 'You should not go there.' I try to get loose and I hit the umpire . . . actually I just touch his uniform."

No one was visibly moved over his protestation of innocence, so Clemente began corresponding with Giles, noting that when notorious bad boy Leo Durocher had repeatedly kicked umpire Jocko Conlan in the shins in an early-season episode, he had been suspended for only three days. Perhaps the fact that Conlan, who was wearing shinguards at the time, had retorted in kind against Durocher, who wasn't, mitigated against a more severe penalty. In any case, Giles condescendingly wired back, "Even though you may be very angry, you must try to control your temper in the presence of umpires."

Clemente again took to the U.S. mails, to the effect that if there were true justice, ballplayers would be able to write reports about umpires.

"It is unfair to take me away from my team for ten days," he said as the incident died away. Later, so advised by a dying brother, he would repent. "Only a hardheaded man would not admit he has been wrong. I see lots of fellows like that. Take Don Hoak. He used to get mad at everything. But he cooled off, did not use up all of his energy. We Latins get more excited than Americans. We have a lot of pepper blood. Sometimes I don't think Americans understand this."

One American did. Danny Murtaugh also had pepper blood. His Pirates were floundering before the 1963 season had reached July. The fans were staying away in droves— the attendance would drop more than three hundred thousand that season. Tempers were fraying. On a West Coast trip, playing with the flu, Clemente performed erratically in San Francisco. On the flight to Los Angeles, he ate shrimp and steak, and later got sick in his hotel room. His roommate, a young catcher named Elmo Plaskett, called the doctor, and the following morning before he reported to the ballpark, Clemente had his stomach pumped out.

"Murtaugh asked me how I felt," Clemente said. "I said, 'How do you think I feel? Very bad.'"

Murtaugh asked team captain Bill Mazeroski to report on Clemente's condition just before game time. "Bad," was the diagnosis Clemente passed on to Mazeroski.

"Stick around," Mazeroski replied.

Murtaugh reappeared moments later. "Maz says you can play," he told Clemente. "You play."

Don Drysdale, who often tried to intimidate Clemente with inside pitches, was on the mound for Los Angeles. Clemente singled the first time up—"I don't know how I did it"—then struck out twice—"I had no swing at all; you can imagine."

When the Pirates moved on to Houston, Murtaugh called Clemente to his office in the ballpark. "You let me know when you are ready to play again," Murtaugh said. "You're making too much money to sit on the bench. The next time you feel like playing, you'll play, and you'll play everyday until I say you won't play."

"You talk like I don't want to play," Clemente countered.

And that was the crux of what was between them. Murtaugh didn't believe Clemente wanted to play daily, and Clemente was incredulous before such thinking.

20. Only one of them was a thoroughbred, and he didn't eat hay. Named Campeon Bate (Champion Batter), the racehorse given Clemente by Pirate owner John Galbreath lured hundreds of two-dollar bettors to their fiscal deaths. But the only batting champion in the stable had two legs.

21. The 1970 return of manager Danny Murtaugh signaled an uneasy but lasting truce.

22. Vera Clemente wasn't the only one who felt affection, and Luisa and Melchor Clemente weren't the only ones applauding, on Roberto Clemente Night in 1971.

23. Clemente offers another piece of evidence to fortify his claim that "no one plays better than me," a home run off Baltimore's Jim Palmer in the 2–1 game that decided the 1971 World Series in Pittsburgh's favor and testified that, indeed, Roberto was the mightiest of them all.

24. If the smiles seem pasted on, they were for real later when the two most valuable Pirates in the 1971 World Series would embrace on the airplane en route home, and Steve Blass would smile affectionately, "I didn't know what to say. I just held on."

25. The hero and his lady sit on an automobile Clemente received for being named MVP in the 1971 World Series. But the real prize had come earlier: "Now the whole world know how Roberto Clemente plays baseball."

26. During spring training, 1972, the spirit was willing; the flesh needed encouragement, as it always did.

27. The eyes, which had proven him a liar when he scorned their importance, closely follow Clemente's three thousandth major league hit.

No. 3,000 had been for them for him, but mostly it was a ıd arrow buried deep in the ıs of the nay-sayers.

29. Crashing Chicago's walls of ivy in painful testimony to his assertion "I break my ass out there trying to get anything that stays in the park." On this June 1969 afternoon, Clemente fractured nothing save his pride.

30. On opening day 1973, her husband's uniform jersey was retired; Vera's memories would not be dispatched so easily.

31. The original and five copies who would, because of one man's persistent dedication to an idea, have a place to play all their own.

32. The first Latin in the Hall of Fame. Deep inside, he never had a doubt.

33. "Now you will not swell the rout of lads that wore their honors out . . ."

"That was the thing," Roberto said later. "He didn't believe anything was wrong with me."

In a mixture of oil and water, both men were true to their own values. But their values were completely dissimilar. Murtaugh's ethic insisted major league baseball players did not speak of their injuries, did not rub where it hurt, at least in public. To do so was cowardice. If you had real heart, they had to cut the uniform off you. And here was this stripling, blessed by a rare talent, complaining endlessly about his ills.

Clemente talked about his injuries for a simple reason: They hurt. He spoke of them as naturally as he did of the weather. Black and white. No grays. The traditions of his youth placed no premium on suffering stoically, as American Puritanism did, and does. Courage was running into a brick wall to catch the ball, not denying you were bleeding later. Did this strange, harsh tyrant not understand something so simple?

"If I am sick, I do not deny it," Clemente said. "If my back is hurting and I am forced to punch the ball with no power, I tell the truth."

The truth hurt—Murtaugh. Late in the year, after being told by the team doctor to soak his elbow in the whirlpool bath, Clemente sat in the dank Pirate clubhouse at Forbes Field.

"You think you're an honored guest?" demanded Murtaugh, locating the absent player. "Do I have to tell you everything to do?"

"We had another argument," Clemente sighed days later.

It wasn't their last, but the following year they had no

open battles. What manager could fight with a two-time batting champ? Clemente had a banner year in 1964, drawing more than twice as many votes as Henry Aaron for the All-Star team in a year when Aaron hit .318. But Clemente batted .329 and had a career-high 211 hits, tops in the majors. He scored 95 runs and drove in 87, his strongest such showings since 1961. And he played in 155 games. Once more the whisperings ceased.

In 1964, with the Pirates no better than a fourth-place, .500 ballclub, Clemente altered his style and tethered the wanton swing a bit, walking fifty-one times. Word spread that asking umpires to move him out of his favored position deep in the batter's box would inflame him. It didn't. He was maturing. When Ken Boyer of St. Louis won the MVP trophy and he finished ninth in the balloting, although he had outhit each of the first eight choices by at least forty-five points, Clemente held his tongue. Surely, no man was ever more ready for marriage.

On November 14, 1964, Clemente married Vera Christina Zabala, a tall, bright, strikingly beautiful girl he had first seen while en route—irony of ironies—to the drugstore for some medicine.

They were married in the picturesque San Fernando Roman Catholic church, where Clemente had been baptized; where his mother and the Zabalas attended regularly; where he later would be eulogized. More than fifteen hundred people attended the reception; thousands of Carolinians milled in the city's main plaza waiting for a glimpse of the newlyweds. The marriage was performed by Monsignor Orlando Rodriguez, a Cuban priest beloved in Carolina, and was duly recorded on page 519 of the heavy black ledger that sat on a table, under a picture of the Virgen de Guadalupe and just to the right of an ashtray advertising Dewar's Scotch Whisky, in the church secretary's office. A time of change had arrived.

During the winter of 1964, Roberto Clemente busied himself with the normal duties of a bridegroom. He socialized. He performed civic duties, visiting hospitalized children as he did regularly in Pittsburgh "not because the club want me to but because I want to." He supplemented his income, managing the San Juan club in the winter league against the Pirates' better judgment "because the people want me to" and because it was an opportunity "to earn extra money." And he did some household chores, washing windows, carrying out the garbage, cutting grass. That was what he was doing in December when the mower blade sucked up a rock and whipped it against his right thigh with sickening force.

At that moment, Roberto Clemente should have retired to his bed and remained there until the year 1965 had safely passed. A few weeks later, in a winter league all-star game, his leg collapsed while he was running out a base hit. A ligament was torn and he couldn't walk. On January 15, Clemente underwent surgery to drain a pool of blood from his right thigh. The doctor claimed the operation an unqualified success; the Pirate front office proclaimed it likewise, saying that Clemente would appear, as fit as he ever was, in spring training camp on March 1. He did not appear on March 1. Piqued, the Pirates issued a further communiqué. Clemente would be fined one hundred dollars each day until he did appear. The fine was never collected.

Word came from Puerto Rico. Clemente was in the hospital with a temperature of 105 degrees. He was suffering from malaria—contracted on a trip to the Dominican Republic—or a paratyphoid infection—contracted from the hogs on his new farm. Or both. The doctors were uncertain. In any event, he was a very sick man. Nobody offered the opinion he was jaking, which was nice, if surprising.

For days, Clemente shivered through the chills, sweated through the fever, and swayed in and out of a coma. "If I am not so strong, I might be dead," he explained. When he finally reported to the Pirate camp at Fort Myers, twenty pounds underweight, it was against the advice of his doctor, Roberto Buso, and after much soul-searching. Dr. Buso advised Clemente to sit out the 1965 season; his wife offered similar advice. Clemente was sick and bone-tired, and it mattered not a damn whether anyone believed him or not.

"I was tempted to retire," he admitted after arriving in Florida. "Malaria make you really sick. My wife said, 'Why don't you retire for a year, then come back?' But I said, 'No, I go and try it.' She said, 'You can't play like this or you'll kill yourself.' But I like baseball. I love baseball and I know I have to play. It is my life."

Fortified with daily shots of vitamin B-12 and heavily dosed with other vitamins, Clemente played. And talked. A winter physical had revealed that Murtaugh had a heart problem. His wife, Kate, and closest friend, Joe L. Brown, talked him into taking a less strenuous job with the club, and to remain in that capacity until such time as Brown decided that other future managers were inadequate.

The new man was Harry Walker. The Hat. A Punch and Judy hitter who had led the National League in hitting one year with a torrent of singles, and probably knew as much as any man alive about the difficult art of placing a round bat against a round ball, squarely.

In spring training, Walker suggested that Clemente adopt an idea of Brown's and pull the ball more often. The theory was that Clemente had hit twenty-three home runs when he batted .351 in 1961, so he should be able to hit with greater power without losing much from his average. Walker also proposed a lighter bat to quicken the wanton batting stroke. Such a radical departure, suggested by Murtaugh, would have gotten short shrift from Clemente. Walker easily sold him on it.

Harry Walker could peddle George Wallace bumper stickers in a Haight-Ashbury commune. He is Alabama-born, honeysuckle dripping from the string of words that spill from his mouth in an unending stream. He is now a sportscaster; Job was no better suited for his role as sufferer. Walker shakes hands like a Rotarian, sincerity pools in his large brown eyes, and he calls almost everyone "pardner." To converse with Harry Walker is to hear the uneven flatness of the River City High School band.

Roberto Clemente, Harry Walker determined from the outset of their relationship, would be his pardner.

A bright man, Walker understood Clemente's deep-seated need for national recognition, perhaps from hearing himself referred to on numerous occasions as "Dixie Walker's brother." In Florida, Walker began beating the drums for Clemente and he never ceased, though the season began treacherously, the Pirates ever streaky. Clemente was in the lineup from opening day, but the Pirates lost twenty-four of their first thirty-three games, were as frustrated as they had been since the redemptive year of 1960, and, finally, the atmosphere became conducive to disharmony. Harry Walker and Roberto Clemente crossed swords, for the first and last time.

"I want to be traded . . . I cannot play for this man," Roberto Clemente said. A few days later, Clemente and Harry Walker agreed: There had been a misunderstanding. And probably there had. Walker had said during a radio interview with St. Louis sportscaster Harry Caray that "superstars such as Stan Musial and Ted Williams played with injuries." It was a tactless remark, Clemente sidelined at the time with an injury.

Clemente didn't hear the interview, but was told of it by—who else?—a doctor. Hopefully the man was a better physician than reporter. "The doctor say to me, 'Walker say there is no reason for you not to play,'" Clemente related. "I say, 'That cannot be right. Walker tell me yesterday to rest, that Yogi Berra tell him I am not swinging the bat right.' I tell the doctor, 'If he say that, I do not play for him.'"

One fact was startlingly clear. Clemente was unhappy on the bench. On the road trip he had been benched in favor of left-handed Jerry Lynch, who had produced seven hits in ten at-bats while Clemente was striking out in his only two appearances.

Walker and Clemente met under a white flag at breakfast. "It was a misunderstanding," Walker said. "We tried to start him too soon after the malaria and then rest him. It was the wrong way to do it."

The air cleared, the Pirates immediately blew out of Tap City, winning twenty of their next twenty-two games without Clemente and Bill Mazeroski, who had broken a foot.

As the Pirate fortunes improved, so did the relationship between windy Harry Walker, who obviously knew a good thing when he saw it, and Roberto Clemente, delighted with a manager with whom he could talk. And everybody could talk to Walker.

"They say he talks too much, but he has done a good job," Clemente defended the new kid on the block. "To me, he makes sense. He knows baseball and he wants us to know it. We haven't had as much pitching as we did in 1960, that's what's the matter."

Certainly, Walker appeared to be a miracle worker. Under his easy-rider approach, Clemente, who had known every ill mortal man can suffer, caught fire at midyear and dragged the Pirates with him to Fat City.

His average climbed steadily from a low point of .257 on May 21, when the Pirates were 13½ games off the lead and out of contention, to .329 on the last day of the season, when they were 7 games behind champion San Francisco and only 2 out of second place. Clemente hit safely in 33 of 34 games during the Pirate resurgence and, after the first miserable month of the season, Pittsburgh won 81 and lost 48, a record unmatched in the National League during that span.

Where Murtaugh had poured vinegar on Clemente's wounds—real and imagined—Walker used syrup. "I thought he deserved credit," Walker said. "People always talked about what he didn't do, but for every one thing he didn't do, there were ten he did. You always heard he wouldn't play—but he played for me."

They had their little squabbles, Walker and Clemente did. After a tough loss in Chicago, Walker chewed out his right fielder, and there was some hollering reminiscent of the Murtaugh era.

"He missed throwing a guy out at the plate because he didn't come up on the ball quickly enough," Walker said. "I told him, 'There's nothing wrong with your legs. If you had charged the ball, he wouldn't have challenged you and you wouldn't have had to make the throw.' The next day, he came up to me and said, 'Don't feel bad about yesterday. I know you were just doing your job. I play for you. You are the man.'"

And in the National League in 1965, despite malaria and/or a paratyphoid infection; despite the torn ligament; despite the surgery; despite his normal state of rack and ruin, Roberto Clemente was the man. His .329 mark beat out Henry Aaron's .318, and no one in baseball hit so well.

Clemente played in 152 games, only three less than he ever had, and had 194 hits, which was worth a $15,000 raise, to $65,000 for the coming season. "I had a terrible year," Clemente explained. "I was sick most of the time, and I had to push myself all year."

Los Angeles Dodger pitcher Jim Brewer didn't doubt it. "Clemente will hit .320 the year after he dies," Brewer sighed.

Chapter 10

DR. CLEMENTE

"Hallo, Roberto? You are awake? This is Roberto. How you feel this morning?"

"Aaagh!"

"What is the matter?"

"I only sleep two hours last night."

"What time you go to bed?"

"Eight o'clock in the night."

"It is ten o'clock in the morning. How you only sleep two hours?"

"I was thinking. Thinking. Always thinking."

Roberto Marin, the scout who discovered him, smiled wanly on those winter mornings when his phone calls would nudge Roberto Clemente from his restless reverie. "He always sounded like an old man in the morning," Marin chuckled.

To know Clemente at all was to know that in the best of health, he was terminally ill. *Sports Illustrated* magazine ran a page-long sketch of Clemente in 1965, describing his various and sundry ailments. It took sixteen captions, scattered at various points of his anatomy, to list them all.

Roberto Clemente suffered no flesh wounds; each injury or sickness he viewed as mortal in conception. "He would sit around reading these big, thick medical textbooks he had," smiled a friend, Pittsburgh psychiatrist Mort Aronson. "The next day he'd have something new."

No subscriber to *Reader's Digest* knew more about medicine, or uncovered and adopted more symptoms than Clemente. The list of his more fugitive ailments ran from tension headaches to tired blood to disappearing bone chips to stomach disorders to insomnia to fear of nightmares. Fortunately for the medical profession, other of his maladies were more easily traced and treated: wayward discs, dozens of severely pulled muscles, a blood clot of the thigh, bruised Achilles tendons, infected tonsils, damaged insteps, curvature of the spine, osteomyelitis in both shoulders and neck, and others too numerous to mention.

He was considered, without doubt, baseball's prize hypochondriac; his suffering a source of humor, a conversational respite from the boredom of the dugout, the tedium of the press box. Players who hadn't run hard on a routine ground ball since their Little League days would watch a straining Clemente give himself completely to the baseline sprint and grin condescendingly, "He's hurt, huh?" Unimaginative sportswriters would suck their bellies away from the space bar and write, "Roberto Clemente didn't look like he was ailing yesterday when he . . ."

It was widely held that he had a low threshold of pain, which upon investigation appears not to be true. It was also widely held that Billy Graham spoke of his religion no more fervently than Roberto Clemente did of his health, or the lack thereof, and of this there can be no argument.

"He always had something wrong with him," said a longtime teammate, who is neither an unkind nor an insensitive man. "He made a lot bigger issue of his injuries than any player I ever knew. He loved sympathy, being made over. But he played when he was hurt most of the time."

In fact, there were few moments when Clemente was not hurt or sick, or both. The world took little note of his discomfort, save to smile patronizingly. We are a nation that laughs when people fall down. We don't know why we do, but we do. "I know I shouldn't have laughed but . . ." is a common phrase. So, when Roberto Clemente's health went sprawling, there was laughter:

"The thing about Clemente is that he's the only guy to receive get-well cards after going four for five, throwing two runners out at the plate, and stealing second standing up."—Jim Murray, sportswriter.

"I think I am the best hitter in baseball . . . when I am feeling right."—Roberto Clemente.

"He could hit .299 in an iron lung."—unidentified National League pitcher.

"My bad shoulder is good, but my good shoulder is bad."—Roberto Clemente.

"Every time I hear he has an ache, I expect him to go four for four."—Gil Hodges, manager.

Nowhere was Clemente's discomfort funnier than in Pittsburgh. One day when Pirate manager Danny Murtaugh taped a blank lineup card to the dugout wall prior to a game, a Pirate player penciled in the cleanup position: "The late Roberto Clemente." In 1965, when Clemente complained of being weakened by malaria, a teammate predicted, "He'll win the batting title by twenty points."

To look at Roberto Clemente—he looked a lot like Harry Belafonte singing the blues—was to believe he had never even been personally acquainted with a pimple. "He wasn't born, he was mined," a writer once observed. Such an appraisal seemed accurate. Clemente's shiny, mahogany skin was stretched tight, 180 pounds of sinewy muscle in a 170-pound container. A muscular neck tapered into the wide, bulging shoulders of a big middleweight, and he had the rippling waist of a prima ballerina overly preoccupied with situps. He would've given Charles Atlas an inferiority complex.

Clemente's teammates, with whom he had little meaningful contact, were less than indulgent, his love affair with infirmity grating on them, limiting the degree to which they sought him out socially. "People say I am moody, that I don't have much to do with the other players," he acknowledged the tension. "But if I don't take care of myself, I have a bad season. I'm stealing people's money. My conscience wouldn't stand that."

A few Pirates accepted Clemente's idiosyncrasy for what it was, a human frailty housed in a man with other redeeming virtues; similar to other players' conversational leanings toward sex or hunting or clubhouse gossip or sex.

"Robby likes to talk about how he feels," Pirate pitcher Al McBean said one afternoon in the gloaming of the 1965 season. "He complains a lot, wants you to talk to him, makes him feel good. When he says he feels terrible, I tell him he looks good, that he will go four for four that day. He'll say, 'I feel weak,' and I'll tell him he is strong. He doesn't like noise, likes to rest. 'The more you rest, the prettier you become,' he says."

And rest was the kingpin. Roberto Clemente—hypochondriac or not, public agonizer or not—didn't sleep worth a damn.

"It's always like that," he'd sigh, the carved features losing their tautness, intensity draining from his face at the thought of sleep—blessed, restorative, tension-relieving, wonderful old sleep. "I see the sun rise. I try to think of the nice things about my childhood. But my mind run like a movie. I can't stop it. I worry because I don't feel strong.

"I am tired, tired, tired. I am always tired. I never sleep. I know my wife want to go out, my kids want to go to the zoo, but I got to say no. I got to rest."

The choreography of Roberto Clemente retiring for the night in a strange hotel room would require the talents of a Fred Astaire. The telephone would be propped up on a stand at exactly arm's length from the bed. Rooming alone—the Pirates accorded him this privilege when he complained that returning teammates rattled clothes hangers and kept him awake—afforded him the time to leisurely study the room. He would memorize the floor plan. Where is the bathroom? Windows to the right, door to the left, dresser there, floor lamp here. "Suppose I have a nightmare and jump up? Hoo! I'm screaming and I rush through the window and the room is thirteen floors up."

Most critical, however, was the placement of the telephone. Should it ring, and hotel operators were instructed otherwise, it was vital he be able to pick up the receiver without lifting his eyelids. Once his eyes opened, he explained, tears welled up in them and he could not go back to sleep.

Still, there were many mornings when he greeted the dawn bleary-eyed, when even sleeping pills had been rendered powerless by his insomnia—"they keep me awake."

"One morning he looked like a corpse," McBean told a friend. "I said, 'You'll never make it.'"

Ironically, on the nights he had nightmares, Clemente often dreamed of dying—in an airplane accident.

"For the three years that I knew him, he never slept a wink," laughed Noreen Green Williams, a Pittsburgh housewife who as a teen-ager was a Pirate fan and friend of Clemente's. "He would sit around and talk with my girlfriends and I about his health . . . he was a wonderful guy, but he was a health nut. I remember him once saying he hadn't gotten any rest for so many nights he'd taken to sleeping on the floor. He worried so about his health. He always kept a large bottle of honey in his car, and he'd take it for energy—but he always looked just perfect."

A Puerto Rican doctor who treated him theorized that Clemente was his own worst enemy, a victim of his own fears. "When I don't sleep, I don't feel like eating and I lose weight," Clemente told the doctor.

"So, he wind up with a stomach trouble," sighed the doctor.

For years, insomnia and a nervous stomach parlayed into excruciating headaches. "I was having headaches . . . headaches . . . headaches . . . the pain split my head," Clemente grimaced. "The doctors said it was tension; that I worry too much. They say, 'Don't worry so much.' They gave me tranquilizers, but they didn't work."

Headaches, insomnia, stomach disorders. Shadowy ailments, as difficult to trace as a campaign contribution. But, Clemente would shout, they hurt. A few years after an automobile accident sent two discs fluttering loose from his spine, doctors examined Clemente and shook their heads in dismay. All of his vertebrae were accounted for, and in proper alignment. "I know something is wrong; it hurts," the doctors were told. In 1957, his elbow "swollen like a softball," he was shipped to Johns Hopkins Hospital, where Dr. Richard Bennett diagnosed bone chips that would be removed when the season ended. When the season ended, the bone chips had slithered off, disappeared. "It hurts," Clemente insisted. Modern medicine, on the brink of breakthroughs in a dozen crippling diseases and recent conqueror of polio, could not come to the aid of Roberto Clemente's right arm or his back.

Aha, baseball people nodded knowingly, he was jakin'. Arturo Garcia did not think so. Arturo Garcia was not exactly a doctor. Arturo Garcia was not exactly even a chiropractor. Arturo Garcia, it was suggested by those who did not know him, was a quack. Roberto Clemente did not think so. When Clemente insisted that Garcia be allowed to treat him, the Pirate team physician lost patience, perhaps because he had also lost face. "I'm fed up with the guy," the Pirate doctor fumed. "Let him go to that witch doctor of his."

If Garcia was not exactly a doctor, he was neither a witch doctor nor a quack, as Pirate pitcher Bob Veale and San Francisco manager Clyde King, both of whom had back problems alleviated by Garcia, were willing to testify. Garcia had dropped out of his last year of medical school but, Clemente was adamant, "he knows about muscles and bones." Wealthy and practicing chiropractic as a hobby, Garcia once asked Clemente to perform a simple exercise. "I make a face once and he look at me and say, 'You have bad disc,'" Clemente said triumphantly. It was Garcia who then showed Clemente how to manipulate the disc back into place. And for the rest of his career, Clemente sought out Garcia when in severe pain.

Considering that at thirty-eight Clemente played with more abandon and was more supple than most of his twenty-five-year-old teammates, it might be argued that his faith in Garcia was justified. In any case, it existed, and he became Garcia's chiropractic protégé, also coming to know about muscles and bones.

For years, the son of the law partner of Clemente's attorney, Elfren Bernier, had only been able to turn his head twenty degrees or so in each direction. "The boy had been taken to many doctors, but they hadn't done him much good," Bernier said. "Roberto told me one day, 'Bring him to my home. I will fix him.' He put the boy on a special table and twisted and pulled his neck."

After a few minutes, Antonio Perez, Jr., sat up, blinked, and turned to look over one shoulder at his father. "The boy was very straight after that," Bernier said. "Roberto was always bringing some kid to his house to fix his neck or back. I used to get angry with him, tell him, 'You are not licensed to do that. You are going to get in trouble.' But he would not listen."

Among other of Dr. Clemente's patients were ex-teammate Don Hoak, whose neck problem was corrected, and Pirate president Dan Galbreath, whose ailing back was improved, and—sweet, sweet vengeance—Danny Murtaugh.

"Danny criticized me a lot when I played for him because I say I have a sore back," Clemente recalled one afternoon. "Then he develop the same trouble I had: lower back spasms. So I ask him, 'You want me to help you?' He said, 'Yes.' So I give him two treatments, and right away he felt better.

"He said, 'You know what? This is the best I have felt in five years.' I said, 'Now you know how I feel those years when you criticized me.'"

Shortly, Clemente became his own physician, which

had figured from the beginning. One afternoon in late 1964, he explained to *Sports Illustrated* writer Myron Cope how he could arise each morning only after treating himself.

The treatment—Clemente gladly demonstrated it to Cope—consisted of laying on his right side, crossing his left leg over his right, digging his fingers deeply into the soft flesh above his left hip, grimacing, pushing, and awaiting the sound that informed him his wandering disc was back home.

"Boop," Clemente shouted for Cope's edification. "Every morning you can hear it from here to there, in the whole room." Two boops, actually, for an adventurous disc at the top of his spinal cord had to be repositioned daily.

Cope returned to Pittsburgh and wrote a hilarious, bantering story that suggested if all of Clemente's ills were genuine, the only reasonable course of action was euthanasia. Clemente did not speak to Cope for four years.

Cope could hardly be blamed for having fun with Clemente's profession of mortality. Humor had long been the handmaiden of his misery. "Reports of Clemente's birth were greatly exaggerated," and "when he reads about a disease, he wants it," and "he looks as if he just stepped off a Michelangelo pedestal and sounds as if he just stepped out of a TB ward."

But the intensity with which he pursued all things, large and small, turned a lock on Clemente. He was his own prisoner in a very real world of injuries; insomnia; pain; and draining, self-imposed pressure.

And who is to say how much the other guy hurts? And

how heavy is his burden? Reach back for a moment of some agony you've suffered. Childbirth? A knee in the groin? The throbbing of an impacted wisdom tooth or an ear infection? Whatever. Could you have explained to any living thing how tormented you were? Could your vocabulary have done justice to searing, knifing, all-encompassing pain? Not unless your name is Shakespeare.

Roberto Clemente hurt. Who could honestly say, "Forget it. It is not that bad. Be an Oriole. Rub dirt in it and play." Or any of those thousand worthless phrases the pain-free lay on the pain-racked in the name of comfort?

It is the professional opinion of two doctors who knew him that Roberto Clemente did not writhe without reason.

"Even if the pain was psychogenic, it existed, was real," said Mort Aronson, the Pittsburgh psychiatrist who rarely ever missed a Pirate home game. "My feeling is that he had real pain. His body was everything in life to him. But I wouldn't say he was morbidly preoccupied with his ailments."

Dr. Roberto Buso, who treated Clemente for malaria in 1965, agreed. "I wouldn't call him a true hypochondriac. If his back hurt, he worried. If he had a little diarrhea, he worried he had a serious stomach difficulty."

Nostrils dilating, his voice climbing for C above high C, Clemente would deny hypochondria in a tone of voice, and with a depth of feeling, that, well, must have hurt his ears.

"That's a person who cannot produce . . . imagines sickness . . . look at my body; look, I have the scars," he would shout.

Dignity and honor and pride, they were the stuff of

Latin manhood; of Roberto Clemente. "I am a man," he would say, possessed by the *machismo*, challenging anyone who dared to question the physical ailments so skillfully camouflaged by the physical skills. "I have so much God-given ability I can play even when I ache so bad."

Simple braggadocio? The delusions of an overblown ego? Perhaps. More likely less of an excuse than a simple truth. "He's better at 75 percent than the rest of us are at 100 percent," Bill Mazeroski said.

If Clemente had accusers—and he had many, and mostly they were cruel and lacked the courage to speak out publicly—he also had defenders: Pirate trainer Tony Bartirome, who would peer down his nose at charges of Clemente's malingering and bury them in a torrent of expletives; General Manager Joe L. Brown, who grew weary of defending a man who averaged 136 games per season for 18 years and was the most exciting player in the game at an age when his contemporaries puffed running out pop-ups at the church picnic. And there was, through the years, an occasional teammate willing to understand someone who was different, someone who marched to his own drummer.

Tony Bartirome's clear, dark eyes—black olives floating in a pool of champagne—flashed angrily whenever Roberto Clemente and hypochondria were mentioned in the same sentence.

"They called him a hypochondriac," Bartirome sneered, moving about his training room with the quick, sure movements that conjured up visions of the truly brilliant-fielding first baseman he once was. "He played more games than any player who ever wore a Pirate uniform. How the hell could he have been a hypochondriac?

"He played with injuries other guys wouldn't have come to the ballpark with because he knew his presence made a difference. I've seen him play with Achilles tendons stretched tighter than a drum. One year he had a bad knee, all swollen and stiff. I told him not to play, that he could be out for weeks if he did, or jeopardize his whole career. 'No, we need a few wins,' he said. And that kind of thing was not unusual."

Bartirome was Clemente's close friend—"dumb dago" . . . "stupid spic"—so it is to be expected he might defend him against all comers, all charges. Bartirome does so, but indignantly—Carrie Nation swinging a righteous ax against the speakeasy door.

"He got hurt by the drive he put into a game—any game. He didn't know how to pace himself. He played every game the same: hard. A lot of guys played winter ball, too, but for them it was a vacation. Good money, their wives came down, a chance to sit in the sun. They don't give a damn, win, lose, or draw. He played a whole season down there every year, and for him there wasn't any difference between the winter league and the big league. Hell, he played twice as many games as Aaron or Mays. Aaron's one of the greatest, but I've seen him hit a thousand ground balls and then trot down the line. You ever see Clemente do that—even once?"

And the answer had to be "No." Not even once. Not even when he had a pulled leg muscle or hadn't slept a wink. He played without any reserve. What you got was what he had. And all of it—every day, winter league or in the bigs, on every play.

"I told him once, 'You are a fool to play down here, you're going to break a leg,'" said Omar Cordeiro, his lifelong friend. "He say, 'No, I play hard, but I won't get hurt.' Once he told me about a game. The Pirates needed a run bad. He was on base and he explained what he did. He got so enthusiastic that he stood across from me and showed me how he slid by the catcher.

"We were on his concrete patio.

"I said, 'You'll break your leg.' But he said he never got hurt sliding. That's how wrapped up he was in baseball. On the patio, he slides."

Even the Clemente apologists, however, referred to his low threshold of pain. "Hell, it was higher than most players," sneered Bartirome.

In Florida one year, Bartirome had applied a hydroculator pad to one of Clemente's aching shoulders. The pad is standard equipment in training rooms and is used to apply wet heat. It's heated to more than two hundred degrees in a sterilizing unit, and towels are placed between it and the skin.

"I put a hydroculator pad on his shoulder this day and I told him if he wanted another towel under it, to holler," Bartirome said. "Well, he and some guys got talking and suddenly he says, 'Hey, you damn dago, you burned me.'

"I took the pad off and it had burned clear through two folded towels and his jersey, and had left a big star-shaped burn on him. Hell, anyone with a low tolerance for pain would've thrown the thing at me. It left an awful-looking scar. He didn't even make a fuss.

"Hypochondriac . . . shit."

"A lot of that stuff was easy copy for the writers." So said Pirate pitcher Steve Blass. "He was our No. 1 man, and when there was something wrong with him, people wanted to know about it. And that kind of thing was easier to write about than taking the time to get to know him and understand him."

Understand him. Joe L. Brown thought he did. "The local press felt he was a malingerer," Brown said. "It wasn't true, but even some of the players, the managers, and the coaches didn't want to recognize that his injuries were real. He played a good many times when most players wouldn't have. And everybody who played as hard as Clemente was bound to get hurt. But I saw him run into a wall, bust his chin open, take eight stitches, and be back in the lineup the next day."

The man himself, as he had with the press, gradually quit worrying over the disbelievers. "If a Latin or an American Negro is sick," Clemente would shake his head from side to side in resignation, "they say it is all in his head. Felipe Alou once went to his team doctor and the doctor said, 'You have nothing wrong.' The next day he go to a private doctor and the doctor tell him, 'You have a broken foot.'"

The charges that he was faking injuries, or inventing them and letting them affect his performance, never really ceased. They would haunt his career, suck away some of the joy he felt, and embitter him, coloring his play, overshadowing his classic grace and impeccable credentials. In the years to come, golden years, they would impede the obvious: that he was perhaps the finest complete talent the game had known.

He would often rail against such thinking publicly.

"I don't give a damn if people don't believe I am hurt," he would say one day, another kind of pain in his eyes. "They don't know how I feel inside. Only I know when I am hurt . . . and only I know how much I want to play."

And play, the man did. On and on, until even the most obtuse fan or cynical player could see how very much Roberto Clemente wanted to play baseball. And how very brilliantly he could do so.

Chapter 11

MOST VALUABLE AT LAST

What makes one man a leader and another a follower? Why will soldiers follow one officer over the top into treacherous crossfire, and grovel in the dirt in defiance of another? Why did thousands trail Martin Luther King, Jr., as he marched against the snarling police dogs and fire hoses and cattle prods of a Birmingham desperately struggling to preserve its most cherished traditions? Why did thousands starve to death at the gentle command of Mahatma Gandhi?

Perhaps because the true leader never looks back?

In 1966, Roberto Clemente quit looking back. And quietly, possibly without realizing it, he became leader of a baseball team, a band of men who, amid the tensions of September, need leadership as they do skill. The reasons behind Clemente becoming a leader are as unclear as those that had to do with King and Gandhi becoming men among men.

Certainly change had something to do with it. By 1966, Clemente had changed noticeably, was more able to compromise with his life, better able to accept the vast grayness that separates the black and whites, the absolute goods and the absolute evils. In truth, age seemed to have absorbed the harshness of his ideals, as it does all men's. He was thirty-two, and perhaps the years had bent him toward the realization that living a life of absolutes was painful and not necessarily productive. For more than a decade, he had danced to only his own drum; perhaps he stumbled upon the awareness that other men, good men, heard a different tune. And perhaps he merely tired of the fight and wished now to live and let live. To desert one's ideals, the poets have written, is to sacrifice one's youth. Perhaps that was it. Roberto Clemente had gotten older, decided to channel his energies instead of flinging them about. At any rate, he changed, and if the change was gradual, it did not seem so to those around him in the spring and summer of 1966.

And by then, the Pirates had changed, new players replacing the ones from whom Clemente had grown estranged. The manager had changed: His longtime antagonist Danny Murtaugh had been replaced by the irrepressible Harry Walker, rapidly becoming his champion.

And the time and the conditions were prime for Clemente to become the Pirate leader, as Mazeroski was the captain and pitcher Vernon Law the quiet elder statesman. Clemente was by now earning eighty thousand dollars a year. Baseball players, like other men, fall in line behind him who carries the heaviest load to the bank. In addition, the Pirates had lacked a natural leader since Don Hoak had been traded, a fact that general manager Joe Brown had not overlooked.

"Bob, you're one of the best players in the game today, but we want you to be more of a leader," Brown had suggested when the nucleus of the 1960 championship team had been dissolved by trade or attrition.

But leadership can't be bestowed. Players who enthusiastically slap teammates' backsides are not leaders, but cheerleaders; players who hustle hither and yon in testimony to their own desire are not leaders, but poseurs; players who assure every sportswriter within range that the Pirates or Yankees or Maple Terrace Bombers are united in a bond of brotherhood last witnessed in the balmier days of Romulus and Remus are not leaders, but aspirants.

Leadership evolves slowly; it demands not affection or friendship or admiration, only respect. And in the early 1960s, Roberto Clemente correctly sensed that he did not own his teammates' full respect, that they laughed at, rather than with, him. He had fought with a man they still held in esteem, Murtaugh. And when he had spoken out, trying to inspire, it had purchased only further disharmony. He balked at Brown's request.

"How can I be more of a leader?" Clemente asked. "I talk to everyone when they have a good day or a bad day. I try to help everyone out there. What more can I do? I break my neck for this team and I do not get so much as a thank you from Murtaugh."

There were other reasons, uncertainty among them, that

restrained Clemente. "I always talk to the young players, give them advice," he would say later. "But I didn't feel I should speak out much because no one would listen. When I try to do that, Murtaugh put me down. How could I be a leader?"

In a variety of ways. Let the years mature you, eat away the rigidity of your ideals and leave a residue of tolerance. Let new contemporaries replace those with whom you had no common ground or understanding. Let time provide the condition for your acceptance of the role. Let confidence replace your fear of rejection. All of these.

And all of them led, in some measure, to Clemente becoming a leader, paved the way for his conversion from a loner fired by only his own needs and desires to a colleague able to accept injustice and failure and weakness for what they are, merely intrinsic parts of the human condition.

Under the auspices of Harry Walker, Clemente's personality changed, and he became, covertly, a company man. So said two Clemente watchers of 1966, Joe Brown and the pitcher-turned-broadcaster, Nellie King.

"The turning point in Roberto's career was Walker," Brown said. "Some people Harry didn't reach, but Roberto he did. The two years under Walker were Clemente's best. He convinced Roberto he could become one of the great players of all times."

King agreed. "Clemente's personality changed under Walker. He knew he was a hell of a ballplayer, and he started to open up as a person. He got respect under Walker. Everyone in the league started realizing all the stuff about him not playing when he was hurt was a lot of bullshit. And when you search for recognition so long, when it's suddenly there, you are freed."

And this was Murtaugh's failing. He hadn't freed Clemente so that he might live up to his self-image—that of a man striving passionately and honestly to be not good, but great; a man who did his best under the prevailing conditions and expected, when those conditions were ill health, to receive compassion, as he would give it.

Clemente saw himself as unique—in talent, temperament, ambition. He demanded to be treated as an entity; more than just a part of the whole. This was irrational heresy to Murtaugh, a product of the baseball tradition that at least seeks to treat every man equally. To elevate one man is to court disaster, or at least defeat. No man is above the team.

Walker's code was less rigid, and perhaps more self-serving. Where Murtaugh had insisted fatigue was no fit reason to absent oneself from the arena, Walker let Clemente take the odd day off. "I know he's putting out for me," Walker explained. "I told him to tell me when he didn't feel like playing." Where Murtaugh insisted that all his outfielders take pregame practice, Walker's approach was different, more subtle. "Robby, go out and shag for a while. You don't need the work, but the others do. If you're not out there, they'll loaf."

"He goes out and busts his butt," Walker said. "I wish I had a dozen like him. He's high-spirited, a thoroughbred. He needs to be treated differently. But things mean a lot more to him than people ever realized."

Such a realization began to dawn in spring training of

1966. During the previous winter, Clemente had played just two innings of winter ball and spent the majority of his time relaxing and playing with his year-old son, Roberto, Jr. When he appeared at Fort Myers, despite the lingering effects of malaria, he weighed a solid 180 pounds. Walker immediately gave him a twofold task: reach prearranged hitting goals, and serve as a batting coach with one pupil.

"I want you to get 25 home runs and drive in 115," Walker told him. "We'll need that to win the pennant."

In the busy days of spring, Clemente appeared less tense, even amiable. "How do you feel today?" big pitcher Bob Veale would leer, openly agitating. "Ooh, I feel terrible," Clemente would grin, at ease with the by-play and what it suggested, where short months ago he would have been chilled or enraged.

"He had changed," admitted Mazeroski, Clemente's teammate for a decade. "Since Walker's been here, he's been different. He talks a lot more, hollers it up. Maybe it stems from not getting along with Murtaugh. Maybe it's the different players we have now. Maybe he's the one who has changed. I don't know."

Now, Mazeroski was "Hey, you dumb Polack." Now Clemente was easing from behind the wall he had thrown up in the years when there was misunderstanding, when he'd been able to sense rejection, when nobody wanted to hear of the troubles he had known.

"It seems like he wants to win more now," Mazeroski theorized in a moment of candor. "Maybe that's not right to say. But now it shows more."

It also showed that the Pirates were beginning to understand what Harry Walker had immediately understood—that here was a man unlike most. "Latins are very temperamental," Mazeroski acknowledged. "They don't think like we do. Something goes wrong, we say, 'Aw, shit.' They get all worked up."

This was no great dramatic breakthrough, merely Mazeroski giving voice to his thoughts on a sleepy March day. But no Pirate was better liked or more respected than Mazeroski, and his attitude heralded a new acceptance of Clemente, a fresh awareness of him. "He joins in the agitation that always goes on now. He's a lot looser . . . happier."

"And the ballclub had changed," King said. "The guys he broke in with, the guys who had bitched about him not playing, were gone by then." An older, tireder Mazeroski held a like opinion. "Hell, everyone needs a rest now and then," said the peerless second baseman, who in ten years had rarely rested and whose daily presence in the lineup, injured or not, had accentuated Clemente's absences. "Sometimes we get so mentally tired, we might as well not be in the game. You go to the plate thinking, 'I can't hit,' and you don't."

So 1966 was a beginning—Roberto Clemente was now less inclined to joust with windmills. The leader that Joe Brown had sought was about to emerge.

"I knew the one thing in life that he wanted was to be the MVP," Walker said. "I told him some things: that he was our leader now . . . that he should set the example . . . that if he did, he would win the MVP award. I think he learned to believe in me—know I was in his corner."

The new chain of command went into affect in Florida.

The Pirates had made a determined charge before finishing third in 1965, and Walker was convinced they could win the pennant in 1966. If. If Clemente could provide the long ball, and if he could convince tiny Matty Alou that a 5-8, 155-pound singles hitter was never destined to threaten Babe Ruth's memory. Before the Pirates had acquired him in 1966 in a trade, Alou had spent 6 years with the Giants trying to pull the ball into the gale-force winds that could and often did carry baseballs beyond the right-field fence at Candlestick Park as though they were feathers. For his troubles, Alou hit exactly 14 home runs in San Francisco.

No one better understood the art of hitting than Harry Walker, and it was obvious to everyone, with the exception of Alou, that the little Dominican would pump precious few drives out of expansive Forbes Field, the largest park in baseball.

If he knew hitting, Walker also knew the Latin psyche. "I want Alou to hit to left field," he told his new team leader. "The pitchers are working the outside corner on him, and he's become an easy mark trying to pull everything. Talk to him about it."

"I'll tell him," Clemente nodded.

Every day of spring training, Clemente told Alou, "Don't pull the ball." He would station himself in left field during batting practice and scream at Alou in Spanish, "Hit the ball to me. . . . Hit the ball to me. . . . Hit the ball to me."

Alou came to hear the command in his sleep, and soon sharply struck line drives began buzzing over the heads of shortstops and dying at the feet of left fielders. Clemente had been an excellent instructor. Matty Alou would succeed him as the National League batting leader.

From the outset, the 1966 season was a study in the reasons behind baseball being known as the national pastime. Before it ended, it would become a siege, Pittsburgh, Los Angeles, and San Francisco furiously fighting for the pennant into the last two weeks of the season.

In the coolness of April, Clemente tried to give Walker the power he'd requested. And, as usual, he tried too hard. By mid-May, his average had tailed off to .285 and he had hit but three home runs. Frustrated, he insisted the batter's box at Forbes Field was the culprit.

"For years I have been pleading with them to put in clay instead of sand," he wailed. "Sand make my feet slip. Batters dig holes, I come to the plate and scrape dirt loose to cover them up."

Perhaps, confronted with such a theory, Murtaugh would have torn at his hair. Walker smiled patiently. The batter's box was dug up, and clay replaced sand as a base. Clemente went on an immediate tear, hitting at a .444 clip and hammering 6 home runs during an 11-day home stand in June. Two of the home runs disappeared over a huge, iron exit gate in right-center field, 436 feet from home plate. No veteran observer of the Pirates could ever recall another man hitting 2 home runs in that location, and Roberto Clemente had begun to put another Pirate immortal, Paul Waner, behind him. Paul Waner could not have propelled a baseball 436 feet to the opposite field with a bazooka.

Pittsburgh had known baseball heroes other than Clemente. When an all-time, all-star team was announced in the 1960s, Pittsburgh was well represented by shortstop Honus Wagner, an eight-time bowlegged batting champion of the 1900s, and Pie Traynor, a giant of the 1920s who retired with a .320 lifetime average and the acknowledgment that he was, indisputably, the finest third baseman who had ever played the game. But it was Waner, a more proficient copy of Matty Alou, to whom Clemente had long been compared, usually unfavorably.

Waner was called "Big Poison"; he had a younger brother, Lloyd, who was referred to, as might be guessed, "Little Poison." Paul Waner was a brilliant right fielder and a slashing hitter who finished his career with a .340 batting average—a legend Roberto Clemente could approach, but never quite equal. Always the "but."

"I am tired of playing in Paul Waner's shadow," said Clemente, the surfacing power-hitter. "Everything I do, they compare me with Waner. Always Waner. I have talked with people who saw him play. They say he was good, but not great."

It wasn't the ghost of Paul Waner that Clemente lashed out at; it was his failure to acquire the status of superstar, with its hundred-thousand-dollar contracts and the attending publicity; its acknowledgment that no player was greater.

"I think I can hit better than any of those fellows, with the exception of power," he said in the summer of 1966. "I don't try to use power in this park; I can help the club more with line drives. I know I can field as good as any of them. And I know I can throw better than anyone."

What hurt most was a lack of recognition at home.

"They think Mays and Aaron are supermen. I say, 'I can hit with them.' They say, 'If you was that good, we'd see your name in the papers.'"

That day was fast approaching, but now the talk was of one of the closest pennant races in the National League in years. Before a month of the 1966 season had expired, it was apparent that three teams would duel through the long summer. The Pirates had inconsistent starting pitching; the Dodgers very little of anything else; the Giants hit for power but not for percentage.

As the race evolved, it became a question of relative weaknesses rather than strengths. The Giants were shaky afield; the Dodgers had Sandy Koufax and several regulars who could not hit as well as Koufax; the Pirates would have to make hitting and defense atone for the sins of the pitching staff. Otherwise, it would come down to the supermen: Koufax, Mays, Clemente.

The pressures of such a prolonged struggle asserted themselves in the heat of early summer. Walker rudely jerked Al McBean from a game for a mental lapse; chewed out catcher Jesse Gonder on the field in Houston for calling a poor game; and according to a story that appeared in the New York *Post*, was punched by catcher Jim Pagliaroni, although both men denied it, and Pagliaroni later filed a libel suit.

None of these incidents resounded quite like one involving Clemente and a fan. On the night of May 6 in Philadelphia, the Pirates scored four runs in the top of the eleventh inning to take a seemingly insurmountable 7–3 lead over the Phillies. In the bottom of the inning, Philadelphia scored five times to win the tense game.

As the shaken Pirates boarded their team bus, a group of young Phillie fans from the nearby Stevens Trade School approached. One of them asked Clemente for his autograph, and witnesses said there was scuffling. When it ended, Bernard Heller said Clemente had struck him. Newspaper accounts said the nineteen-year-old Heller had three loose teeth and a sore jaw. Five days later an oral surgeon amended the damage to four lost teeth and a broken jaw.

Clemente said he was trying momentarily to board the bus before signing autographs—which he did after the incident—when someone pushed him from behind. He said he threw his arm back and hit young Heller. "I saw someone coming at me with his hands up, like he was going to hit me. I reached up to push him away. I wouldn't hit anyone without provocation."

The story sounded like the product of a publicity man's fertile imagination, but the incident ended without court action. One thing seemed incontestible. Roberto Clemente —the malingerer who wasn't supposed to care—had reacted violently to the loss of a single ballgame in 1966.

As the pennant race deepened, the Pirates fought the pressure in novel ways. Pagliaroni, a free spirit, helped organize the Black Maxers, proudly announcing "there isn't a sane guy on the team": the Green Weenie was brought out of retirement.

The Maxers were a parody of a popular World War I aviation movie, *The Blue Max*. The Pirates adorned themselves in World War I aviation headgear, chalked up absurd signs in the clubhouse, and posed for ridiculous pictures. The Black Maxers helped draw off the tension as three teams moved inexorably toward a September showdown.

The Green Weenie was restored to unnerve opposing pitchers. In the summer of 1960, trainer Danny Whelan had bought a huge, green, plastic frankfurter and leveled it at enemy pitchers. When Whelan brought out the Green Weenie, Pirate bats seemed to come alive. Six years later, the Pirates locked in even combat with the two West Coast teams, Son of Green Weenie appeared. Perhaps even its predecessor would have failed to overcome the presence of Harry Walker, something of a jinx in his own right, as it turned out.

The 1966 Pirates, with the noteworthy exception of Clemente and a few others, finally tired of Walker's southern twang; his demands for victory and the tirades that followed when it was not forthcoming.

The year before, Walker weighing heavily on their nerves, the Pirates had discussed mutiny. In last place in May and—the indignity of it all—trailing the ninth-place circus known as the New York Mets by 4½ games, Pirate veterans, organized by pitcher Bob Friend, gathered in a Chicago hotel room to discuss the club's plight and what might be done about it. Something obviously had to be done. Even Clemente the disciple was wearying of Walker, although he told his teammates, "I am not mad at him; I play for Walker."

It was decided to allow word of the meeting to drift back to Walker as a sign of some Pirates' unhappiness. When it did, he met with the entire squad in a frank, revealing session. What was revealed was that the Pittsburgh Pirates, or a majority thereof, thought Walker was overmanaging, too scientific in his approach, too demanding, too nitpicking, and was creating unnecessary pressure. They were not all, they informed him, Matty Alous awaiting only Walker's educational genius to blossom into superstars.

One year later, in the cauldron of a pennant race, few had altered their thinking. Harry still talked too much. And the Pirates had other problems.

An arm injury had shelved fireballing rookie left-hander Bob Veale for five turns; shortstop Gene Alley, enjoying his finest year, was beaned; Pagliaroni, who had wielded a hot bat earlier, hurt his leg, and his average fell off sharply. Through it all, Clemente, hampered by a sore shoulder, carried on. He was hitting .330 into August, when the three front runners could have been covered by a blanket.

For most of the Pirates, the pennant would be worth eleven thousand dollars; to Clemente it was far more valuable—quite probably it would mean receiving the Most Valuable Player Award that had come to represent so much to him. To become the MVP would be to silence all of the critics down the years, cleanse his honorable name, prove his worth to the most cynical of doubters, and give evidence to Murtaugh that he had been wrong, wrong, wrong. And it would, most important of all, testify to Puerto Ricans that, like Mays and Aaron, Roberto Clemente was a superman, too. No Puerto Rican had ever won the award.

On the night of September 3, the sprint for that award had come down to two men: Clemente, and Koufax, enjoying his finest hours despite a painful left arm. On this warm fall evening, with all of the drama that had marked his career, Roberto Clemente authored base hit No. 2,000.

His thousandth hit had come in a meaningless 1961 game against Cincinnati, a single that was buried amid a four-run, first-inning uprising that excused a young Reds' pitcher named Ken Hunt for the remainder of the afternoon. Umpire Mel Steiner momentarily called time and presented the baseball to Clemente with little ceremony. Only a thousand? It seemed like Clemente had been banging out hits since sometime in the Dark Ages to Cincinnati relief pitcher Jim Brosnan. "That's Clemente's thousandth hit," he remarked to teammate Bill Henry as Steiner flipped the ball to Clemente.

"Did he get 'em all off us?" the laconic Texan replied.

In fact, the Dodgers, ironically, had been Clemente's biggest victims. He hit an aggregate .375 against the Dodgers during his first decade in the majors.

The setting for his two thousandth hit was ideal. Veale, clinging to a 1–0 lead over Chicago, scratched a hit off shortstop Don Kessinger's glove to open the Pirate fifth. Matty Alou attempted to sacrifice, but Cub pitcher Ferguson Jenkins overran the bunt, and both runners were safe. Alley sacrificed them ahead, bringing Clemente to the plate.

On the mound, Jenkins dug nervously at the rubber. Clemente girded tired, aching muscles and tensed at the plate. The lanky young right-hander came over the top with a fast ball, and Clemente lunged for the outside pitch, his bat sweeping through a huge arc. The ball leaped from the plate in a pale blur and crashed against a seat back in Section 203, high in the right-field seats.

A crowd of 13,677 leaped to its feet, and wave after wave of applause rolled from the stands and washed over distant walls. Ernie Banks followed the flight of the home run with mixed emotions. It would cost Chicago a game, but he knew the feeling Clemente carried with him around the bases, having experienced his own two thousandth hit just two months before.

"It's something you remember a long time," Banks explained. "I know he had a wonderful feeling of satisfaction. When you get 2,000 hits, it sort of puts you in select company."

It did that. Only 8 players active in 1966 had managed 2,000 hits; only 115 in baseball history. No. 116 was jubilant in the Pirate clubhouse, recalling that when he had thought of leaving the game a decade before, a love affair with the fans had changed his mind.

"When my back got worse in 1957, I said to myself that I would quit," Clemente smiled. "I called my father in Puerto Rico, and he encouraged me to stay. But I was still undecided until I remember what the fans write to me. That clinched it. If it wasn't for them, I would not be playing today. They told me to keep trying, they said they understood. That's why it was such a thrill to get the two thousandth hit here. I couldn't have wish for anything better."

In fact, he did wish for something better. A pennant. Twelve days later, the Pirates moved into Dodger Stadium 1½ games behind their hosts, 3 ahead of the third-place Giants. The race had not loosened a notch since June. Clemente was hitting .327, and Harry Walker's power goals were just over the horizon. At the height of the stretch drive, Clemente had 23 home runs, tieing a career high, and 110 rbi's, the first time he had breached 100. Still, with Clemente having his finest year, the Pirates could not overhaul Los Angeles, and their pennant hopes were roped to this final series. Roberto Clemente loved it. The limelight was right here, the attention of the nation's baseball fans sharply focused.

"I never get nervous," he said. "I love this, in September, when you are in first or second, and each game mean something, and there are lots of people watching me. Who want to play when the game mean nothing?"

The games of September 15 and 16 meant everything. In the first one, Don Drysdale survived a ninth-inning home run by Clemente to win, 5–3; in the second, Koufax, the pain in his arthritic left arm bringing beads of cold sweat to his forehead, dominated the Pirates, 5–1.

Pittsburgh's pennant hopes died, although they would not officially be buried until the night two weeks later when Koufax recorded his twenty-seventh win, beating the Pirates at Forbes Field to clinch the championship. The Giants trailed Los Angeles into Pittsburgh and swept the final series of the season to edge the Pirates out of second place. Roberto Clemente's finest season had ended in disaster.

He hit .317, fifth best in the league, and delivered the power Walker had requested, 29 home runs and 119 rbi's, second in that last department to only Aaron. He reached personal levels with the bat previously unattained: 355 total bases, second highest in the league; 71 extra-base hits; 13 intentional walks, another league high. During the year of his two thousandth hit came his hundredth triple and three hundredth double. He played in all but 8 games. He joined the power elite of Mays and Aaron. But when the season ended, he was not the favorite to capture the MVP award.

Koufax had been nothing short of sensational, with 27 victories, a microscopic 1.73 earned-run average, 327 strikeouts, and an incredible 27 complete games. All of this with an inflamed arm. Clemente, the perennial bridesmaid, was offered little hope, some solace. "That he has never won the award is, of course, as big a crime as if Spencer Tracy never won an Oscar," one writer observed. And Walker growled, "If he doesn't get it, it will be criminal."

No crime was perpetrated. On November 16, it was the published opinion of his old, old enemies, the Baseball Writers Association of America, that Roberto Clemente had been more valuable to the Pittsburgh Pirates than Sandy Koufax had been to the Los Angeles Dodgers, 218 votes to 208. Rarely had a player on a third-place club won the award.

No one else was in hailing distance, Mays, Richie Allen, Felipe Alou, Juan Marichal, Phil Regan, Aaron, Matty Alou, and Pete Rose filling out the first ten. It was a source of great pleasure for the winner to note that four of the top ten vote-getters were Latins.

True to his own code, Clemente was painfully honest in his thoughts upon being notified he had attained his most cherished goal. Among the things he said after being informed he had reached the summit, there to gaze down upon the prostrate remains of his enemies, real and imagined, were:

"It is the highest honor a player can hope for, but I was expecting it," and, "Sure I am still bitter about 1960. I carried the club the whole year."

Yet he meant it when he said he would rather have had a pennant. "If I had not won the MVP, I would not have been mad because Sandy Koufax was a great pitcher and he deserved it. Besides, I know I would have been close and not been snubbed like I was in 1960.

"And I tell you one thing, I didn't win the MVP alone. I was sad because we didn't win the pennant, but I thought that the MVP was something the ballclub could be proud of because it gave our whole team recognition." Only the cynics laughed.

"He won the MVP because he did so many little things," said the man who had campaigned for Clemente the hardest, Harry Walker. "He did the things so many stars don't: hustling on routine ground balls, breaking up double plays, taking the extra base. He has pride, wants people to know what he has accomplished."

Walker was proud, too. His cultivation project had been a huge success. Pirate fans were proud. Their main man had reached the stars, and now everyone knew what they had known for years: Their pride and joy was the best of the very best. But no one was prouder than Roberto Clemente. The kids of Puerto Rico would no longer be caught short when yelling in sandlot games, "I'll be . . ."

"When I was a kid, I felt baseball was great for America," Clemente said. "Always they used to say Babe Ruth was the best there ever was, that you would have to really be something to be Babe Ruth. But Babe Ruth was an

American. What we needed was a Puerto Rican player they could say that about, look up to, try to equal."

The kids of Puerto Rico, at long last, had their very own Babe Ruth.

Chapter 12

THE LEADER

The huge, square room, deep in the bowels of Forbes Field, always seemed damp. On the hottest July day, the sun blistering the green paint from the grandstand and sending fainting fans off to Presbyterian Hospital in wailing ambulances, the dungeon of a clubhouse remained cool and dank.

Dressing cubicles, each fronted by a three-legged stool, marched in orderly procession around the high walls. Their pattern was broken only by the doorway to the clubhouse, a tiny foyer that housed the hallway running between the manager's office and the cramped training room, and the entrance to the equipment room.

Space was parceled out on an ethnic-racial basis, Latins along one wall, white veterans taking up the middle walls, the black Pirates and the younger white players splitting a wall. Entering the dreary, damp home of the 1967 Pittsburgh Pirates, a stranger might have deduced it to be a house divided into warring clumps of men banded together against one another.

In fact, this was not the case, although in the past there had been rumblings of racial tension in this room, and in two years they would rise briefly again. But in the spring of 1967, there was harmony here.

"Hey, you," José Pagán, the veteran utilityman, cried to Roberto Clemente, the neophyte superstar. "Everytime I see you, you like Cassius Clay, yak, yak, yak. Don't you ever stop?"

"He wouldn't want to talk to you," Roberto Clemente smiled, pausing in the middle of the interview. "There wouldn't be anything to talk about."

"Sure there would," broad-faced relief pitcher Pete Mikkelsen cackled across the room. "Joe could tell them about the time he was in the Army in Puerto Rico."

"Nah . . . Pagán was never in the Army. He's a cripple."

Pagán grabbed a pot from the table in the training room and hoisted a broom to his right shoulder. "Hut . . . hut . . . hut two-three-four."

"You were never in the Army," Clemente jeered, "but you should be in the nuthouse."

Roberto Clemente immersed in clubhouse horseplay? The man who so recently had snarled, "My teammates know better than to get on my ass; they do, and I will kill someone. I no fool around with them, and they know not to fool around with me."

But times and men change, as has been noted. And this was 1967, twelve years after Roberto Clemente had come to Pittsburgh, scared and black and proud, to live among the relaxed and white and humble.

The winter of 1966 had for him been an ambivalent time. He signed a six-figure contract, becoming one of only five hundred-thousand-dollar players in baseball and joining an elite group that included Mays, Aaron, Mantle, and Frank Robinson. But shortly after the first of the year, Clemente was enveloped in sadness. His oldest brother, Osvaldo, succumbed after a long, torturous duel with cancer. Weeks later his youngest brother, Vicente, also died. And, as often happens, death came in threes. A favored aunt passed away.

"Osvaldo was the head of the family, and I sort of had to take over for him," Clemente said. "And then Vicente and my only aunt. We are a close family, and it was sad for all of us."

Clemente spent the winter grieving, improving a small farm he owned twenty miles east of San Juan, and opening a restaurant amid the pastel affluence that was fast replacing the worn frame homes of Barrio San Anton. The restaurant was called El Carrertero, Spanish for "the man who leads the ox-drawn cart." The name held deep meaning for him, for it was the Jibaro peasants, his people, who led carts flowing with sugar cane to the processing plant of Don Pepito Rubert in Clemente's youth.

The restaurant was located in the shallow hills beyond Carolina, a rambling, buff-colored building of Moorish design surrounded by a low stone wall. An intricate wrought-iron fence guarded a short path to the building, which sat peacefully in a shady grove of banana and mango trees. It thrived for a few years, but was situated too far from Carolina and finally was forced to close, Clemente losing thousands of dollars.

When Clemente arrived at spring training in 1967, his goals were fourfold. From the press he would seek, if not unconditional surrender, at least the acknowledgment that he was the game's finest pure talent. From the fans he wanted merely a continuance of their affection, which he hoped to repay by giving them another heady ride, such as the one they had taken in 1960. From management should come money and more of the freedom of choice he had acquired under Harry Walker; from his teammates, more of the true camaraderie he had first experienced the previous season. Not all of these goals would be fulfilled.

That the bulk of the Pirates had come to forgive Clemente's vices and embrace his virtues was apparent in 1967. No three men in the Pittsburgh clubhouse could have been more diverse than Alvin O'Neal McBean, Vernon Law, and Jim Pagliaroni. McBean was a festive master of the King's English from the Virgin Islands, ebullient, candid, emotional. Law was a quiet Mormon, reserved, shy, candid to the point of intervention by the Golden Rule, a man loved and respected by all who entered this cool room. Pagliaroni was a delightful paradox, thoughtful, chief pilot of the wacky Black Maxers, swinger and man of principle, student of his fellow man, and leader by reason of personality rather than accomplishment. Each admitted to respect for Roberto Clemente; each saw a different Roberto Clemente.

On a gray April day, McBean described a close friend, a changeling burdened by heavy responsibility, a uniting force. None of the trio knew Clemente as well. McBean had chosen him as his best man, visited him in the off-season, was familiar with his family. And he had the special feeling one outsider has for another in a strange land.

"We colored are supposed to be different," McBean philosophized this day. "And the Latins are so far from home and have a responsibility the others don't. We have to live up to a little more because our people look upon us as their representatives. But there comes a time when, even if we bust our butts time and again, we fail. But Clemente loves to play, so even when he was hurt he would play. Then people would say, 'See, there is nothing wrong with him. He is faking.'

"For a long time he was a loner. People would ask, 'Why doesn't he go out with the rest of you?' Well, Clemente doesn't go out, period. He watches TV, orders room service, sleeps. He enjoys that; that's the type of guy he is. This year he's changed some. We took him to a Chinese restaurant in Chicago, and he looked so happy I think he was surprised he had such a good time. I said, 'Momen, you have to do this more often.' But he's the kind of a guy who'll go out when he wants to . . . you can't influence him. He's too independent.

"For a long time he impressed me as an individual; now he is more of a team player. Maybe he was that way before and just couldn't get it across to the other players. I thought he was playing for himself, but now he works with all of us, the young players, and he's our intermediary with the front office. And that's what a superstar's supposed to do, spread himself around. Robby has realized his importance, taken control, looked after us. Now he's everybody's player. He's come into his own.

"This is the new Clemente. We admire him, look up to him. And he'll do anything for us. A lot of guys on this team are outspoken. Me, Bob Veale, Mazeroski . . . we have various views. But we're still a team. And Clemente epitomizes that team feeling."

Law, the tall, somber man of the cloth from Utah, was light-years removed in personality and background from McBean or Clemente. It was not in him to be harshly critical; neither was it in him to be dishonest for the sake of flattery.

"Clemente was moody and temperamental at first," said Law, as phlegmatic as McBean had been verbose. "And I can understand why. He was away from home. He had quite an effect on the rest of the players until he felt his way around and got a sense of belonging. His whole way of life was different than it was here in America.

"He matured last year after he really proved his point. He was deserving of the MVP award in 1960. I've always believed that. After he got a couple more batting titles and so on, he had proved to everyone that he deserved it in 1960. But it's taken him a long time to get any recognition.

"When there was something seriously wrong with his back and his elbow, people wouldn't accept it. He didn't use those things to jake it. It was hard for people to accept that. I know that from experience, because I went through a time with a bad arm.

"As far as I'm concerned, he's one of the finest men I've met in this business."

Pagliaroni felt Clemente had won an inner struggle by the time 1967 had rolled around. "He was fighting a battle within himself for recognition, for himself and for players from his country. He knew he had the desire and the ability, but he was perplexed when some people didn't recognize that. He's a devoted individual, an inspiration, really.

"He's for the little guy, and that's something a lot of people don't realize. When a man like him tells me how he goes through Puerto Rico giving kids half dollars . . . he's telling me this in a serious discussion about his country. He's not getting any publicity telling me this. If it's publicized he'll be mad at me."

Three varied observations with a common theme: The war between Roberto Clemente and his teammates was at an end.

The war between Roberto Clemente and National League pitchers was, however, to reach new heights. The Pirates and Clemente both broke fast from the gate in 1967, Pittsburgh winning sixteen of twenty-six and Clemente hitting .390 when the club pulled into Cincinnati on May 15.

The following night it was Cincinnati vs. Clemente. Cincinnati very nearly lost. As he would remind writers afterward, it was the "biggest" game of his career, but "not the best."

Milt Pappas was pitching for the Reds. Traditionally, he fared well against the Pirates, and in later years he would somewhat dominate them, a heady, determined right-hander with a fine, darting curve ball.

In the opening inning, Clemente lunged wildly for an

outside breaking pitch, and the ball seemed to float from the end of his bat, a routine fly ball that right fielder Tommy Harper would catch in his tracks—except the ball didn't descend until it had cleared the right-field bleacher fence. The Pirates had a 2–0 lead.

Clemente built upon that margin in the fifth, sending a Pappas pitch screaming over a nine-foot wire fence in right-center to make it 4–0 and give Bob Veale, who hadn't allowed a hit, a comfortable working margin. Immediately, Veale gave it up, Cincinnati scoring three times in the next inning.

In the seventh, with two on and two out and Darrel Osteen on for the stricken Pappas, Clemente pulled a line-drive double over left fielder Pete Rose's head to rebuild the Pirate edge to 6–3. Back came the Reds to make it 6–5 in the bottom of the inning. Back came Clemente, this time lashing a Gerry Arrigo curve ball over the leftfield fence with two out and no one on in the ninth. No Pirate but Clemente had a base hit after the fourth inning. He failed to overcome the Reds single-handedly when Cincinnati tied it in the ninth and won it in the tenth on a home run by Tony Perez.

Clemente trotted slowly from the field, head down. In the visitors' clubhouse at Crosley Field, a narrow, steamy room, he revealed he had conjured up just such a performance the night before while having a nightm . . . uh . . . dream.

"I had a dream I would hit three home runs in one game," he explained, "and it came true." Ironically, his finest individual performance in twelve years came down to an ultimate test of skills between two Puerto Ricans, and Clemente wasn't involved. Perez of Caguas had homered off his own neighbor, Juan Pizarro.

"I never hit three home runs before, but it doesn't make me happy," Clemente said. "It was my biggest game, not my best one. I don't count this one. We lost."

Nevertheless, it was a *tour de force*. Three home runs and a double. Seven runs batted in. And he had made the extra inning necessary by leaping high above the fence in the Reds' ninth to swat Arrigo's bid for a game-ending home run back onto the playing surface.

The loss in Cincinnati was something of an omen. All of the Pirates but Clemente continued to stagger, and in the following month Pittsburgh was forced to battle relentlessly for fourth place. But Clemente thrived, hitting .385 in a bid for his fourth batting championship, a feat equaled by only six players in baseball's ninety-one years.

Off to his finest start ever, Clemente was envisioned as the reincarnation of a supposedly extinct species.

"He can be a .400 hitter," Cincinnati infielder Chico Ruiz theorized, as much out of awe at Clemente's skill than ethnic loyalty. "He hit better later in the year, no?" Yes, but baseball had not known such a hitter in twenty-six years, or since terrible-tempered Ted Williams had rammed a .406 season down the throats of the Boston sportswriters in 1941. It would not have another one in 1967, not even with such a noble purpose of watching the sporting press squirm, Clemente insisted.

"A player who hit .350 now is like a .400 in the old days," he said one day near the middle of the season. "You could do it for maybe 100 games or so, but not for 162. "When I started in 1955, you'd see a lot of older pitchers, pitchers near the end of their careers. Now you see more kids. They have live arms, live fast balls. They throw curves on three and nothing. I don't think they did that in the old days."

The ax of unemployment hung heavily over Harry Walker's neck as the Pirates failed to challenge for the pennant, but he never lost his gift for inspiring Clemente. "He's just exceptional," said the Pirate manager as Clemente's bat smoked through June. "Counting what he did last year, he's the best I've ever seen."

But even the best Harry Walker had ever seen couldn't surmount the trials 1967 had yet to reveal. At the All-Star break, Clemente led the National League with a .368 average and was the top vote-getter in the balloting, but he celebrated his eleventh appearance in the classic by striking out no less than four times. The indignity of his performance at Anaheim brought out the bitterness he had husbanded since his conquering role in 1961.

"I was the hero of that game, but to the press, Mays was," he said. "They were talking to him and he kept telling them, 'I didn't do it. This man next to me did. Talk to him.' But they wouldn't listen to Mays. I did everything I could, but the writers didn't care. They wrote about everything else but me. I knew then how the American writers stand."

From such small seeds of bitterness, large plants bloom. His successes ignored, his failures burning a hole in him, Clemente would ignore both. "I don't think about those games," he lied. "I don't think about World

Series games, either. I know they happened, but I am a funny fellow about remembering. Nothing stands out."

Everything stood out, though, when his pride was at stake. In July, the Pirates were playing in New York when a movie company filming Neil Simon's huge Broadway success, *The Odd Couple,* moved into Shea Stadium. One of the featured roles in the film was that of a sportswriter, and several of the Pirates and Mets were hired, at a fee of a hundred dollars each, to participate while some footage was being shot. Clemente, who didn't understand the purpose of the filming, was supposed to hit into a triple play.

"They going to pay me one hundred dollar," he explained to Matty Alou the night before the scenes were to be filmed.

"You should get a thousand dollars for hitting into a triple play," Alou laughed. "They're going to make a lot of money on that picture."

"You are right!"

Clearly an act of impertinence had been committed, and Clemente fumed over it. No one had informed him this was to be a commercial venture. "I thought it was for the kids, a documentary, something like that. Then I find out from Alou that it will be a big movie, that they will show it all over Latin America. They insult me.

"One hundred dollar! One hundred lousy dollar, that's what they want to pay me. Who they think they try and fool? They think Roberto Clemente born last week? I would be in a movie for nothing. But not for a hundred dollar. Would they ask Cary Grant to play baseball for a hundred dollar?"

Presumably not. "What would fans in Latin America say if they see me hit into triple play?" Clemente demanded. Probably the same thing palpitating mid-America housewives would say if Cary Grant, lips poised over Ingrid Bergman's mouth, were to sneeze: that such an act was unthinkable.

The next day at Shea, a director, baseball cap perched jauntily on his head and megaphone securely in hand, strolled over to Clemente and laid a possessive arm across the broad shoulders.

"Hiya, Roberto, how's my old buddy?"

Clemente stiffened as though shot. "I am not old," he said frostily. "And I ain't going to be in your bleeping movie. How you like that, old buddy?"

Someone else hit into the triple play.

Recalling the incident the next time the Pirates played at Shea, Clemente still seethed. "The nerve of that guy. Old buddy, huh? I'll give him old buddy."

Stepping into the cage during batting practice, he jerked a pitch 440 feet over the left-field fence and strode royally from the plate to confront an innocent cameraman. "Hey, movieman, take a picture of that bleeping home run and put it in your bleeping movie."

"You can have it for nothing."

But his pride was not trampled often, and when it was, Walker was there to sustain it. As the Pirates lurched into mid-July, Clemente continued to threaten to make a prophet of Ruiz.

"Walker treats me like a human being," said Clemente, crediting the Pirate manager for his startling success and instantly raising the question of what Murtaugh had treated him like. "Walker makes me feel wanted, important. He gives me peace of mind."

Alas, the great love affair went on the rocks two weeks later. Harry Walker had succeeded into talking himself out of work. The Pirates playing exactly .500 baseball, Walker was fired on July 18 despite Clemente's earlier efforts to save his job.

On June 8, Clemente had called a team meeting. "No coaches, no manager." Grabbing the horns of leadership, he had lectured the Pirates sternly for forty-five minutes. "I know there are some of you who don't like Walker, and there are some of you who don't like me, but Walker is our manager, and we must do what he tells us whether we like him or not. I hear the things some of you say behind my back. Maybe it's the salary I get. Maybe it's the attention I get. Maybe it's the things I do. But I called this meeting to talk things out. If you have any gripes about the manager, about me, or about anything else, speak up. We can settle it here. We owe something to the fans who come to the ballpark. We have only ourselves to blame; we must stop blaming others."

While the meeting was going on, Walker sat in the dugout by himself, a forlorn figure. It had been for him a summer full of trouble. Outside Forbes Field the night before, he had been loading his golf clubs into his car when a fan wandered past.

"I hope you can play golf better than you can manage," the passerby had said. It was clearly the wrong comment—the Pirates had just lost a doubleheader to the New York Mets—and Walker nearly throttled the man.

"I didn't punch him . . . I just grabbed him and shook him a little," Walker explained.

The Pirate fans had been in a nasty mood in the final weeks of the Hat's reign. A few weeks before, Clemente and his friend Phil Dorsey had been accosted by two men outside Forbes Field.

"Hey, Clendenon, you big nigger," one of them had yelled at Clemente.

"I am no Clendenon, I am Clemente."

"You aren't worth a damn, you big nigger."

"I am Clemente. Go away. We want no trouble."

"I'm going to punch your lights out, nigger."

The fans, both of whom had been drinking, rushed Clemente and the husky Dorsey, who threw one of them to the ground and sat on him. "Roberto tried to back away from the other one, but the guy swung at him," Dorsey said. "He swung back. Once. The guy was out cold. He cut his hand and we went back to the park to have the doc take a look at it."

Such was the mood of Pirate fandom in July 1967. Something had to be done. It was. Walker was dismissed. The meeting called by Clemente hadn't been able to arouse the Pirates, as Walker hoped it would. "Say you're walking around in a daze," Walker said on June 8. "If I clap my hands, it might wake you up." But the Pirates slept on, as Bill Mazeroski had predicted. "All the talking in the world won't get you a base hit. If it wasn't for Clemente, we'd be in eighth place. He's the only one doing the job."

When the fateful day came, Walker was replaced by the last man Roberto Clemente wished to see in the

Pirate clubhouse. Danny Murtaugh had been working for the club in a semiretired state as a special-assignment scout. His health had improved and perhaps his wife, Kate, felt as the wife of New York Mets' general manager George Weiss had when her man retired. "I married George for better or worse, but not for lunch," Mrs. Weiss offered when her husband went back to work full-time.

In any case, Murtaugh was recalled by Joe Brown to jolt the Pirates off their second-division treadmill and calm the waters stirred by Walker. By a freak of timing, Clemente was at that time being quoted in a national magazine saying some hard things about his old manager.

His views appeared in a *Sport* magazine story by Lou Prato, a young, talented Pittsburgh sportswriter with a penchant for drawing personal beliefs from usually reticent professional athletes.

Clemente told Prato he blamed Murtaugh for labeling him a hypochondriac, a tag he felt the press then exploited. An older Clemente would have rebelled, he informed Prato. "If I knew then what I know now about Murtaugh, things would've been different. He either would've been gone a lot sooner or I would have been playing on some other club. There wouldn't have been room for both of us on the same team."

The question in 1967 was: Would there be now? Murtaugh picked up the torch hours before the Pirates were to play a twi-night doubleheader against San Francisco. Immediately the answer appeared to be, no, Murtaugh and Clemente couldn't coexist.

As several players strolled into Murtaugh's office prior

to the doubleheader to renew old acquaintances, Clemente remained in the training room just across the narrow foyer. A brief clubhouse meeting was held, and all of the Pirates except Clemente left for the field. Both men must have been embarrassed by Prato's story. A meeting of the minds was clearly necessary. Clemente went into Murtaugh's office and the door was closed. When it reopened, neither man would discuss what was said in any depth. But the facts seemed to speak for themselves.

Pirate infielder Maury Wills had been feuding with Walker and had not played recently, claiming a leg injury. The night Murtaugh took over, he played both games, returning to the lineup much sooner than expected. "The leg got better," he explained tersely.

Clemente had been playing for a month with a leg injury. He did not play the night Murtaugh took over. "I'm paid to hit, not to decide who's going to manage the club," he snapped, but obviously his sympathies were with Walker, of whom he had recently said, "I play for him until I am dead."

Beyond his obvious unhappiness at Walker's fate, Clemente would not comment, although elaboration was hardly needed. "Murtaugh was not on my side," he had told Prato. "I know he felt that way. No one has ever had to pat me on the back to play baseball, but when I needed a pat on the back between 1956 and 1960, I never got it. I never tell anyone this before because I respected him because he was my manager. No matter what happened between us, I wouldn't put him down. But most of the bad reputation I got was because of him. He wouldn't stick up for me. When he left, he didn't come to see me or anything. I went to him and said I was sorry to see him go. I had nothing against him personally, but I did not like him professionally. I do not talk to him much now."

The awaited explosion never occurred. Clemente sat out a third straight game after Murtaugh's return, but the next day a reasonable explanation was offered. He had reinjured his leg the previous Monday night, but soon would return to the lineup. Clemente had made a subtle point: Times had changed during Murtaugh's absence.

"Bobby is too much of a team man to let his differences with Murtaugh keep him from going all out," one Pirate had predicted. He was right. Clemente and Murtaugh had aired their differences and come to an agreement, never again to feud openly.

"That was all in the past," Clemente said a few days later. "And you can't live in the past. I don't have anything against him. How can I feel that way? He just got here. We haven't had any trouble, and if it's up to me, we won't.

"I told him I said the things in the [Prato] story. But I also tell him I am a professional and I will play my best for any manager. I never cheat. If I can play, I play. And sometimes I play when I shouldn't. I have only one thing on my mind. And that is to win."

This time around, Murtaugh rested Clemente periodically, and after each respite he came back like a hurricane. The Pirates did not noticeably improve under Murtaugh, finishing a dead-even .500, 81–81. But that was in no way the fault of Roberto Clemente. He ran off the competition by hitting at a sizzling .385 clip during the final month to finish at .357, the highest average in the majors since Stan Musial's .376 9 years before. Clemente led the league in base hits (209) and drove in 110 runs, just one short of Orlando Cepeda's league high. It was also his most productive defensive season, as he threw out 17 runners to lead National League outfielders in assists for the fifth time.

Only 6 other men had ever won four batting championships: Ty Cobb; the old Pirate, Honus Wagner; Rogers Hornsby; Stan Musial; Ted Williams; and Harry Heilmann.

During the daylight hours of 1967, Clemente was virtually unstoppable, batting .411 in 68 day games. He had 2 5-hit games, 4 4-hit games. At 33, he continued to swing the bat freely, walking only once every 14 times at bat, eating the bad pitch alive.

"Roberto can hit any pitch, anywhere, at any time," Sandy Koufax sighed. "He will hit pitchouts. He will hit brush-back pitches. He will hit high, inside pitches to the opposite field, which would be ridiculous even if he didn't do it with both feet off the ground."

Clemente closed his most successful season—"my greatest year but my biggest disappointment"—as Clemente would. Days before it ended, he blistered some of his teammates for the Pirates' sixth-place finish.

"They know who they are," he said. "There is no reason we should be where we are today. It's one thing not to like a manager and another not to play your best for him. I said when Murtaugh took over, not to blame him for what happens. I didn't know what was going to happen, but I knew it would not be his fault. It was ours."

In years past, such rhetoric might have driven a wedge between Clemente and his teammates, mortally wounded a ballclub. This time it wouldn't. A small dynasty was building, and the next three years would prove that occasionally an old dog can learn new tricks.

Chapter 13

WHO RETIRES AT .350?

He never got used to the winters, really. When mid-October had dropped its multihued curtain on the season, he would fly home to San Juan and seek a hundred ways to occupy the mind that ran like a movie. Often the slow tempo was infuriating. Age had made a demand he could not deny, and by the mid-1960s he had curtailed his activities in the Puerto Rican winter league, playing only enough to keep his countrymen from the doors of his home, managing when not to manage would have been disheartening to all the Puertoriqueños who in the summer had anxiously asked one another, "¿*Qué hizo Clemente?*"

What Roberto Clemente did each day of the spring and summer was to abandon himself to baseball; what he did each winter was to chafe from inactivity. He was among the most restless of men; his principles would not permit inactivity.

"Anytime you have the opportunity to accomplish something for somebody who comes behind you and you don't do it, you are wasting your time on this earth," he would remind each group to whom he spoke, and he spoke to many, because no ribbon-cutting in Puerto Rico was considered quite complete without his presence.

So each winter he cut ribbons and made speeches and used his entree with men of power to better the fortunes of men of poverty. And when there were no ribbons to cut or speeches to make, when the work of sweet charity was at a standstill, he would gather his friends about him or drop in on them unexpectedly. "He would suddenly appear in your office and say, 'Let's take lunch.' And then sit and talk with you for two or three hours," a friend recalled.

His avocations, and they grew unceasingly, received the attention he devoted to his vocation. "When he plays, he does it from the heart; he does everything that way," Vera Clemente would smile when visitors would inquire of the ceramic figurines in the living room, or the abstract driftwood carvings in the game room, or the hundreds of bottles in the storage shed, or the organ in the dining room.

On long winter days, Clemente would stroll the golden sands searching for driftwood. "That's just wood," his friends would say. "There is wood all over the place like that. Why do you waste your time with it?" And Roberto Clemente would draw himself up indignantly, because in the leavings of the sea he perhaps saw something of himself. "You are crazy," he would shout. "Yes, it is wood, but you don't see what I see. You don't feel about it what I feel. No piece is just like another. You can take it and shape it, and it is you. You can make it more than a decoration. You can make it part of your personality." And he would drag the pieces of driftwood home and smooth and polish them until they glistened.

"His hands, they always had to be busy," explained Roberto Marin, the scout. "And what he wanted to do, he wanted to do right now. One year he brought some bottles back from a trip to Italy and told me, 'I'm going to buy them by the thousands and then sell them.' I told him, 'What you need that for?' He said, 'I need to keep busy.'"

To keep busy, Clemente taught himself to play the organ well enough that his songs were recognizable. To keep busy, he invested in a ceramics factory, which he envisioned as one future day providing a source of employment and recreation for thousands of Puerto Ricans. "This is something entire families can do together, it will unite them," Clemente told his attorney, Elfren Bernier. To keep busy, he found no household repair too large or too small. "One day I see him working on a sink and I say to him, 'Pay a man ten dollars to do that,'" Marin said. "But he tell me, 'No, I like to do these things.'"

So it was natural that when some small repairs were needed on his patio in the winter of 1967, Roberto Clemente eagerly undertook them. And almost killed himself.

Actually, there were two patios in his home, one sitting above the other in a tiered effect at the back of the house, which preened majestically atop a steep hill.

Clemente was climbing from the bottom patio to the one on top, pulling himself up hand-over-hand on heavy, four-foot iron bars imbedded in the wall between the terraces. Just as Vera Clemente stepped onto the top patio, the bar her husband was clinging to pulled from the wall. Instinctively, Roberto Clemente thrust the seventy-five-pound bar away from his chest, and man and the piece of iron tumbled down the steep bank. Only a low wall, seventy-five feet down the hillside, kept Clemente from hurtling over a cliff.

"I landed on the back of my neck," he explained to the doctor. "I went over on my shoulder several times, but the bar didn't hit me. If it had . . ."

The doctor in San Juan informed him a muscle was torn in his right shoulder, but nothing was broken, and suggested Clemente wear a brace for several months. When Clemente reported to spring training in 1968, he finally disclosed the accident to Joe Brown. "I didn't telephone you, because I knew you would worry," he told Brown, who really began to worry when Clemente went 0-for-29 during one stretch in Florida.

In early May, the entire organization was worried, and no one more than Larry Shepard, who had been signed to replace Danny Murtaugh after the taciturn Irishman had taken over from the fired Harry Walker.

Shepard was an introspective, uptight veteran of the baseball wars getting his first chance to manage after eighteen seasons of minor league barnstorming. He sang "Ol' Man River" in the shower in a wonderful, resonant baritone, but most of his other pronouncements lacked equal conviction. He was a slightly tragic figure, the epitome of the grizzled organization man who keeps the faith for nearly two decades, enters the kingdom of heaven, and immediately falls through a cloud to his extinction.

From the outset of the 1968 season, Shepard should have switched to "The Old Rugged Cross." Clemente, the man who had hit .357 one year before, was hitting .214 in May. Gene Alley and young slugger Willie Stargell couldn't get untracked at the plate. Pitchers Al McBean and Bob Veale had arm miseries, and Jim Bunning, acquired in a winter trade and widely billed as the pitcher who would assure a pennant, pulled a groin muscle. "I can't believe this team can't hit," Shepard told a friend. "We keep losing by one run, and now we've got a lot of guys banged up."

Shepard tried the Harry Walker method of inspiration: "Yes, I think Clemente is so great he could hit .400; he could do anything he wants; he is the greatest player in the game." It didn't work. Nothing worked. Even Arturo Garcia, who flew to Pittsburgh to treat his prize patient, failed. Clemente was hitting .216 the last day of May, and the nature of his injury and its severity were revealed to the public. "The ballclub told me not to say anything," Clemente told reporters. "They said, 'Shhh. Don't mention it.' But I shouldn't have played in Florida."

By Independence Day, two things were clear. Clemente, hitting .245, was not going to repeat as the National League's most prolific hitter. And the Pirates were a .500 team. "It hurts to swing, and when it does, it bothers me mentally, and I wince when I think of hitting the ball," he said during the All-Star Game break, not on the team for the first time since 1960.

When the regular schedule resumed, Clemente pulled his average up to .275, slumped again in August, and finished at .291 as the Pirates were, measurably, one game worse off under Shepard than they had been the year before guided by Walker and Murtaugh. They finished sixth, 80–82. The future did not look promising. The right fielder was talking about quitting.

"I don't want to stop playing baseball, but if my shoulder aches this winter, I won't be back in baseball in 1969," said Clemente, having failed to bat .300 for the first time in eight seasons. Only a few people took him seriously, Clemente having scotched a rumor of his retirement the week before by demanding, "How could I ever quit? I have thirteen people to support."

And, of course, how could he ever allow sportswriters the pleasure of realizing that, as it does to all mortals, age was overtaking Roberto Clemente? Obviously, he could not. "Some reporters will say I'm through," he sneered before returning home in October. "Fine, let 'em say it."

Joe Brown was not upset at Clemente's hints at retirement. "I don't think he'll quit," Brown said. He was unexcited because he knew Clemente was merely frustrated by the caliber of his performance. He was loyal to many things, but none more than his self image. He was the *primero pelotero,* not some journeyman .290 hitter with a bum arm masquerading in the uniform of greatness.

"Anytime you're not doing your best, you are stealing

the fans' money," he said. "And I don't call myself a thief."

He would not make mockery of the past. "My first responsibility is to do my best in the playing field," he said. "These people, in Pittsburgh and Puerto Rico, have been wonderful to me . . . have pushed me to accomplish what I have. I try to pay them with the same treatment they pay me."

No, only the real Roberto Clemente would play in 1969. He would be loyal to himself and those who watched him, for he regarded loyalty as perhaps mankind's chief virtue. One was loyal to the things that enriched him—"Someday I will put a sign outside my home and it will read 'To God, Mother, Father, and baseball.'" One was loyal to country—"I was born in Puerto Rico and my wife goes home to have our children because I want them born there."

And one paid allegiance to old comrades, as he would a few years later when teammate Bill Mazeroski was being honored before a game, and Clemente momentarily returned to the clubhouse to find several Pirates playing cards. "I give you bastards four minutes to get outside. They are honoring the greatest second baseman the game has ever known, and anyone not out there in four minutes will have to fight me."

Clemente's loyalty was tested in 1969. For the very first time in fifteen years, the fans of Forbes Field, who had loved him long and without equivocation, who seemingly had understood him when his teammates and the press couldn't or wouldn't, booed Roberto Clemente.

His shoulder still ailing, Clemente had swung a mediocre bat through spring training and into the first week of the season. In a Sunday afternoon game on April 13 against the Phillies, he could do nothing right. In the first inning he struck out; the next two times at bat he grounded into rally-squelching double plays. In the top of the eighth he allowed a routine single to go between his legs, and the error gave the Phils two runs. When he came to the plate in the bottom of the inning, an audible buzzing began. Someone booed; the Bronx cheer took hold. The boos tumbled from the stands, and the sound was so foreign that a sportswriter in the press box said, "It took me two minutes to realize they were booing Clemente."

The subject was much quicker. He looked up at the unfamiliar sound and then gave a frivolous wave with his batting helmet. Half the boos melted into applause, many of the 14,981 patrons immediately regretful.

Later, Clemente smiled wanly at the experience. For fourteen seasons they had cheered his every move; his loyalty to them was unshaken. "I was not trying to be smart when I waved my helmet," he said. "I was just trying to tell them they could do whatever they want. The fans of Pittsburgh have cheered me a lot through the years. There's always a first time for the booing. But I don't say 'to hell with the fans' because of this. In 1956 when I had trouble with my back, they were the ones who gave me the lift I needed."

Then came the supreme compliment from a man who gave them sparingly. "I'll never play for any team but this one. I could never come to Pittsburgh and play before these fans in another uniform."

The fans of Pittsburgh immediately returned Clemente

to their bosom; about the rest of the cast they were undecided. The second straight sixth-place finish in 1968 had convinced Brown he was running a team with tired blood. Six young Pirate farmhands were promoted. Bob Robertson took over at first base until he couldn't stem the challenge of another rookie, Al Oliver. Dave Cash split playing time with second baseman Mazeroski, whose legs and batting eye were fading. Dock Ellis moved into the starting rotation, Manny Sanguillen shared the catching, and young Richie Hebner was installed at third. Still, callow youth and injuries to Clemente and shortstop Gene Alley couldn't conspire to trouble the Pirates in Shepard's second year, and they became pennant hopefuls once more.

Clemente severely pulled a thigh muscle in April and then reinjured the ailing leg. He could not play for short stretches during the first two months, and he was sorely missed. In May, however, he had almost been lost permanently.

Following a night game in San Diego, his shoulder was throbbing and he was deeply depressed. He had been thrown out of the game for one of the few times in his career, and the world was, indeed, a gloomy place. He called Vera in San Juan and told her his baseball career had just ended. He was going to retire on the spot.

"Finish the road trip," she told him. "Then if you come back to Pittsburgh and you don't feel any better, it will be all right to quit. That's a promise, O.K.?"

"O.K., you're the boss. But if I don't feel better when I get back to Pittsburgh, then it is all over."

Tired and hurting, Clemente left his room at the Town

and Country Hotel and ran into teammate Willie Stargell in the lobby. Stargell was carrying a small brown bag in his hand.

"What's that?" Clemente asked.

"Chicken. There's a place you can get some just down the road."

Clemente was returning from purchasing a bag of chicken when a car pulled up along what is known as Hotel Circle, which runs parallel to a San Diego freeway. There were four men in the car. One of them waved a gun. "Get in."

Clemente was taken to an isolated part of the countryside overlooking Mission Valley and ordered to remove his clothes. The men took his wallet, his All-Star ring, and about $250 in cash.

"That's when I figure they are going to shoot me and throw me into the woods," Clemente said when he revealed the story fifteen months later. "They already have the pistol in my mouth."

Clemente talked for his life, told his abductors he played for the San Diego Padres. One of the men spoke Spanish, and Clemente recognized any port would do in a storm. "If you really need the money, take it," he pleaded, "but don't kill me. Don't kill anybody for money."

It was a supreme performance. Clemente's clothes were returned, and he was allowed to dress. "Don't forget to put your tie on," one of the men said. "We want you to look good."

His money, wallet, and ring returned, Clemente was driven to within three blocks of his hotel and released.

The car pulled away, only to return a minute later. "I started looking for a rock," Clemente recalled.

"Here," said one of the robbers, handing a package of fried chicken through the window. Clemente threw it across the street and returned to his hotel room.

He didn't reveal the story for more than a year, perhaps accounting for the disbelief with which it was greeted. However, San Diego police later verified it. But San Diego baseball fans remained skeptical. One of them dropped a rubber chicken near Clemente on a later Pirate trip.

Strangely enough, the kidnaping had the effect of immediately hypoing Clemente's average. On May 21, he was batting .226. One month later he was hitting .314, and the Pirates trailed front-running New York by only 6½ games.

But in July that old Pirate bugaboo, poor pitching, began making itself felt, and veteran catcher Jerry May was injured, the burden of guiding a shaky staff through a pennant fight falling to the rookie, Sanguillen.

A vivacious young Panamanian of fervent religious beliefs, Sanguillen struggled for weeks until one Pirate said wistfully, "I think pretty soon he's gonna' quit smiling."

But the grin remained pasted across Sanguillen's wonderfully expressive features in spite of a series of gaffes both behind the plate and on the bases. In Houston, at the tag end of a disastrous road trip, Shepard blurted in a postgame interview, "Sanguillen's killing us." When the quote reached his ears a few days later, it became clear that Clemente would be the rookie's champion.

Blaming the channel rather than the source, Clemente

lashed out at the sportswriters. "So Sangy's killing us, huh? Well, the writers can kiss my nasty black ass."

From that day forward, Clemente sustained the young catcher. When Sanguillen was twice picked off base in one game, he returned to the clubhouse to find Clemente manipulating a broomstick that had been punched through a large piece of cardboard.

"It is a new machine," he confided with a grin at Sanguillen. "I have just bought it. I am going to use it to take control of your body whenever you get on base." After another of Sanguillen's base-running errors, Clemente informed the entire clubhouse, "I am going to buy a shotgun, and when he gets on base, someone can shoot him so he don't get picked off."

"Here he was, the big superstar, and he was trying to make a kid comfortable," said pitcher Steve Blass. "When he was a rookie he had to struggle. He identified with Sangy and went out of his way to help him learn the things you have to know: how to get acclimated to the big-league atmosphere, how to handle yourself with the news media, how to dress, where to eat. I guess he wished someone would've been around to help him that way. And he taught Sangy something very valuable—that nobody blames you if you blow a game. A lot of rookies spend a couple of years worrying about that, don't understand no one actually blames them."

Sanguillen's rookie miscues were not the only thing that plagued the 1969 Pirates. In August, they no longer posed a real threat to the Mets, the clowns who suddenly were for real. But Clemente, sore shoulder, ailing leg, and all, inched his average up and began dueling Cincinnati's

Pete Rose for the batting title. Through the last two weeks, he played with the flu, and day by day inched nearer Rose, who had led the chase all year long.

During the last night game of the season, it seemed hopeless. Rose owned a .348 to .343 lead. Clemente would need four hits and Rose to be shut out in the final game for Clemente to win his fifth batting championship.

The Pirates played Montreal at home; Cincinnati was in Atlanta. Clemente singled twice and doubled in his first three at-bats, while Rose was blanked in three appearances.

In the eighth inning, Clemente chopped a ground ball to Montreal third baseman Kevin Collins and streaked for first. The throw beat him easily. In the Forbes Field press box, the ticker from Atlanta clicked madly. Rose had beat out a bunt in his final turn to claim the batting championship.

For Clemente, if not the Pirates, it had been a respectable season. The Pirates finished third in the newly realigned six-team National League East. Clemente hit .345 and drove in ninety-one runs.

Shepard was fired. For months he had implored Brown to trade the thirty-five-year-old Clemente for a young pitcher and some added infield help. Brown demurred. In the spring he had delivered an ultimatum of sorts to Shepard; win or go. The week before the season ended, Shepard went. For the third time in eleven years, Brown turned to an old friend with a request. And, yes, Danny Murtaugh would be glad to help.

When Murtaugh had replaced Walker, there had been a truce, and Clemente upped his batting average thirty points during the second half of the 1967 campaign. Peace would remain in force. "I can always get along with a .340 hitter," Murtaugh smiled. "I play for any manager," Clemente repeated.

Getting the rest of the Pirates in a proper frame of mind would be Murtaugh's main task in 1970. In the final months of Shepard's tenure, there had been rumblings that the Pirates were racially tense. Pitcher Dock Ellis, a product of the mean streets of Watts, openly alluded to it. Lockers in the Pirate clubhouse at Forbes Field had been distributed so that the team was racially grouped. In 1970, a sportswriter would make note of that, and the locker assignments would alternate a black player and a white one so obviously that Ellis would giggle, "It looks like a piano."

But there were never more than rumblings, due in part to Clemente's cohesive force. The black players—twelve of twenty-five—were led by the gentle giant, Willie Stargell, the non-Latin Pirate perhaps closest to Clemente. No white player was more respected than Bill Mazeroski, who had shared the clubhouse with Clemente for sixteen summers, and in the last few had swapped the outrageous insults that connote friendship in baseball. Clemente was the uniting factor.

And if real racial disharmony had erupted, he would not have hidden it, for nothing, not even qualifications of his athletic prowess, so provoked his outrage as did prejudice.

He had never failed to roar in anger at it. Early in his career in Florida, during a series of exhibitions between

Pittsburgh and Kansas City, he and the Athletics' Vic Power had gone into a restaurant in Texas to eat.

"I'm sorry," said a waitress, "but we don't serve Negroes."

"That's O.K.," a customer drawled, "these boys are Spanish."

"No," Clemente replied. "You serve one man, why you no serve all men?"

The following year, Florida was still hoarding its antebellum memories. One day a group of white Pirates left the team bus to enter a restaurant. "Fellows, you want anything to eat?" one asked the black players who remained on the bus.

Clemente told him, "You ever accept anything for us, and you and me, we are going to fight, because I think this is unfair. If this is going to be the way it is, then we are going to suffer."

Clemente never lost his hatred of bigotry. One afternoon during the 1969 season, he explained to a reporter how it was possible to have much of what this world is willing to concede to a man—wealth, respect, a beautiful wife and family, a fine home—and still have the taste of ashes in your mouth.

He and Vera had gone to a furniture store to shop while the Pirates were in New York. "A salesman ask us, 'What do you want?'" Clemente said. "I tell him, 'We want to see the furniture you have in the showroom.' He say wait a minute, they are sending a man to the last floor to see what they have.

"I tell him we want to see the furniture in the showroom. He say, 'You don't have enough money to buy that.'

I say, 'How do you know?' He say, 'Because it is very expensive.'"

He and his wife had been planning a trip to Europe, and Clemente was carrying five thousand dollars in cash. "I showed them," Clemente said. "So they want to know who I was and all that. They said, 'Oh, you are Roberto Clemente the ballplayer. Oh, that is different.'

"I said, 'Look, your business is to sell to anybody. I don't care if I am from Puerto Rico or Jewish or whatever you want to call me. Because I am Puerto Rican, you treat me different. Why you don't treat all men the same? My money is the same as anybody's. But I have a different color skin, huh?'

"I got so mad, I walked out."

For all his ferocity when angered, there was no real hatred in Roberto Clemente. In the pursuit of what he considered just, he would curse and revile the subjects of his wrath. But the heat was always in his words, not in his heart. The eyes would flash and his muscles would bunch up, but it was not in him to leap for the jugular.

"I can hate no man," he would say, and in his voice you could hear the regretful acknowledgment that Roberto Clemente lacked the killing instinct; was, in fact, a pussycat. True, he carried bitterness, but as a gonfalon, not a weapon. Self-cast in the role of redeemer of the unrightable wrongs, he was seen as a humorless man. In fact, he had a talent for mimicry, and in the twilight of his career was one of those players baseball writers refer to as having the ability of "keeping the club loose."

When he realized he was considered lacking in humor, he invented a silly, touching defense. His face, he said, was constructed in such a manner as to preclude the broad smile. "Roberto, you got to smile more, people will get the wrong idea," Luisa Clemente had told her son a dozen years before. It was, Roberto proclaimed, a physiological impossibility. Others, hearing his explanation over and over, adopted it. "He just had one of those faces that couldn't smile," trainer Tony Bartirome explained, believing his words devoutly.

Still, an unsmiling Clemente was not devoid of wit. When Pirate announcer Bob Prince had casually used the word "bomb" while entering an airplane in Houston, he had been detained by police and missed a Pirate flight to San Francisco. Taking a later flight after the matter had been cleared up, he arrived just before a game at Candlestick Park and rushed to the field to offer an explanation. Clemente listened to Prince give a description of his detention and then walked over and whispered into his ear, "Tick . . . tick . . . tick."

And Clemente appreciated wit. He was ejected one night by umpire Lee Weyer, who said, "The way you're goin', you'd be better off out of the game anyway."

"When he said that," the slumping Clemente remarked later, "there was not anything left for me to say."

Clemente's imitations were so realistic as to be painful to those being imitated. Pirate doctor Joseph Finegold, a small, roosterish man, has a high, nasal voice. He was never seen to applaud when Clemente would spot him in the clubhouse, hold his nose, and wander about crying shrilly, "Hey, Bobbee . . . you know me, Bobbee . . . trust me, Bobbee."

Neither was ex-teammate Joe Christopher delighted

with Clemente's impressions. One night the phone rang in Christopher's hotel room, and a high, sultry voice said, "Joe, this is Lisa." Christopher warmly greeted his old acquaintance, and Lisa proceeded to make several interesting recreational offers.

On the team bus to the ballpark the next evening, Christopher was peering out of the window, perhaps contemplating further involvements later that night, when a falsetto voice sang out, "Joe . . . dis is Lisa, baby."

In 1969, Clemente reached his height as a clubhouse entertainer a few days after it had been announced that Larry Shepard would be replaced. Holding court among the Pirates one night before a game, his monologue featured a mythical conversation with Joe Brown and the events that would take place after Clemente signed on as manager.

"I weel manage thees ballclub for nothing, Mr. Brown," Clemente said, exaggerating the Latin accent for effect. "I weel not take even a penny. It would be a pleasure to manage thees fine ballclub with thees fine young men. We weel go to spring training and we weel all smile and laugh and we weel learn thee fundamentals and we weel win. When I go home at night in Florida, I weel put all thee names in a hat and pick out a batting order; weeth thees great club it will not matter."

(The Clemente-managed Pirates lose five in a row.) "Yentleman, do not worry. We weel smile and work on thee fundamentals. We weel be all right."

(Losing streak reaches ten straight.) "Do not be afraid, yentleman. We weel laugh and smile and work harder on thee fundamentals."

(Losing streak reaches fifteen in a row as Pirates blow a five-run lead in the ninth.) "Yentleman, my ass!"

Humor was the byword of the 1970 Pittsburgh Pirates. They were, in the vernacular, loose. The kids had matured. Sanguillen hit .303 in 1969, Richie Hebner .301, and Al Oliver .285. Ellis and Blass and Bob Moose were the hub of a good, young pitching staff, and during the winter of 1969, Pittsburgh had acquired a fine relief pitcher, Dave Giusti, along with back-up catcher Dave Ricketts in a deal with St. Louis. And both Roberto Clemente, the Pirate player representative now, and Murtaugh had mellowed. "The only difference between this club and the 1960 club," Matty Alou said, "is that the manager is a lot smarter." This Pirate club would make a run for the pennant.

History had reversed course. In May, Clemente had been playing with a bruised heel for three weeks. Murtaugh couldn't keep him on the bench. "I wanted to rest him, but he insisted on playing because we haven't been winning," Murtaugh said. "Finally, I get him out of the lineup one day and he goes back in late in the game for defensive purposes. He's doing everything he can to get us rolling."

On June 28, the Pirates played their final game in Forbes Field. The lovely old park was being torn down and would be replaced by the new Three Rivers Stadium, located near the downtown section. For Clemente it was a nostalgic moment, and after the Pirates had stretched their winning streak to six games and handed another contender, Chicago, its ninth loss in a row, he said, "This ballpark mean a great deal to me. I spent half my life here. I told some of the fellows, 'You been married to your wife this long and suddenly something happens, you going to be hurt by it. Maybe the new park be like finding another wife.'"

It was like finding you were married to Raquel Welch. The new stadium and new skin-tight double-knit uniforms must have inspired a redoubled effort, and Clemente and the Pirates made it. Before the new park had been in use two weeks they had crept past New York and into first place, Clemente hitting a sparkling .350.

On July 25, a cool, lovely evening, the Pirates had the National League East firmly in hand, fitting because this was Roberto Clemente's night.

For his years of matchless skill, for his easy grace, for the excitement he created, and because the city loved him, and the word is not used inadvisedly, the Pirates were honoring Roberto Clemente.

Hundreds of Puerto Rican poor, wearing the boat-shaped straw *pavas* that shielded their eyes from the sun, had come from the island. Clemente's parents, wife, and children were there. Melchor Clemente, a wisp of a man now, stared straight ahead, and his face still held the look of eagles. One Pittsburgh reporter referred to him as a man "in his seventies." He was ninety.

The ceremony began with the Pirates' Latin players approaching Clemente, singularly and in solemn procession, to place a hand on his shoulder, and bend forward slightly, not quite touching his cheek. He blinked back the tears, and after they had paid their respects, spoke in measured phrases, expressing dignified gratitude. Gifts were presented and the game, ironically against a Houston team now managed by his *compadre* Harry Walker, began. And Roberto Clemente offered his gratitude in the best way he could.

He had two base hits and made two beautiful, skidding catches of line drives. In the ninth inning, with two out and the Pirates ahead by nine runs, Danny Murtaugh removed him from the lineup. As he slowly trotted in from right field, the applause was deafening, mad affection thundering through the night in wave after wave.

In the clubhouse, Clemente acknowledged the emotion of the evening. "In a moment like this you can see a lot of years in a few minutes," he said. "You can see everything firm and clear. I don't know if I cried, but I'm not ashamed to cry. But we are a sentimental people. I don't have the words to say how I feel when I step on that field and know that so many are behind me, and know that I represent my island and Latin America."

Later he thought of the night and said, "If it wasn't for these fans, I don't know what would have happened to me."

His back continued to plague him the rest of the way, along with a surfeit of minor but nagging injuries. But the Pirates, who in years gone by might have used his ailments as an excuse to fold, made a brace of them in 1970. Murtaugh juggled his lineup with the precision of Merlin; and when he played, Clemente made his presence felt.

In September, the Pirates stretched their lead over second-place New York to five games and held on through the stretch to claim the National League East pennant.

Clemente hit .350 but did not accrue the necessary 502 appearances at the plate to qualify for the batting title.

In the final month, he played in only four games, and in one of them reinjured his back while hammering the game-winning hit. But nine days before the playoffs began, a young Pittsburgh doctor, Charles Murray, gave him a series of treatments, and when the playoff series against Cincinnati began in Pittsburgh, Clemente was in the lineup.

His presence was never felt. The power-mad Reds used brilliant pitching to sweep the series in three straight games and capture the pennant. Clemente was a factor in only the second game, driving in the one run the Pirates managed in a 3–1 loss to lefty Jim Merritt, who had beaten them for the seventh time in two seasons.

When the playoffs had ended, two questions were posed by the press: Would Murtaugh quit? Would Clemente quit? The first answer was affirmative. To the second, Clemente answered, "Let's see. I hit .345 last year and .350 this year. No, I don't think I want to quit now."

It was a wise decision. In 1971, the "whole world" would discover "how Roberto Clemente play baseball."

Chapter 14

THE GREAT ONE

There was a little of Willy Loman in Roberto Clemente. Willy, the poor soul searching desperately after a lost vision of the man he saw himself to be, trying to dredge up the final shred of courage that would allow him to peer unwaveringly into some buyer's cold eyes and make that one, big, killing sale that would bring his self-respect winging back.

There was a terrible, huge gap between what Willy Loman thought of himself and what others perceived him to be. So it was with Roberto Clemente, who waged Willy's war, constantly measuring his self-image against a public image that increasingly saddened him.

By the winter of 1970, a lack of national recognition had ceased to be an irritant to Clemente, a stabbing of his pride; rather it had become a riddle he found insoluble. Age had captured the great Mays, ruined his once-marvelous skills. Injuries had driven Mantle, limping, out of baseball. And for all of his power, Aaron had never been the total ballplayer Clemente had proved himself to be. Why then wasn't Roberto Clemente widely acclaimed the greatest player in the game; why wasn't he referred to in Walla Walla and West Palm Beach as the Great One, as he was in Pittsburgh? Why the omnipresent, maddening "but"?

By 1970, Clemente's public image nationally was something of a monster, too evasive to corner and conquer, a gossamer thing upon which he could bring no weapon to bear. There were moments when he seemed to be crying out, as Willy Loman had, "No . . . no, you do not understand about me."

"I play as good as anybody . . . but I am not loved," he said one night, his tone wistful rather than petulant, merely marveling at the fact that his extraordinary talents had somehow become lost to anyone residing beyond the Pittsburgh city limits. "I don't need to be loved. I just wish it would happen. There are many people like me who would like that to happen. Do you know what I mean?"

Clemente's meaning seemed clear. He had done and said things that caused a stranger to be projected to the public; now he was sorry the world didn't know the man he saw himself to be.

"People misunderstand you quickly," he philosophized. "I don't try to be better than anyone else. I'm as good, but I don't try to be better. I try to accomplish something, yes. I want to be the best there is. I have pride. It's like the movie Oscar. To win, you really have to put out. That is what I try to do."

But, after sixteen summers, Roberto Clemente hadn't really won an Oscar, and his reaction to being an ignored superstar had run the gamut from bitter anger to melancholy. "I need recognition. . . . I need people to respect me," he admitted. "That is what I play for, not money."

But respect and recognition are the province of adults, and Clemente's natural affinity seemed to be for the very young and the very old. "I have good relations with a lot of people, but there are very few people who understand me," he was willing to concede in 1970.

Children understood him perfectly. To the young, he was not Roberto Clemente, the oft-injured, or Roberto Clemente, belligerent battler of sportswriters, or Roberto Clemente, passionate crusader, or Roberto Clemente, intemperate seeker of truths large and small.

He was simply Merlin, bringer of magic to the ballpark; Pan, flinging himself about effortlessly; No. 21, performing the feats that spread gaiety among the adults, and drew from them indulgent smiles at pleas for peanuts and hot dogs and ice cream and piggyback rides back to the car. He was Roberto, and he made the stadium come alive.

To kids he was not the austere, unsmiling, unapproachable man many adults saw; an impeccably controlled zealot. "Once I left my three-year-old daughter outside the Pirate clubhouse while I ran inside to check something," Pirate scouting supervisor Merrill Hess said. "When I came back, I found Clemente on his hands and knees in the hallway, playing a game with her. He seemed to have a feeling for children."

No, to kids Roberto Clemente was not a stranger, and with them he was infinitely gentle. Before a game in Houston, Pirate broadcaster Nellie King introduced him to a deaf teen-ager. Many ballplayers, young and lithe and powerful, become uncomfortable when confronted by intimations of their own mortality. Clemente talked with the boy for fifteen minutes, using gestures and smiles. A few minutes later he carried one of his bats fifteen rows up into the grandstand, handed it to the deaf boy, and smiled. On the barrel of the bat was the message: "Jamie, you don't have to be able to hear to play baseball and enjoy the game. Best wishes, Roberto Clemente."

"He has a little trouble hearing," Clemente explained when he returned to the dugout.

This is not to say he wouldn't ignore his share of autograph seekers, was never gruff with young, pestering fans. He was. But he was also generous with them.

"He is generous with everyone," said his attorney, Elfren Bernier. "A friend of the Clementes in Carolina, Marita Sanchez, was killed in an automobile accident. The litigation to settle her estate was very complicated. She had been the sole support of her family, and Roberto supported them for a long time until the case was settled."

The Sanchez family was one of a myriad of things Roberto Clemente had to deal with in the winter of 1970. Melchor Clemente became seriously ill and had to undergo surgery. "You can make it better this year," he reminded his son before the operation. Clemente smiled, "You go and make it better this year."

In January, a group of influential San Juan citizens came to the House on the Hill and asked Clemente to run for mayor. "There's no use for me to say 'Yes,'" he told them. "Say I was elected and a situation came up where I had to compromise. I cannot compromise." They left with the reminder that the door was not closed if he should ever change his mind.

Clemente spent that winter managing San Juan in the Puerto Rican winter league and dealing with financial matters. Neither was particularly beneficial. On the opening night of the season, the lights failed at Hiram Bithorn Stadium. The next night in Mayaguez, another power failure struck. A few weeks later Clemente bumped an umpire and was fined and suspended for a week. Five of his Pittsburgh teammates were on the San Juan roster, and a month into the season all had been sidelined by injuries. Badly in need of pitching, San Juan signed Baltimore left-hander Mike Cuellar. Immediately, manager and star pitcher clashed. Clemente removed Cuellar from a game in the sixth inning, and they argued on the mound. In Cuellar's next appearance, he was shelled, and Clemente suggested the bullpen. This, he insisted, was not training ground for spring training. Cuellar could help the club in the bullpen. Cuellar quit in a huff, and San Juan eventually finished the season at .500.

When Clemente went to Florida in the spring of 1971, he quit talking about retirement and began talking about a two-year contract. But he didn't ask Joe Brown for it and it was not forthcoming. The spring was uneventful, Clemente having no particular injury problems. Much of the discussion in Florida, of course, centered around the teams who would war for the divisional titles. In the National League West, Cincinnati's Big Red Machine was given a wide edge; in the East, thought the experts, the Pirates should hold off New York and Chicago.

In Pittsburgh, a day or two before the 1971 season began, Clemente was trying to hold off an indomitable foe, the Internal Revenue Service. The Pittsburgh IRS sniffed that no player could spend as much money on medical expenses and remain ambulatory, much less perform, the way Clemente did. And further, it cast a suspicious eye toward Clemente's listing clubhouse tips as unreimbursed business expenses. When each road series ended, he would leave the visiting clubhouse attendant a twenty-dollar bill.

"When you get into my salary range, you are expected to tip big," Clemente argued. Further, he must pay taxi fares to the doctors' offices in every city the Pirates visited. After negotiations, a settlement with the IRS was reached, but Clemente would continue to be pestered by financial matters.

He was generous to a fault. A former Pirate farmhand needed money to start an auto dealership; Clemente wrote him a check for $10,000; a friend in New York was organizing a Little League team; Clemente bought 4 dozen gloves. The gas company laid off his brother Martino; Clemente wrote a check. The Pirates visited Los Angeles; Clemente bought trainer Tony Bartirome 6 silk shirts. "He'd always do stuff like that," Bartirome explained. "Once he asked me to hold a cashier's check for him. I stuck it in an envelope and put it in the pocket of one of my white uniform shirts. A week or so later, when the shirt was going to the laundry, I found the envelope and gave it to him. He grinned and said, 'Look at the check.' It was for $15,000."

Clemente didn't lack money. In 1971, he was making almost $150,000 a year; his home in Rio Piedras was worth more than $100,000, and a business acquaintance said he had more than $500,000 in savings. He merely had trouble keeping track of it. Of course, there were those who tried to help. "He was an easy touch," sighed Bartirome. "Yes, people were always after him for money," agreed his friend, Omar Cordeiro. "And usually he gave it to them."

No one found Clemente an easier mark than did one of his uncles. When Clemente was a young boy, one of his father's brothers had disappeared under mysterious circumstances. After months had passed and the man had not been located, it was assumed he was dead, and a memorial service was held in a Carolina church.

One evening in 1970 at Shea Stadium in New York, Clemente was standing near the right-field stands, chatting with teammate José Pagan, when he saw a familiar face and paled. "José, you see that man sitting there, the one that looks like my father?"

"Yes, I see him."

"I think he is a ghost. He look exactly like my dead uncle. Go talk to him; see who he is."

Pagan walked over and talked to the man briefly. "He say he is named Clemente."

"That cannot be. He is dead. Tell him to come to the clubhouse after the game. I want you to ask him some more questions."

When the game ended, Clemente lingered until the clubhouse was all but deserted, while outside Pagan held an inquisition. Yes, the man was from Carolina. Yes, he had a brother named Melchor. "He is your uncle," Pagan told Clemente. The next afternoon the man appeared at the Pirates' hotel and left $500 richer.

Clemente's superstitions were part of the clubhouse humor in 1971. And, ironically, it was in the clubhouse where Roberto Clemente had the greatest effect on the 1971 Pirates.

The experts had been wrong about the 1971 National League season. Cincinnati's Big Red Machine broke down after a pennant year, and the Pirates would not hold off New York and Chicago, but rather peer down at the Cubs and the Mets from a high perch.

In 1971, the Pirates needed Clemente not on the field, but off. They immediately grabbed control of the National League East. Willie Stargell set a major league record for home runs in the month of April, and Dock Ellis was virtually unbeatable as the Pirates leaped atop the standings. They were young and resilient and cocky. From April on, they never looked back. Even their ills were a source of bantering good humor. Bartirome ran not so much a training room as a stage.

"The swelling on Oliver's knee isn't as bad as the swelling on Robertson's hand, which proves all along what I've been saying about this game," the trainer would set up an innocent bystander.

"What's that?"

"That baseball is a game of inches."

Their laughter was contagious, centering around Bartirome's elaborately planned practical jokes and Clemente. Visitors to the clubhouse would be told Bartirome, all of 5-9 and 175, was a man of great strength, that his most marvelous feat was picking up 3 men at once. The visitor would lay down on the carpeting and be flanked by 2 of the larger Pirates, the men's legs entwined. Bartirome would appear and go about flexing his arms theatrically. At the moment of truth, he would grasp the helpless visitor's belt, heave mightily, and then spray the man with a hidden can of shaving soap.

Certainly, they had to claim the pennant on the field, but when the Pirates showed signs that their grip on the race was slackening, it was Clemente who renewed their spirit.

"A big thing about playing is enjoying coming to the park," explained batting coach Bill Virdon. "If you don't like to come to the park, chances are you won't be happy after you get here, and then you're going to have some problems."

Clemente kept the problems to a minimum in 1971. Baseball teams are rarely united beyond the ballpark, but victory comes much easier if a feeling of unity prevails in the clubhouse. In 1971, the Pirates' unity could be traced back to Clemente.

"He had something going with everyone on the club," Bartirome said. "There was something special between him and each of the other guys, me included. Like everyone knew Sangy was a very religious man. He'd come in the training room reading that little Bible he always carries, and Roberto would motion at me to get the telephone book. I'd open it and pretend to be reading, say, the Twenty-third Psalm. 'Yea, though I walk through the valley of the shadow of . . .' Clemente would start to sing 'Rock of Ages' and parade around the training room, and Sangy would be going crazy by this time, saying, 'God is going to punish you all for blasphemy,' and Bob would be laughing his head off. He'd kid everyone."

As the Pirates swaggered through the early summer, they ran into a bad slump, and rumors spread about dissension, fights in the clubhouse, and all other sorts of maladies. Occasionally, if such stories are persistent, a team can be disrupted and real tension can develop. It didn't in 1971.

"You'd walk into our clubhouse and hear guys screaming, 'You nigger son-of-a-bitch,' or, 'You dago bastard,' but there wasn't any animosity," Bartirome said.

"Everything in the clubhouse would center on Roberto the last ten or fifteen minutes before a game," said pitcher Steve Blass. "Only the club would be in there then, and you're there with people you really trust, twenty-five men going through the pressure cooker of a pennant race. That was Roberto's time. He and Dave Giusti used to really get going, screaming at each other about really serious subjects. He'd say, 'That's what happens when you let an Italian in. I been here seventeen years and he comes in and in one season take over. That's the Mafia for you.'

"But he helped keep us together."

And when the Pirates threatened to come apart on the field, as they did a couple of times through the summer, Clemente was also there. "We lost a few on the Coast and then we dropped one in Montreal and we were going horseshit," remembered Dave Giusti. "He started saying, 'Hey, we're not doing this,' or, 'Hey, we're not doing that.' He didn't do it often, mostly when we were down. Other guys tried to do that. But, hell, who were you going to listen to? He'd get on us and then suddenly we'd be on our way."

When talk wasn't enough, Clemente provided inspiration on the field. In the eighth inning of a game in Houston in mid-June, he made an incredible catch to prevent the tying run from scoring. One Houston sportswriter called it "a catch for the ages."

Astro outfielder Bob Watson smashed a high drive down the right-field line, a bullet that seemed destined to hit above a yellow line painted on the Astrodome fence for a home run. Playing Watson to pull, Clemente sprinted for the corner, soared high into the air, and snatched the ball just as he crashed into the brick wall with sickening force.

As Clemente fell to the cinder warning track, Watson stood frozen at first base and applause rolled from the stands like a thunderclap, 16,307 fans standing and cheering a robbery clearly comparable to the Brinks heist.

"When you get held up by Jesse James, it's not so bad," Watson sighed later. Others were more effusive. An 80-year-old retired Texas sportswriter said, "It was the greatest catch I ever saw. I was sitting maybe 75 feet away, and I could almost feel the impact when he hit that wall. What guts . . . and to have held the ball."

The catch—and Clemente's 2-run homer—won the game for Steve Blass. "That's what he does for us . . . he keeps us in games," Blass said. "With him around, you're never out of it."

But no one man made the 1971 Pirates. At midseason, Stargell already had 30 home runs. Clemente was hitting .342, Dave Giusti was the premier relief pitcher in baseball, and Blass and Dock Ellis had been superb starters. On July 23, the National League East race seemed over, the Pirates commanding the division by 11½ games.

But one of the beauties of baseball is its uncertainty. On August 16, St. Louis had climbed to within four games of the Pirates, and if panic was going to ruin the season, now was the time. Pittsburgh clung to first place, but on the Pirates' final swing to the West Coast, in the midst of a streak where they would lose twenty of thirty games, they suffered a mind-blowing loss in the first game of a series in Los Angeles.

The relief pitching, which had been brilliant, failed. Mudcat Grant gave up a ninth-inning grand-slam home run to Bill Buckner that gave the Dodgers an 8–5 win and cost Ellis a thirteen-game winning streak. It was the sort of loss that can set even a division leader to questioning itself, and no one had to tell Grant it was a painful defeat with possible serious ramifications.

In the tomb of a clubhouse, Grant sat slumped on the stool in front of his locker, eyes frozen to the floor, unmoving for perhaps twenty full minutes.

Clemente looked across the room at the dejected veteran, who had been a big help to the club the previous year but had struggled throughout 1971 trying to sustain his career. He walked over to Grant and spoke quietly.

"Forget this game; it is gone," Clemente said. "You

can't change it. You helped this ballclub last year and you will again. I know you can still pitch."

Grant never forgot the incident. "I was crushed," he said later. "You don't want to drag your career out. You want to contribute, especially with a club like this one. It was a dumb pitch. I felt terrible. Everyone got dressed quickly—I guess they wanted to leave me with my misery. But Clemente came over and talked to me. All he did was spend twenty minutes holding my hand because he knew I was suffering. He's a guy who's been in baseball for so long, and he had three hits that night, and he came over to help. It's the warmest thing anyone's ever done for me in baseball."

The Pirates swept the next two games from Los Angeles and shoved the Cardinals back into the pack in early September, clinching the Eastern Division championship on September 22 in St. Louis.

Stargell, who had carried the club most of the way, finished with 48 home runs and 125 rbi's. Clemente hit .341 and drove in 86 runs. Manny Sanguillen batted .323, and the rest of the young Pirate hitters—Richie Hebner, Dave Cash, Al Oliver, and Bob Robertson—had productive seasons. A kid named Rennie Stennett came up from Charleston of the International League and hit .353 in the last 50 games. Outfield spares Gene Clines and Vic Davalillo hit .308 and .285, respectively. *Sport* magazine ran a story on the Pirate reserves entitled, "Thunder from the Bench," such were the feats of the Pirate irregulars. Suddenly, the Pittsburgh Pirates were the most feared hitting team in baseball.

They were nothing less in the best-of-five playoffs

against San Francisco, champions of the National League West. The Giants won the opener, 5–4. But then Pittsburgh blew them out of the series with three straight victories: 9–4, 2–1, and 9–5.

Clemente had three hits in the first Pirate win, powered by Robertson's three home runs, and two in the third triumph, his second hit putting Pittsburgh ahead to stay. But Stargell had gone 0-for-14 in the playoffs, and it was now time for someone else to pick up the big stick.

Baltimore had ripped the American League East apart in the final weeks of the season and then run over Oakland in three straight in the playoffs to carry the momentum of a fourteen-game winning streak into what was once aptly described as "that autumnal madness," the World Series.

These Orioles were baseball's most recent dynasty. They had won three consecutive pennants, four in six years. They had the Robinson boys: the celebrated Brooks and Frank. They had a slick glove at short in Mark Belanger, and a renowned power-hitter at first in Boog Powell. They had four twenty-game winners. (The Pirates' last twenty-game winner had turned the trick eleven years before.) They had bench strength to rival the Pirate thunder, they had a vast edge in Series experience, and they had irrepressible manager Earl Weaver, who had a big mouth. The latter was an insurmountable handicap, despite odds of 9–5 on Baltimore and cracks about the Orioles sweeping the Series in three straight.

The World Series really doesn't involve baseball. Nothing consequential is decided by having teams that have already played 162 games trying to settle the issue of superiority by meeting in a 7-game series during the football season.

The World Series' primary functions are to shunt football off the sports pages for another two weeks or so, and give the fans something to talk about on those winter evenings when other men of reason are wondering why Wilt Chamberlain can't shoot free throws or who will play in the Super Bowl.

Hordes of sportswriters descend at World Series time to greet old friends, consume free booze, and give the old typewriter a final workout before hibernating until spring training begins anew in March.

The World Series demands controversy to sustain interest the way waffles demand syrup to sustain flavor, so the reporters ferret it out. It was not difficult to locate in October of 1971, and Clemente was at its hub.

During a spring game between the clubs at the Pirate complex in Bradentown, Florida, Earl Weaver had belittled Jackie Hernandez, whom the Pirates had acquired that winter from Kansas City and who played eighty-eight games for Pittsburgh due to regular shortstop Gene Alley's knee and shoulder problems.

"Hernandez is a loser," sneered Weaver, an effervescent barrel of a man with the countenance and proclivity to stir excitement usually found in a gremlin. "If the Pirates are going with him at shortstop, they'll never win the pennant."

When Hernandez, championed by Roberto Clemente, had aided in the Pirate pennant drive, Weaver changed course without so much as a shame-faced grin. "Tell those

Pittsburgh writers to come ask me about Hernandez," he reminded a Baltimore sportswriter, eager to make amends lest an inspired Hernandez extract heavy vengeance.

As Weaver so graciously admitted, he "had been wrong about Hernandez." The slender Cuban had played well, hitting .260 and making spectacular plays afield to compensate for a habit of blowing the easy chances, which had brought about Weaver's low opinion of him.

Although he denied it at the time, Hernandez had been stung by Weaver's spring remarks. He had been a fringe player with Kansas City and a throw-in on the trade with the Pirates. When Alley had to be sidelined, the man who replaced him was not loaded with self-confidence.

As he had with Manny Sanguillen two years before, Clemente came to Hernandez' aid, laughing with him at the shortstop's triumphs, commiserating with him at his failures. "After Alley got hurt, you could see Roberto walking in the clubhouse after games and spending time with Jackie," said Steve Blass. "He bolstered Jackie's confidence; day after day he made Jackie feel a part of the club. He was just sensitive to the fact that he could help Jackie contribute." Hernandez was not a consistent player—after once costing the Pirates a game he wept—but neither was he considered a liability when the World Series began.

When Hernandez vs. Weaver had been duly reported, Clemente kept the pre-Series pot boiling. "It is terrible out there," he said after a workout at Baltimore's Memorial Stadium the day prior to the Series opener. "This is not a major league field. You cannot run without fear of tripping or falling. I would rather play in a coal mine."

Baltimore's pro football team had played two exhibition games on the turf, which had been weakened by heavy summer rains that had caused nineteen postponements, including one during the recent playoffs. But Baltimoreans loyal and true bridled at the remark, and it brought further discussion midway in the Series.

After years of seeking a national forum, and aware that at age thirty-seven he might not again have such an opportunity, Roberto Clemente made the most of it —before, during, and after the 1971 World Series. The Oriole book had it that Clemente's bat had slowed, that he no longer could pull the ball with consistency. "See if I can pull the ball," he needled Baltimore catcher Ellie Hendricks, and the first time the Orioles pitched him anywhere but low and away, he tripled into the left-field corner.

Reporters who had long heard of his tirades and believed the myth that he was not a good subject for in-depth interviews prodded him for fiery, headline-making remarks. They were not disappointed. Clemente told them, over and over, "Nobody in this game does anything better than me." However egotistical it might have seemed, it was true. And the evidence would soon become available. Roberto Clemente would close the gap between what he knew to be true and what the public had been led to understand. He was the very best there was, and, by God, in a fortnight every baseball fan in the world would be made to realize it.

Finally, after Danny Murtaugh had observed that the

9–5 odds and the reams of newspaper stories that had all but dug the Pirates' grave had caused him to wonder "why we even bothered to show up," the World Series of 1971 began.

Despite recurring elbow problems, Dock Ellis started for the Pirates against Baltimore's clever left-hander, Dave McNally, who overcame some wildness and uncharacteristically poor fielding by the Orioles to win the opener, 5–3. Clemente singled and doubled, but the Pirates had only one other hit, a single by Dave Cash, and scored only through McNally's early lack of control and Baltimore's generosity.

Laboring, Ellis gave up a three-run homer to Merv Rettenmund, and when Don Buford homered in the fifth, it was all the Orioles needed to wrap up their fifteenth consecutive victory and set knowing heads to nodding.

Earl Weaver switched to a right-hander, Jim Palmer, for game No. 2, after rain had delayed the Series a day. Like McNally, Palmer experienced control problems, walking eight men. The walks mattered little; Baltimore singled the Pirates to bits and breezed to an 11–3 triumph. Clemente had two more hits—he hit safely in all seven 1960 games—but in Pittsburgh, Pirate fans were bravely recalling the 1960 classic when their heroes had suffered bludgeonings of 16–3, 12–0, and 10–0, only to triumph on Bill Mazeroski's historic home run.

Astronomical odds weighed against the Pirates repeating that world championship when the teams moved to Pittsburgh. Only four clubs had lost the first two games and then rebounded to capture the Series.

The day of the third game, a headline in the Pittsburgh

Press read: "Will the Real Pirate Team Please Stand Up?" In the first two games only Roberto Clemente, who had gone 4-for-9, seemed to be himself, and manager Danny Murtaugh insisted, "You haven't seen the real Pirate team yet."

In the third game, Baltimore got to see the real Pirates. Steve Blass throttled the Orioles on three hits, including a bases-empty home run by Frank Robinson. Clemente accounted for the Pirates' first score, his headlong dash nipping a double-play relay that would have canceled the run. In the seventh, Clemente led off by tapping a routine bouncer to pitcher Mike Cuellar, his old winter league antagonist. Clemente sprinted madly down the first-base line, and hustle was rewarded as Cuellar's hurried throw pulled Boog Powell off the bag for an error. Unnerved, Cuellar walked Willie Stargell to bring Bob Robertson to the plate. With no one out and runners at first and second, Murtaugh decided a sacrifice was the percentage play, and Robertson was given the bunt sign by third-base coach Frank Oceak. Clemente was surprised to read the sign, and wanting to make sure Robertson had understood he was being asked to sacrifice for the first time all season, screamed, "Time! Time!" He was too late. Robertson took a full cut at Cuellar's screwball. It disappeared over the left-field fence to account for the 5–1 final score.

"I thought the hit-and-run might be on, so I wanted to make sure what the sign was because I was going to have to be moving on the pitch," Clemente explained his near-*faux pas*.

Pirate strategy charted before the game had taken

effect. "Our pitchers had been throwing too many good strikes, so it was decided to try and make them hit everything to the opposite field," Clemente explained. "It worked."

Almost everything worked from the third game on. Game No. 4 was played on a Wednesday night, the first World Series game ever under the lights. An estimated 61 million people watched it on NBC television. When it was over, 30.5 million argued Roberto Clemente had been a victim of outrageous larceny.

Baltimore led, 3–2, when Clemente came to bat in the third inning with a man on first base. Baltimore right-hander Pat Dobson fed him an outside fast ball. That was the Baltimore book. Low and outside. But Dobson got the pitch up too high, and Clemente slashed it on a curling arc toward the right-field seats and the yellow painted line that served as a foul pole.

Pittsburgh's shining Three Rivers Stadium has everything. Plush red seats; huge, flashing scoreboard; a posh, glass-fronted dining emporium. Everything but a plain, old foul pole. Depending on your persuasion, Clemente's blast ricocheted off the yellow painted stripe, meaning it was a home run, or hit an inch or two to the right of the yellow stripe, meaning it was a very well-hit, exciting foul ball.

Stocky, red-faced John Rice of the American League, working the right-field line, immediately threw his arm toward foul territory.

"It was fair, 60 million people saw you blow it, John," raved Pittsburgh first-base coach Don Leppert. Rice shook his head. Murtaugh waddled into the fray. Rice continued to shake his head. The argument raged for 5 minutes. As might be expected, Rice prevailed. Clemente returned to the plate and singled. Al Oliver followed with a single that tied the game and placed it in the tender hands of a pair of young roommates, Bruce Kison and Milt May. Kison replaced a shaky Luke Walker in the first inning and threw 6⅓ innings of zip at the Orioles, yielding only 1 hit. In the seventh, May pinch-hit for him and singled in the run that gave the Pirates a 4–3 win and deadlocked the Series.

Nelson Briles unraveled it the next day with a magnificent two-hit shutout. Clemente drove in the last of the Pirates' four runs to maintain his record of hitting safely in every Series game he played. The smart money had become uncertain and the Orioles irritable. Two reporters snared the Orioles' Frank Robinson as he was about to enter the shower following the fifth game.

"Clemente says your park is lousy," said one reporter.

"If he's supposed to be such a great outfielder, he should adjust to it," Robinson jeered. "Where does he get off knocking any park? He's played all of his career in a coal hole. If he doesn't like our stadium, let him buy a ticket and watch from the stands. I'm a professional. I don't cry about parks. I get out there and do the best I can. Now I'm going to take a shower."

In fact, the Orioles were already all wet. They had fielded sloppily, and suddenly they had quit hitting. And, Frank Robinson notwithstanding, they had not been able to handle Clemente. He had nine hits in twenty-one times at bat in the first five games. He was spectacular afield. In the second game, he had grabbed Frank Robinson's sinking liner on the run at the foul line and in the same motion unloaded a strike to third base that very nearly retired Rettenmund and did serve as a warning to the Orioles for the remainder of the Series.

"You watch Roberto and you can't help getting all psyched," said Pirate outfielder Gene Clines. "There's the old man out there busting his ass off on every play of every game. Look, I'm twenty-five. If he can play like that, shouldn't I?"

October 16 was a travel day, and a Baltimore newspaper featured a story that revolved around the Oriole report that Clemente, for all of his greatness, still lacked the bat speed to pull the ball. It was like squirting gasoline on a fire.

"He was storming around the batting cage before the game . . . ranting about what he had to do to prove what kind of a hitter he is," said Brooks Robinson after Baltimore had again stalemated the Series with a gutty 3–2, tenth-inning win. Clemente homered for the second Pirate run and tripled. In the ninth inning, he made a throw from the right-field corner to home plate, a rocketing, knee-high arrow that was called the biggest nonplay of the Series, although it prevented the winning run from scoring. "It's got to be the greatest throw I ever saw," said Oriole second baseman Davey Johnson. "One second he's got his back to the field at the 390 mark, the next instant here comes the throw, on the chalk line."

Even Frank Robinson offered grudging respect after Baltimore's dramatic victory. "Clemente's good, but even Clemente can play only one position at a time," he said.

Baltimore sent the Series to a seventh game in the tenth when Frank Robinson took some liberties with Vic Davalillo's arm and slid home with the winning run. When the game ended, Danny Murtaugh unleashed a barrage of hot words at plate umpire John Kibler, who had been charged by Pirate starter Bob Moose and others with "squeezing" the strike zone. Murtaugh rode Kibler viciously throughout the game and ultimately was fined $250.

The day of the seventh and deciding game did not dawn brightly for the Pirates. On their way to the stadium, Jackie Hernandez and José Pagan were almost seriously injured when their taxi struck another automobile at an intersection.

In the clubhouse before the game, Clemente spotted Howie Haak, the Pirate scout who had befriended him during the dark days of Montreal. "Sit down, Howie, I want to tell you something," Clemente said, drawing up a stool. "Howie, you have been a good friend of mine, so I want you to be one of the first to know. If we win today's game, I am going to retire."

Steve Blass, hero of the Pirates' first Series win, opposed Cuellar in what might have been Clemente's final game. Blass was superb, and in the fourth inning, Clemente extracted a particularly sweet piece of revenge, driving a Cuellar pitch high over the left-center-field fence for the game's first run. In the eighth, the Pirates scored another run and Blass, although giving up a run in the bottom of the eighth, held on with a four-hitter.

Pandemonium reigned from the final out. Blass leaped into catcher Manny Sanguillen's arms, and the Pirates fought their way from the field. Roberto Clemente decided to unretire before he reached the dugout. "I saw my wife as I ran off the field," he explained later. "She said, 'Don't quit now. Baseball's your life.' She was crying. I changed my mind."

Reporters pressed against Clemente in waves and, in the baseball idiom, he let it all hang out. They asked about leadership, and he told them, "For me I have to produce to be a leader. You can't be a leader with your mouth. I just say some things in the clubhouse after we lose the first two games. I tell everyone not to worry, that we'll be all right when we go to Pittsburgh. When fellows have their heads down, you have to pep them up.

"If I put my head down, they say, 'Why try?' A man they trust, if he quits, everyone quits."

Clemente did not quit. He batted .414, made two remarkable catches, ran like a man possessed, hit two home runs, and maybe a third. The voting for the automobile to be given to the most valuable series player had been conducted in the nation's newspapers after the fifth game, and the announcement that Clemente was the recipient was anticlimactic.

No reporter left Clemente's locker following the seventh game without some variation on a singular theme. "I want everyone in the world to know that this is the way I play all of the time," he said over and over. "All season, every season, I gave everything I had to this game. The press call me a crybaby, a hypochondriac . . . they say I'm not a team player.

"Now everyone knows the way Roberto Clemente

plays. They saw me in the World Series. Mentally, I will be a different person now."

When television intervened and Clemente was hauled atop a storage locker to tell millions of people how it felt to have won a war, he said, "Before I say anything, I want to say something in Spanish to my mother and father."

Watching on television in Puerto Rico, Melchor and Luisa Clemente were paid true homage. "On this, the proudest day of my life, I ask your blessing," Roberto Clemente said.

Later, in the training room, Clemente was again surrounded by reporters when Dave Giusti roared into the room, tugging the cork from a bottle of champagne and aiming it at Clemente.

Clemente ducked his head. "Don't, I got a bad eye," he yelled with a perfectly straight face.

In the larger room beyond, the floor made treacherous by spilled wine, Willie Stargell held forth at length on the man who had dominated the Series. "He has supreme pride," Stargell said. "There are people who say he's overpaid, but they don't see him play every day. He never gives less than his best. He runs into the ground. Take a look at the scars on his legs sometime."

On the Pirate charter back to Pittsburgh, where the city was celebrating in a frenzy that would last until dawn and be variously labeled "civil strife" and "an orgy," Clemente and Steve Blass met for the first time since leaving the field in Baltimore.

"He said, 'Where have you been? Let me embrace you,'" Blass said. "And he put his arms around me. It was a very personal moment for me. So many miles . . . so many ballgames, and then having that happen.

"I didn't know what to say. I just held on."

And, ultimately, that's what Roberto Clemente had done. Held on. Held on until he had closed the distance between what he saw in himself and what others saw. Held on until, from Walla Walla to West Palm Beach, everyone knew who the Great One was. Held on until there were no more "buts."

And now there were no more.

Chapter 15

NO 3,001

He had pursued perfection down the long halls of time and, finally, during nine lovely Autumn days, he had run it to earth. There were no more "buts." After seventeen splendid summers, Roberto Clemente had become an overnight sensation, a publicly certified marvel. The summit had been conquered. What he had sought to prove had been proven beyond a reasonable doubt. He was an accredited Main Man; the Guy Who Makes the Difference; the *Ichi-Ban* boy. Now everyone knew exactly how Roberto Clemente played baseball, which was, demonstrably, just a little better than anyone else. "A kind of baseball that none of us had ever seen before," Roger Angell wrote in *The Summer Game*. "They" knew it, he knew it, and most importantly, he knew "they" knew it.

Now the goals would be more restricted. A three thousandth hit. Only ten other players in the long history of baseball had produced three thousand hits, a dividing line between mere greatness and immortality.

Another World Series, to be sure—in case anyone missed the 1971 edition and the man who had so thoroughly dominated it.

A choice of suitable occupation when he decided to hang them up, or, as a few put it, "if." Something that would involve him in the game, for he had said once, "I would be lost without baseball; I don't think I could stand being away from it as long as I was alive."

And the Ciudad Deportiva must be built. For years he had dreamed of a sports city for the kids of Puerto Rico.

And all of these goals would be realized in the year or three that he would continue to display skills the public was now alerted to observe.

But the real struggle had ended; he had banished reasonable debate of his talents during the World Series. He was, suddenly, a cinch to become the first Latin enshrined in the Hall of Fame.

On November 9, 1971, there were two important arrivals at San Juan International Airport. Early in the day, a moon rock was flown in from the Manned Space Center in Houston to be studied by the geologists of Puerto Rico. Later that afternoon, Roberto Clemente arrived from Pittsburgh, to be adored by the people of Puerto Rico. The story and pictures of Clemente's triumphant homecoming were on page one of the San Juan newspapers; the moon rock story was on page two.

But during the winter of 1971, Roberto Clemente discovered that adulation was a heavy burden. Nothing of significance, civically or socially, could quite function without his presence. He attended banquets, meetings, all manner of social events. The governor needed him for this, the parks administrator for that, the Lions Club for the other. When Clemente took to his home in Rio Piedras for shelter, he was rousted by visitors; when he and Vera tried to take a vacation in Venezuela, it was interrupted because Melchor Clemente had become ill again.

"I had a rough winter," he explained. "I didn't get any exercise; just kept going from one place to another. For a month and a half, my wife and I couldn't get any sleep. Our house was like a museum. People flocking down the street, ringing the doorbell day and night. Walking through the house. People from town, even tourists. Then I had so many things going down there, I just couldn't say 'No.'"

In Puerto Rico, Roberto Clemente had made the transition from idol to folk hero. His name was magic; it seemed to guarantee success to any project. Pirate owner John Galbreath, who had years before given him an undistinguished racehorse—named, reasonably enough, Campeon Battey, or Batting Champion—named another of his colts Roberto. Galbreath, who had owned Kentucky Derby winners Proud Clarion and Chateaugay, shipped Roberto, the horse, to England, and in an upset he won the famed Epsom Derby. In Puerto Rico, the name Clemente brought similar results. "And you know him," said a friend of Clemente's, "he wouldn't do anything except 100 percent."

And that, undoubtedly, was the secret to Clemente's success. He did not believe in luck or chance, so he left nothing to their vagaries. For years, teammates had snickered upon discovering him, apparently asleep, on the trainer's table. But there was a reason for his lethargy.

"What I like to do is lay there and think about the game we will play that night," he said. "Say Tom Seaver is going to pitch. I think about him; how he likes to pitch to me. I see myself at the plate. First time up, he throw me a fast ball inside for a ball, then go slider away and I hit it on the line to right for a single. Next time, fast ball away, curve in, and I see the hole between short and third and I pull the ball through it. Next time, low slider, and I hit it hard back up the middle. The fourth time, he go fast ball away again, then change-up, and I see it coming and wait and then I hit it down the right-field line.

"In my mind I have seen all the pitches Seaver has; I have hit against him four times. Then I get up and I go out there and get four hits because I have seen all of his pitches. Some nights, you get four pitches you can hit, and you get four hits. Some nights you only get one pitch you can hit, and I hit it because I have already seen that pitch in my mind."

Like the conscientious Boy Scout, Clemente believed in preparedness. "Early one afternoon I was at the park and Clemente was on the field by himself, standing in the batter's box," Joe L. Brown said. "He'd swing the bat, drop it, and run like hell for first. I said, 'What are you doing?' He said, 'We're playing against Seaver tonight. I know how he will pitch me and I'm practicing what I will do, and how it will be.'"

The attorney, Elfren Bernier, was visiting the Clementes

during the 1971 season. At two o'clock one afternoon, in the middle of a downpour that threatened that night's game, Clemente suddenly informed his portly friend that they were leaving for the ballpark immediately. "The field will be wet tonight," he told Bernier. "I want to try a couple of things."

"He had someone roll the ball on the ground to make it wet and then throw it against the wall so he could practice grabbing it barehanded," Bernier said. "For a long time he did that, and then he ran back and forth, stopping and starting."

And, like any Boy Scout, Clemente embraced all victories, be they gained at the expense of Tom Seaver or a Puerto Rican jailbird.

"One day in the winter, I call him and ask him to play a softball game at the prison," Roberto Marin said. "The prisoners want to see him. He say 'O.K.,' and we go. I am a nothing-ball pitcher, and the prisoners get five runs right away. He comes running in from center field and say, 'I will pitch now.' They don't get no more runs, and in the last inning he hits a double and we win. On the way home, he tell me, 'I no like to lose that game.'"

Because Clemente worked at his craft so painstakingly, in time those who watched him came to conclude that his was an innate grace, a purity of motion born to him. "He makes it all look so easy," said New York Met star Rusty Staub. "He's great at everything. He just beats you, and beats you at everything you can do in baseball. There is no player comparable to him."

The years of practice resulted in Clemente showing

no apparent strain to muddy the aesthetics of his fluid, compact movements; no caution to soil his craft. He seemed without flaw, and he played, always, with an enthusiasm so contagious that you went home from the games and immediately began rummaging in the closet for your own baseball glove.

"This guy plays like he was sixteen," Baltimore manager Earl Weaver had said during the 1971 World Series. "A few years ago, when I was managing in the winter league, he took the first six weeks of the season off. Then in the first game he plays in, he dives for a ball in the cinders along the right-field line and comes up throwing it on the money to the plate."

His style was special. At the plate, his hips would rotate south, his upper torso north, his feet east, and the bat would be flung west. Other outfielders made diving catches occasionally; he made them routinely, one-handed, sliding across the turf on his butt. Others deftly retrieved drives from the concrete walls; he snatched them barehanded and flung them like silvery arrows. Willie Mays made basket catches; he caught the ball nonchalantly at his knees with a self-assurance so brazen no one ever conceived that he might drop one.

So, in the spring of 1972, were you so inclined, it would have been possible for you to draw a portrait in words of the finest player in the game; perhaps the finest pure talent baseball had ever known.

In drawing such a portrait, it is the picture of Roberto Clemente at bat that is the most distinctive, that comes to the imagination most readily. Huddled in the deepest corner of the batter's box, hands held to his chest as a nun might, waiting until the last fraction of a second to swing, shrugging his upper body into the ball, swaying his lower body away from it, virtually swiping the ball from the catcher's glove at the moment it was about to strike leather. In the vernacular, "hitting from the inside out." Finishing the lustiest of swings with his numbers easily observable to the second baseman. No strike zone: "How can it be a bad ball if you can hit it?" Hitting on pure instinct.

"What kind of pitch did he hit?" Don Drysdale of the Dodgers once repeated a question disgustedly. "Ball four." And to correctly envision Clemente at the plate was to understand that he was in no way vulnerable, had no weakness that a pitcher might exploit. "The best way to pitch him is to roll the ball," Drysdale's Dodger teammate Sandy Koufax thought. For a time, Drysdale and others tried intimidation. "You can't knock him down," Drysdale finally admitted.

Said Clemente, "Sometimes you are on fire and your body aches, and you get knocked down and you get mad. Other times, you feel they are just trying to pitch close to you. I don't care one way or the other."

"Even though Drysdale knocked him down, he hit Drysdale," Bill Mazeroski said in the spring of 1972. "To be an exceptional hitter, you must hit the exceptional pitchers, and Clemente does. I think he hit Koufax better than he does a lot of other pitchers. People say he doesn't hit enough home runs, but he lacks the killer instinct. Most big home-run hitters just hammer away, even if a game is already decided; he thrives on the big win-lose situation. What impresses the players is that he hits like he does in spite of almost always taking the first pitch. I've seen him swing at the first one very few times in all the years. And every time he does, he comes back to the dugout muttering, "Why did I do a dumb thing like that? I never do that."

For Roberto Clemente, hitting was warfare. Sometimes psychological warfare. "He takes five bats to the on-deck circle and sometimes changes bats," chuckled Hank Aaron. "He makes the pitcher think he's going to use a heavier bat to punch the ball to right field, and then he goes up and takes a big cut."

Clemente was never concerned about his unorthodox batting style, only in the quickness of his hands, which would have awed a pickpocket. "I have to get in front of the ball to hit it; otherwise pitchers overpower me," he explained. "If you're ready when the pitcher throws the ball, you've got the edge. But I don't look for nothing up there—curve, fast ball, nothing. I don't want the pitcher to know what I like or don't like."

And then there is Clemente the outfielder. No portrait of Roberto Clemente the outfielder would be complete without mentioning that, defensively, he looked for everything. Even bunts. When writers began acknowledging him as the game's finest outfielder, they never failed to cite one indisputable bit of evidence: He was the only outfielder ever known to play a bunt. In a 1964 game with Houston, the Astros had runners at first and second in an obvious sacrifice situation. The Pirate counterstrategy was to have the third baseman rush the plate and field the bunt. The shortstop would cover third, hoping for a force play. So it went, only the Houston batter popped his sacrifice attempt into the air near second base. The runners held up briefly, and suddenly Clemente was skidding across the infield in pursuit of the ball. After recovering from the shock of discovering Clemente in his midst, Houston's Walter Bonds streaked for third base. Clemente's throw preceded him to the base, and the humiliated Bonds was out.

"No matter what the situation is, we're always aware of what he can do," Pirate pitcher Steve Blass said. "If the other team's got a rally going, he'll make some unreal catch to kill it. He's the only guy who turns the other players on. Seeing him come dashing in and sliding across the wet turf on his knees to make a catch with the spray coming up all around him . . . well, that's excitement."

All the instincts of Clemente the hitter didn't materialize in Clemente the outfielder. He got no great DiMaggio-like jump on the ball. Mazeroski felt he didn't need it. "Baseball's more mental than most people think, and he doesn't play it mechanically," Mazeroski said. "The majority of outfielders figure, 'I'll play this guy to pull just off the left of the mound.' They move to a spot and stay there. Clemente plays both the hitter and the pitch. A hitter gets two strikes, Clemente moves, adjusts his position, because he knows now the hitter isn't going to be trying to pull the ball as much."

To adequately describe Roberto Clemente the outfielder, you would first observe that perhaps no other outfielder's arm had such an impact on the playing of a baseball game. Beyond that, you might say he was the only outfielder of his time to regularly throw out hitters on legitimate singles; that as a rookie, manager Bobby

Bragan sternly told him, "Kid, throw slower, the infielders can't catch the ball"; that Dodger announcer Vin Scully used to crack, "Clemente could field a ball in Pennsylvania and throw out a runner in New York"; that quite often he would be photographed suspended sideways in the air, four feet off the ground, as a white blur streaked plateward; that somewhere there is a photograph of an open-mouthed Willie Mays, standing dumfounded ten feet from first base, where he has been tagged out because he made a mistake others had and taken too wide a turn and been gunned down by Clemente.

"He changes the game," Mazeroski said simply. "In almost every one of our games, a runner is afraid to try to go from first to third on a single to right. In a year's time, that makes a hell of a difference in how many runs we give up."

Perhaps you would care to document your description of Clemente's arm with the observations of other knowledgeable baseball folk: "The greatest throw I ever saw"—Leo Ward, St. Louis Cardinal traveling secretary for fifty years. "Never been a better throw in history"—Harry Walker, manager. "I couldn't believe it"—Davey Johnson, Baltimore second baseman.

Of course, each was speaking of a different throw by Clemente.

To finish your portrait of Roberto Clemente, you would probably say that in the spring of 1972, he was the most gifted ballplayer of the day. It would be a poor choice of words, for gift implies bestowal. Mostly, Roberto Clemente had come to be the finest ballplayer alive by working diligently at his trade, as he did at all things.

The word "chance" was not in his vocabulary. Work, Melchor Clemente had explained, equals success. If the commode wouldn't function properly, Roberto Clemente got some tools and repaired it. If you wanted to learn to keep your footing on wet artificial turf, you went out and ran back and forth, starting and stopping, until your balance was secure. There were, he believed, rational solutions to all problems.

When his name had become symbolic with attention, Clemente was asked to tape a commercial on the evils of drugs for teen-agers. A nephew had a serious drug problem; when it was discovered, he was flown to Pittsburgh immediately and lived with Roberto's family for nearly a year. But Clemente took pains with all manner of things. During the taping, he decided that since there were so many Spanish-speaking people using drugs, he would do two commercials.

"But the commercial's written in English only; who's going to do the translating?" the producer protested.

"I am," Clemente announced, spending the better part of an hour rewriting the commercial. The floor beneath his feet was littered with paper before he was satisfied with his translation.

But throwing himself head-first at all activities, large and small, was costly to Clemente in 1972. He reported to spring training exhausted and ten pounds underweight, and worked leisurely as the Pirates tuned the arsenal that was seeking its third consecutive National League East title. Danny Murtaugh had retired again and was replaced by the batting coach, Bill Virdon, a longtime teammate of Clemente's. There would be only harmony between Clemente and this manager.

"He's gone out of his way to help me," Virdon said. "He works twice as hard, so there won't be any letdown by anyone else. We've always respected each other. We're not close because our lifestyles are different, but there's a good relationship between us."

The Pirates were heavily favored to repeat. Virdon had at his disposal a bottomless pit of hitting talent, led by Willie Stargell. The pitching rotation—labeled the "no names" by Steve Blass—was quality. The bullpen, led by Giusti, was superior. Defensively, the Pirates were better than average. There was, in fact, such an abundance of talent that a trio of .300-plus hitters—Gene Clines, Vic Davalillo, and Rennie Stennett—could not break into the regular lineup.

In Florida, Clemente denied that the 3,000-hit plateau, only 118 hits away, held any particular fascination. Noting that he had only once failed to get more than 118 hits in a season, reporters pressed him. "It means nothing," he said one day in earshot of the astonished John Galbreath. "I am playing this season not because I have a chance at 3,000 hits. I am playing because I feel good. And because I can play good and the team has a chance to win. That's the reason I play, not for the three thousandth hit."

With friends, Clemente was more candid, and admitted that he badly wanted to reach the milestone. "He told me, 'I will never live to be old, I want to get that hit this year,'" said Luis Mayoral, Clemente's right-hand man on the sports city project. Later, after a Pirate charter narrowly missed another plane, Clemente told Manny Sanguillen, "I have to get that hit this year. I might die."

During the opening month of the 1972 season, it was the Pirates who almost died. They broke slowly, stung by a poor homestand where they lost 6 straight games, including 2 to Cincinnati, the team that would clip them in a gritty playoff series for the National League pennant when Bob Moose wild-pitched home the winning run in the fifth and final game. In the midst of a 9-game winning streak in May, the Pirates still remained 6½ games off the pace.

But in June the expected resurrection took place. Pittsburgh won 7 in a row on a West Coast swing. A week later, Moose beat the Giants in Pittsburgh to shove the Pirates atop the National League East standings, and slowly but inexorably they began to stuff the rest of the division into the background.

Meanwhile, Roberto Clemente continued to waste away, purple hollows pooling under his eyes. When he dipped to 170 pounds—what he had weighed as a callow youth in Montreal—he was forced to borrow a pair of uniform pants from Rennie Stennett, the 164-pound utilityman.

The Pirates reached high gear on July 14, winning 17 of their next 25 games to command the division by 9½ games and remove most of the mystery from the divisional pennant race. They would win a third consecutive divisional championship, but without much help from Clemente, who by now was under siege. In June, it was discovered he had rheumatic heels—"I could hardly walk for a month." In July, he attracted the flu in New York;

later in the month, a stomach virus in Cincinnati. In early August, he began to suffer from strained Achilles tendons. Such was his state of repair that Joe Brown's assistant, Joe O'Toole, removed a wax figure of Clemente from a stadium display and placed it on the trainer's table before a night game at Three Rivers Stadium. Joey Diven—the onetime world champion streetfighter who had years before debilitated the Pitt football team and had since become a county detective—was sent in search of a coffin for the figure, and a pregame ceremony was held. Clemente was ailing too much to appreciate the gesture—"Get that goddamn thing out of the clubhouse" —although the following day he grinned about the incident.

It was fortunate that the Pirates did not need Clemente badly during the first 3 months. He lacked stamina—he would hit only .214 during the playoffs—and was plagued by a rash of irritating ailments. He missed 47 of Pittsburgh's first 116 games, and by the first week of August it seemed improbable that he would get the three thousandth hit in 1972. He went into the last 26 games needing 25 hits to reach the milestone attained by only Ty Cobb, Stan Musial, Tris Speaker, Honus Wagner, Hank Aaron, Eddie Collins, Nap Lajoie, Willie Mays, Paul Waner, and Cap Anson. And there were moments when Clemente sounded as if he would default on the goal entirely.

"I play as long as I can help the ballclub," he said to questions of retirement. "I think I have accomplished some things not many people accomplish and that not too many are going to accomplish in the future. But I don't want to play badly—that way I hurt the fans and I hurt myself."

In September, Clemente began hurting National League pitchers, and the goal hoved back into view. "I would like to see him going into the last five games at home needing about ten hits for three thousand," laughed Pirate pitcher Dave Giusti. "There'll be so many hits flying around that somebody is liable to get killed."

Nothing quite so dramatic transpired. Clemente began raining base hits over the league's parks, and on the Pirates' last road game he authored hit No. 2,999 off Philadelphia left-hander Steve Carlton. He was immediately removed from the game in order that the big hit might come before the fans of Pittsburgh.

Clemente maintained his pose of indifference to the bitter end, telling Pittsburgh *Press* baseball writer Bob Smizik that he wasn't sure if he would play the following night. He had a doctor's appointment in the morning, Clemente explained. Immortality might have to await the convenience of the medical profession.

But that night he was in uniform, looking for the three thousandth hit against one of baseball's premier pitchers, the Mets' Tom Seaver, himself looking for the victory that would give him back-to-back twenty-game seasons. It was a damp, coolish Friday night, but twenty-four thousand turned out at Pittsburgh's Three Rivers Stadium to see Clemente—whose average had climbed to .313 during the September breakthrough—try to carve himself a piece of history.

They went home disappointed, mostly with the official

scorer. When Clemente came to bat in the opening inning, he received a tumultuous welcome, striding slowly to the plate, as he usually did, with the flair of a Cordobes.

What followed had little flair. Clemente swung very hard and hit the ball very softly. It teasingly hopped over Seaver's outstretched glove, took three smaller bounces toward second, and skipped off the glove of charging second baseman Ken Boswell.

The crowd's eyes shifted to the scoreboard. Nothing. In the press box, official scorer Luke Quay had made his call immediately. "Error, second baseman . . . error, Boswell." The rulebook burdens the fielder with making only "ordinary effort," and it had been Luke Quay's unhesitating opinion that Boswell's effort had not even been ordinary. But his message had not been heard over the crowd noise in the control booth, where a crew operated the electric scoreboard. An "H" blinked, hesitatingly, and disappeared from the board in an instant.

It was on view long enough. The crowd went wild, streamers of toilet paper funneling from the upper tiers. Having seen no ruling on the board, both teams on the field participated in a charade. Mets' first baseman Ed Kranepool retrieved the ball and gave it to Clemente, who passed it on to first-base coach Don Leppert for safekeeping. Leppert patted Clemente on the can.

History then suffered a jolt. Quay's ruling got through to the control booth, and the scoreboard lit up: "Error Second Baseman." Booing resounded through the stadium; it was as though some giant hand had reached down from the sky and intercepted George Washington's silver dollar on its flight across the Potomac.

Seaver, masterful as usual, then thwarted Clemente the rest of the evening. On his last time at bat, Clemente lined a slicing drive toward the right-field corner, guarded uncertainly by Rusty Staub, who owns a reputation of killing the opposition with his bat only to provide it artificial respiration with his glove. Inexplicably, Staub was stationed near the line and in perfect position to make a routine catch. History would have to wait until tomorrow.

A gaggle of reporters surrounded Clemente as he sat immersed in the whirlpool, little more than a wide grin visible above the swirling water. Clemente smiling after what many observers thought was a larcenous ruling that deprived him of the three thousandth hit?

Certainly. What more convincing proof would ever come forth to substantiate his charge that the press had been doing him dirty for years?

"Did you want a little scratcher for your three thousandth?" a reporter inquired.

"Why not? A hit is a hit. I wanted the three thousandth not for the glory, but so I could get out of the lineup and rest for five days before the playoffs."

"Boswell says it was an error . . . that he'd have gotten you if he'd handled the ball cleanly."

"He's full of it." The grin widened. "Anyway, I'm glad they didn't call it a hit. They been screwing me all my life, and this shows it."

"How many hits do you think you've lost in eighteen years?"

"How many hits? You mean how many batting titles. I should have won two more."

The debate wore on. Hit or error? Ironically, it had been Clemente's only close friend among the writers who had made the decision. Luke Quay had covered the Pirates for more than ten years for a small daily paper in McKeesport, just outside Pittsburgh. A warm, witty man, he seldom sought out the sensational story, and over the years had established a bond with Pirate players, especially Clemente. Strangely enough, Quay had arranged that he might be the official scorer the night Clemente got his three thousandth hit.

Legend has it that in his bid for the three thousandth hit, Paul Waner had been awarded a base hit on a play similar to the one on which Quay ruled an error. Waner supposedly waved toward the press box, signaling he did not want the cheapie, and the scorer reversed his decision, Waner getting the historical hit on a later, robust clout. Discovering his friend Quay to have been the guilty party, Clemente adopted a similar philosophy. "I want it to be a clean base hit. I hope I can get it tomorrow so I can rest on Sunday. But if I don't get it Sunday, then I won't get it this season because I won't play after that. Being rested for the playoffs is more important than the three thousandth hit."

Later, Clemente told Quay in private, "If I had known who was scoring, I would never have complained. I really didn't want the hit like that anyway."

At precisely 3:07 P.M. the following day, it became a moot point. The Mets' young left-hander Jon Matlack, who had not allowed Clemente a hit during the 1972 season, hung a curve ball. "Go get him," Willie Stargell had said. Roberto Clemente promptly got Matlack, ramming the curve into the left-center gap. History was made. Each time Clemente's name had been mentioned earlier, the 13,117 fans had roared to life. Now the cheering peaked, and the stadium became a ball of noise that seemed endless, rising and falling like waves against a pier. Clemente stood unmoving at second base and then doffed the black Pirate cap. The noise rose by decibels. It's a wonder he had the strength to acknowledge the applause.

"My wife and I didn't get through talking to people on the telephone until four-thirty this morning," he would later explain, "so I decided not to go to bed. I knew I had to get that hit today because I couldn't afford to go through another night like that."

The historic ball was thrown back to the infield by the Mets' Dave Schneck. The hit would be dedicated to "the fans of Pittsburgh and Puerto Rico and the man who made me play baseball, Roberto Marin"—and umpire Doug Harvey gave the ball to Clemente. As he had the night before, Clemente gave it to first-base coach Don Leppert. And as he had the night before, Leppert patted Clemente on the can.

And as it had not the night before, the scoreboard lit up. Stark numbers reflected the glory of the moment: "3,000."

Sadly, there would be no 3,001.

EPILOGUE

Before he had been dead ninety days, the five-year rule was waived, and Roberto Clemente was voted into baseball's Hall of Fame. Said one of the electors, "He was a very special guy. It is not the Hall of Fame which will honor him; he will honor it."

There would never again be equivocation about what he was as a baseball player. Kenny Smith, director of the Hall, had never doubted that Roberto Clemente's memory would come to be housed in his institution. "Are you crazy?" Clemente asked Smith years before, when the director mentioned he would be the first Latin so enshrined. "No," Smith smiled, "you'll be in here some day."

The date was August 6, 1973. The machinery for Clemente's election had been put into gear just days after his death. Joe Heiling, president of the Baseball Writers Association of America, called for a meeting of several prominent BBWAA members to discuss waiving the five-year mandatory waiting period. There was limited dissension on the basis that a precedent might be set. Dick Young of the New York *Daily News,* one of the most respected writers in the business, wondered if they weren't rushing things. Heiling didn't think so. "Do I have the authority as president to call for a ballot?" he asked the night before the New York BBWAA's annual dinner in New York City. He did. "Then, that's it. We'll ballot."

More discussions were held with various baseball people. Heiling's view held sway. The ballots were mailed out. On March 20, at a dinner at which a Roberto Clemente Award was donated to "a ballplayer of high reputation," Vera Clemente presented a trophy to Al Kaline. Then it was officially announced that Roberto Clemente had received 393 votes—75 more than required—and would be enshrined at ceremonies in Cooperstown in August. A total of 29 BBWAA writers eligible to vote—those who had been members for 10 years or more—voted nay, most of them because they were worried that a dangerous precedent was being set.

"I don't know if I can say I am happy . . . make it proud," Vera Clemente said at the St. Petersburg announcement of the results of the voting. The new governor of Puerto Rico, Rafael Hernandez Colon, also used the word "proud." "We have so many things about him for which to have been proud. It is not the least of these that he's the first Puerto Rican, indeed the first noncontinental American, to be immortalized with the all-time greats of baseball. I am sure he would have been very happy to have brought these honors to the land whose name he held so high. He was both a ballplayer and a man of high distinction. The latter has now been officially recognized by his election to the Hall of Fame; the former is enshrined in our hearts."

So now Puerto Rico, an island with no abundance of heroes, has another. To the list of actors José Ferrer and Rita Moreno, and statesman-patriot Luis Munoz Marin, and adopted son Pablo Casals, has been added the name of Roberto Clemente.

But of all the thoughts given voice that day, perhaps the most eloquent one belonged to Clemente's attorney, Elfren Bernier. "The people of Puerto Rico are divided in most things," Bernier said. "Politics . . . economics . . . geography . . . socially. But they are united behind Roberto Clemente."

There were hundreds of eulogies to the lost ballplayer. Commissioner Bowie Kuhn was unusually eloquent, the fan that dominates him coming to the fore: "He gave the term 'complete' a new meaning. He was a man of fierce pride and deep compassion for his fellow man. He was indeed the perfect and classic ballplayer. He made the word 'superstar' seem inadequate.

"He had about him the touch of royalty. Somehow, somewhere, for me, he should have been a king."

However, no eulogy struck at the heart of the loss so sharply as the one that appeared on the Three Rivers scoreboard on opening day, 1973: "Thank you, Roberto. We will never forget the Great One."

Months after Clemente's death, Al Campanis, the Dodger official who had found him in a tryout camp almost two decades before, struggled to sum up the meaning of Clemente's life, but finally could merely reflect what his death would mean.

"He will accomplish things because of the way he died that he would not have had he lived," Campanis said.

And so he will, for on a grassy 602-acre site where the earth is rich and red and flat, a dream will rise, Roberto Clemente's Ciudad Deportiva. In the background will be the fabulously posh San Juan beach condominiums, where the rich pay anywhere from $60,000 to $150,000 for highrise apartments that launch them up and away from the rats and garbage and dead dreams of the slums. But it will be the kids, groups of 1,200 at a time from these same slums, who will learn every sport imaginable from trained professionals; who will eat hot meals; who will get some schooling; and who will leave after 2 weeks aware that they, too, have a piece of the Puerto Rican action.

On the Iturreque Road, ironically just a few miles from the San Juan airport, Roberto Clemente's sports city complex will be built. The government stalled it for years. There was never enough money. A proper location for it could not be found. Later, they told Clemente, later. Only within days after he died, Governor Colon invited Vera Clemente to his office to discuss plans for the project. Money is pouring in, $500,000 from fans alone. The government will donate the land, worth $18 million, and the Puerto Rican legislature has officially petitioned the federal government for funds that mean life or death for the facility. It is a very good bet that the necessary $12 million will be raised. What was once a swamp will become a place where young men can come to collect the ideals that were Clemente's.

He was a bit of a puritan—"fifteen-year-old boys and girls going around holding hands," he once sniffed—but he believed in athletics as a redeeming social value.

"I will work with children; that will keep me in the game forever. I'd like to work with kids all the time, if I live long enough," he had once said. "This is my dream. I do not know exactly what this sports city will be like . . . but it will be beautiful. It will be open to everybody. No matter who they are. And after I open the first one in Puerto Rico, I will open others. I will do this thing because that is what God meant me to do. Baseball is just something that gave me a chance to do this."

The dream of a sports city evolved slowly in Clemente's mind. He was a man with the old country values, a product of the Jíbaro ethic. "In your country the complaint now is that parents only see their children on Saturdays. It is beginning to be that way here in Puerto Rico," said Elfren Bernier. "Values are changing too rapidly here. He could see that. He could see drugs being used, and he hated that. He felt something like the Ciudad Deportiva was needed. For a long time the government just gave him lip service, but he would say, 'I don't give this thing up. It might take a long time, but I am going to do it.'"

An idol, thought Roberto Clemente, was a necessity for youth. He had had Monte Irvin. An idol was a pattern. Choose the correct idol and you construct for yourself a blueprint for success. And to be an idol, he thought, brought grave responsibility.

"A country without idols is nothing," he would say. "I

send out twenty thousand autographed pictures a year to the kids. I feel proud when a kid asks me for my autograph.

"I do it because baseball has given me a good life. I am a human being. . . . I have achieved something. Some players complain. I tell them we do not have to stand in the street with a heavy drill going rat-tat-tat-tat. We come to the park in a clean shirt. We smell from perfume all the time.

"I believe we owe something to the people who watch us. They work hard for their money. When we do not try 100 percent, we steal from them."

So Roberto Clemente tried to pay his tab for living the good life. His children will also pay the price. "I want them to suffer some," he said. "I want them to have what they're supposed to have, but I don't want them to be rich. I want them to be like normal people."

Time will soon fade all these passions of Roberto Clemente; his accomplishments will dwindle and wither with the years; be prostituted out of proportion. His pride and his ailments will go the way of some forgotten wind.

What will be remembered, ultimately, is this: that for a single generation, no one played the child's game of baseball with more grace or dignity or fire.